A History of Women's Seclusion in the Middle East
The Veil in the Looking Glass

A History of Women's Seclusion in the Middle East
The Veil in the Looking Glass

Ann Chamberlin

The Haworth Press
New York • London • Oxford

For more information on this book or to order, visit
http://www.haworthpress.com/store/product.asp?sku=5666

or call 1-800-HAWORTH (800-429-6784) in the United States and Canada
or (607) 722-5857 outside the United States and Canada

or contact orders@HaworthPress.com

The Haworth Press, Inc., 10 Alice Street, Binghamton, NY 13904-1580.

PUBLISHER'S NOTE
The development, preparation, and publication of this work has been undertaken with great care. However, the Publisher, employees, editors, and agents of The Haworth Press are not responsible for any errors contained herein or for consequences that may ensue from use of materials or information contained in this work. The Haworth Press is committed to the dissemination of ideas and information according to the highest standards of intellectual freedom and the free exchange of ideas. Statements made and opinions expressed in this publication do not necessarily reflect the views of the Publisher, Directors, management, or staff of The Haworth Press, Inc., or an endorsement by them.

Cover design by Kerry E. Mack.

Library of Congress Cataloging-in-Publication Data

Chamberlin, Ann.
    A history of women's seclusion in the Middle East : the veil in the looking glass / Ann Chamberlin.
        p. cm.
    Includes bibliographical references and index.
    ISBN-13: 978-0-7890-2983-6 (hc. : alk. paper)
    ISBN-10: 0-7890-2983-9 (hc. : alk. paper)
    ISBN-13: 978-0-7890-2984-3 (pbk. : alk. paper)
    ISBN-10: 0-7890-2984-7 (pbk. : alk. paper)
    1. Women—Middle East—Social conditions. 2. Women—Middle East—History. 3. Women's rights—Middle East. I. Title.

HQ1726.5.C45 2006
305.40956
                                                                2006001664

This book is dedicated to Umm Ismāʻil: I never saw her face, knew her by more than her eldest son's name, nor could I, the night we met, understand a word she spoke. We haven't met again. Yet, her quiet confidence by the light of her dung fire and the obvious reverence in which she was held by husband, children, friends, and neighbors knocked the flimsy supports out from under my brash Western feminism, sending it into a free fall which finally came to rest in this book.

NOTES FOR PROFESSIONAL LIBRARIANS AND LIBRARY USERS

This is an original book title published by The Haworth Press, Inc. Unless otherwise noted in specific chapters with attribution, materials in this book have not been previously published elsewhere in any format or language.

CONSERVATION AND PRESERVATION NOTES

All books published by The Haworth Press, Inc., and its imprints are printed on certified pH neutral, acid-free book grade paper. This paper meets the minimum requirements of American National Standard for Information Sciences-Permanence of Paper for Printed Material, ANSI Z39.48-1984.

DIGITAL OBJECT IDENTIFIER (DOI) LINKING

The Haworth Press is participating in reference linking for elements of our original books. (For more information on reference linking initiatives, please consult the CrossRef Web site at www.crossref.org.) When citing an element of this book such as a chapter, include the element's Digital Object Identifier (DOI) as the last item of the reference. A Digital Object Identifier is a persistent, authoritative, and unique identifier that a publisher assigns to each element of a book. Because of its persistence, DOIs will enable The Haworth Press and other publishers to link to the element referenced, and the link will not break over time. This will be a great resource in scholarly research.

CONTENTS

Foreword

A few years ago I was walking along a street in Milan with a very radical Italian friend—an anarchist, in fact—chatting about this and that, including "women in Islam." "Muslims hate women," said my friend. "They put them in sacks."

I stopped and looked around. I pointed to one, two, half a dozen advertising posters selling who-knows-what commodities by means of huge photos of women, mostly naked, pneumatic babes. "Do these signs indicate that Europeans *love* women?" I asked.

He conceded that I had a point.

The controversy in France about Muslim high school girls who say they want to wear head scarves has been going on for years. I've been impressed by the fact that not one French political tendency, left, right, or center, has expressed any sympathy for these girls—with the sole exception of a few eccentric philosophers interested in "difference." Foucault was condemned simply for trying to understand modern Islam, much less defending it.

French leftists all seem to assume that the girls are lying or brainwashed by their families, and must be forcibly liberated from their own expressed desire for "modesty." Bureaucratic socialism in France retains its ancient loyalty to Bonapartist centralism and secularism—but so do all the conservative parties. As in America, exploitation of women in advertising is defined as "freedom of speech." In France young women must display themselves regardless of whether they want to. Everyone must be *the same*—an ideology that suppresses Occitan and Breton culture as well as Islamic culture.

Personally, I do not defend "the veil." In fact, even the Koran and Hadith offer little support for extreme modern forms of purdah, which certainly oppress women in countries such as Afghanistan or Saudi Arabia. What I object to are the silly misinformed prejudices about Islam that still circulate as "fact" in Western media and literature—and therefore in Western brains.

A History of Women's Seclusion in the Middle East
Published by the Haworth Press, Inc., 2006. All rights reserved.
doi:10.1300/5666_a

For example, the customs of the *zenana,* and the house-boundedness of women, their *seclusion*—these appear to Westerners as indications of powerlessness. I was very surprised to learn that, in Iran in the 1970s, about 75 percent of all cash was controlled by women. Most Iranian men, it seems, turned over most of their salaries to their wives, keeping only enough for occasional tea and water pipes at the café. Liquid cash constitutes real power, especially in a somewhat "backward" economy, does it not?

Most Western women visiting Iran were horrified by the chador and refused to wear it. Some flaunted their sexuality, defending their "right" to wear shorts in the mosque, etc., and then wondered why they were treated as sex objects. A few, however, came to enjoy the mystery of the chador—an impenetrable mask—and also appreciated the chance to meet Iranian women. Something of this spirit suffuses the anthropological work on the Pathans by husband/wife team Chuck and Cherry Lindholm, two old friends of mine: he researched the men, and she the women. Doris Lessing also captured this mood in her little work on Afghan women during the Soviet War. Most Islamology is written by men, who *never* experience the women's world in any way. Thus do old Crusader fallacies still pose for objective scholarship—not to mention "harem" fantasies, etc.

Another aspect of the veil that rarely emerges in Western writing involves mysticism. The veiled beloved acts in poetry as a metaphor (or manifestation) of God hidden in creation, so to speak. This "tantric" aspect of Sufism is rarely explored, but the great Ibn 'Arabi (who was himself initiated by a woman, and later initiated cloistered women by visiting them in their dreams) devotes a chapter of his *Fusus al-hikam* to the esoteric meaning of the Prophet's "love of women."

This symbolism is not simply a masculinist/patriarchalist device for suppression of women. While living in Iran I became aware that a whole feminine sphere of Sufism existed, including at least one reputed living saint—but that it was totally closed to me. A few women writers (Laleh Bakhtiar, Sachiko Murata) have touched on this hidden world, but no one has ever studied it as a whole.

Ann Chamberlin has tried to do something even more ambitious: to study the veil itself, synchronic and diachronic (back to the Stone Age), *from the point of view of women themselves.* She proposes a startling version of feminism that does not automatically value the modern Western secular-rationalist ideal as an unquestioned norm or telos, but offers a more flexible and phenomenological "field" in which difference can be honored as well as freedom, modesty as well as sexuality, mysticism as well as economics.

In other words, this is an almost totally original work—as far as I can tell. As such, it is fated either to be highly controversial and successful, or utterly ignored and forgotten. It annihilates all the clichés. This is a *shocking book.*

> *Peter Lamborn Wilson*
> *Author of* Scandal: Essays in Islamic Heresy
> *and* Sacred Drift: Essays on the Margins of Islam
> *as well as many co-translations from Persian*

ABOUT THE AUTHOR

Ann Chamberlin majored in Archeology of the Middle East at the University of Utah. She spent a summer in Israel excavating the biblical city of Beersheva and reads Hebrew, Arabic, Egyptian hieroglyphs, and ancient Akkadian as well as English, French, and German. She has traveled with her husband across North Africa, Turkey, and Jordan. They have two sons and live in an old farm house near Salt Lake City. Chamberlin is the author of nine critically acclaimed historical novels. Her trilogy set in the sixteenth century Ottoman Empire was a sensation in Turkey where it spent over a year on the bestseller list. Of her current multivolume project set in Joan of Arc's France, *Publisher's Weekly* said, "Chamberlin deserves an honorable place in the company of such writers as Twain, Shaw and Anouilh." She has also had plays produced across the country from Seattle to New York. *Jihad,* produced in New York City in both 1996 and 2000, won *The Off-Off Broadway Review*'s best new play of the year.

Acknowledgments

I would like to thank those who read either parts of or the entire manuscript at various stages over its long history: Curt Setzer, Lavina Fielding Anderson, Betty Chamberlin, Teddi Kachi, Alexis Worlock, David Greenberg, Natalia Aponte-Burns, and Peter Lamborn Wilson. None of them agrees with everything I say, and some with barely a word of it, which makes their continued friendship and support all the more valuable. They all offered many helpful suggestions and are not to be blamed that I didn't follow them. Thanks also to Drs. Yukio Kachi, Giovanni Tata (and his wife Brenda), Leonard Chiarelli, and Lawrence Loeb for sharing their expertise with me.

I would also like to thank all of the authors whose works are listed in the bibliography, with whom I loved to spend time, as well as Linda Barnes in Interlibrary Loans, Ragai Makar in the Middle East Library, their staffs, and all of the other folks at the University of Utah libraries who helped with my research. My sister Dr. Fran Chamberlin pitched in at the last minute to help with the bibliography.

The generous people at The Haworth Press, Peg Marr and Kim Green in particular, without whom this publication would not be possible, my agent Linn Prentis, and my family deserve the conclusive credit for patience and perseverance.

COPYRIGHT ACKNOWLEDGMENTS

A History of Women's Seclusion in the Middle East
Published by the Haworth Press, Inc., 2006. All rights reserved.
doi:10.1300/5666_b

xiii

Excerpts from Hodges (1972), "Domestic building materials and ancient settlements," from P. J. Ucko, R. Tringham, and G. W. Dimbleby, *Man, Settlement and Urbanism* (pp. 523-530). Proceedings of a meeting of the Research Seminar in Archaeology and Related Subjects held at the Institute of Archaeology, London University. London: Duckworth, reprinted by permission of Gerald Duckworth & Co. Ltd.

Excerpts from Pitt-Rivers (1977), *The Fate of Shechem, or the Politics of Sex: Essays in the Anthropology of the Mediterranean,* Cambridge: Cambridge University Press, reprinted with permission of Cambridge University Press.

Excerpts from Wheatley (1972), "The concept of urbanism," from P. J. Ucko, R. Tringham, and G. W. Dimbleby, *Man, Settlement and Urbanism* (pp. 601-637). Proceedings of a meeting of the Research Seminar in Archaeology and Related Subjects held at the Institute of Archaeology, London University. London: Duckworth, reprinted by permission of Gerald Duckworth & Co. Ltd.

Excerpts from Wikan (1978), "The Omani *xanith:* A third gender role?" *Man* 13:3 (September), pp. 473-475, reprinted with permission of Blackwell Publishing Ltd.

This. . . . is the origin and nature of justice; —it is a mean or compromise, between the best of all, which is to do injustice and not be punished, and the worst of all which is to suffer injustice without the power of retaliation; and justice, being at a middle point between the two, is tolerated not as a good, but as the lesser evil, and honored where men are too feeble to do injustice. For no man who is worthy to be called a man would ever submit to such an agreement with another if he had the power to be unjust.

Plato,
Republic

A man is supple and weak when living, but hard and stiff when dead. Grass and trees are pliant and fragile when living, but dried and shrivelled when dead. Thus the hard and the strong are the comrades of death; the supple and the weak are the comrades of life. Therefore a weapon that is strong will not vanquish; a tree that is strong will suffer the axe. The strong and big takes the lower position, the supple and weak takes the higher position.

Lao Tzu,
Tao Te Ching

The partisans of historical culture seem to congratulate themselves on having escaped from cyclic into linear time, from a static into a dynamic and "on-going" world order —failing to see that nothing is so cyclic as a vicious circle. A world where one can go more and more easily and rapidly to places that are less and less worth visiting, and produce an ever-growing volume of ever less-nourishing food is . . . a vicious circle. The essence of a vicious circle is that one is pursuing, or running away from, a terminus which is inseparable from its opposite, and that so long as this is unrecognized the chase gets faster and faster.

Alan W. Watts,
Nature, Man and Woman

If progress is the end, for whom are we working? Who is this Moloch who, as the toilers approach him, instead of rewarding them, only recedes and as a consolation to the exhausted, doomed multitudes, can give back only the mocking answer that after their death all will be beautiful on earth. Do you truly wish to condemn people alive today to the sad role of caryatides supporting a floor for others someday to dance on?

Alexander Herzen,
From the Other Shore

"You do not think it wise to keep sane people inside an asylum and let loose the insane?" "Of course not!" said I, laughing lightly. "As a matter of fact, in your country this very thing is done! Men, who do or at least are capable of doing no end of mischief, are let loose and the innocent women shut up in the zenana! How can you trust those untrained men out of doors?"...
"But my dear Sister Sara, if we do everything by ourselves, what will the men do then?" "They should not do anything, excuse me; they are fit for nothing. Only catch them and put them into the zenana."

Rokeya Sakhawat Hossain,
Sultana's Dream

Introduction

> Resolutely turning her back upon the house, she set out once more down the path, determined to keep straight on till she got to the hill. For a few minutes, all went well, and she was just saying "I really *shall* do it this time—" when the path gave a sudden twist and shook itself, . . . and the next moment she found herself actually walking in at the door. (Carroll, 1871:27)

Inspiration for the subtitle of this study was taken from this scene in Lewis Carroll's *Through the Looking Glass*. As a newcomer to Looking Glass World, Alice is as yet unfamiliar with its rules. She assumes that one can reach a goal—the garden hill or, later on, the Red Queen—simply by walking toward it with plenty of determination. Time and again she fails and ends right back where she started—at the door to her house.

This reminds me of women seeking equality, trying first one seemingly straightforward path (such as gaining the vote) and then another (such as seeking equal pay for equal work) and always ending up where we began—feeling as if we are in shackles. As one Israeli feminist declared, "it's rather like running up a down escalator—a very unequal battle because the speed of the escalator keeps increasing!" (Morgan, 1984:363) In frustration we may be driven to exclaim along with Alice, "Oh, it's too bad! . . . I never saw such a house for getting in the way! Never!" Can it be that we don't yet understand some of the rules of our world, either?

This book is a study of the origins of the seclusion of women in the Middle East. Seclusion is indeed ending up back at the house again. It is running in and slamming the door shut behind us; but, I maintain, we do fail to understand factors that rule our social life and many of the repercussions of modern mechanized high-speed behavior. We understand them no better than Alice did the rules on the other side of her drawing-room mirror. We compound our difficulties when we

A History of Women's Seclusion in the Middle East
Published by the Haworth Press, Inc., 2006. All rights reserved.
doi:10.1300/5666_01

cling to drawing-room visions of the rules. "Victorian" as we may condemn many of the social values of Alice Liddell's day, I would suggest that the most basic—a Protestant work ethic, grandiose notions of Progress, Truth, Freedom, and Equality, and even the White Man's Burden (underline that "man") as a way of viewing the "third world"—are still very much with us, and are part of the problems women face today.

I must state at the outset that I do not share the philosophy of much research[1] which pretends to be unbiased but which generally follows an argument something like this: Our statistics show that the more Western education a Muslim girl has, the more likely she is to throw off the veil and join her merry Western sisters in the (male-dominated, exploitative) workforce. Therefore, an effort must be made to increase opportunities for these girls to attend schools structured on a Western basis.

What is proven by cultural tautologies like this? If you speak nothing but English to a little girl born of Arab parents, her first words will be English, too. That hardly needs proof. Such simplistic calls for seclusion's removal by cultural imperialist tactics shed no light whatsoever on the practice itself except to confirm that it is part—a very important and integral part—of Middle Eastern society. That shouldn't need proof, either. If seclusion does need study in order to defend it, that's another matter. Calling for its removal as a prerequisite to serious study is, however, like studying the carrier pigeon by first rendering the species extinct, hoping all the information one needs may be contained in bones and a few stuffed specimens.

As a matter of fact, the consensus is that "the veil, if one considers the entire Middle East, is probably spreading" (Beck and Keddie, 1978:9). Beck and Keddie wrote this in 1978, before the ayatollah came to power in Iran; before the Taliban's iron grip took hold of Afghanistan; before the rise of Islamic fundamentalism in Egypt, Algeria, and half a dozen other countries.

Seclusion occupies an extreme position "on any continuum of the ways in which societies define a women's place" (Papanek, 1971:517). It seems only reasonable to take every opportunity to investigate cases in which the dichotomy between the sexes is exaggerated, underscored, and emphasized to enable us to see what could or should be done to attain "equality."

Women's history must break the traditional constraints of that discipline to reflect women's experience. A good history of women will have relatively few names and dates, few provable facts. It will interest itself in the rise, development, and nature of cultural institutions over long periods of time. It will investigate phenomena of a collective nature, as opposed to the individual and the single moment. This history should work, as Western women have traditionally done, by intuition when reason fails. World conquerors are tangential characters, disrupters of home life, recruiters of sons and husbands, baby killers, rapists, and enslavers. Great philosophers and artists are ne'er-do-wells who let their children starve. The philosophy and art in women's history is folk wisdom, folk art. They have greater value because they are inclusive (everyone can participate) and because they have a peculiar ability to protect the defenseless.

The story of women, even in the midst of literate societies, is nine times out of ten prehistory—not reflected or reflected only vaguely and unauthentically in what writing we have. I feel justified, therefore, as prehistorian Bruce G. Trigger (1968) does, in making greater inferences from comparative anthropology from many places in the world and over a wide scope of time.

"Once we begin to examine the role and position of women in Middle Eastern society from the standpoint of women," (Nelson, 1974:559), it becomes clear that most categorizations of the confinement or inequality of the practice "are the metaphors of the observers who are recording the actions of men and women in these societies" (p. 560) in their own Western male terms. Such images are incomplete at best, leaving concepts of dominance and exploitation in human history untouched. At worst, they are dead wrong.

When we approach the experience of seclusion in terms that capture its meaning for real-life women, the harem probably "originated as a separate and parallel government of women by women in the temples of the major priestesses" (Boulding, 1976:60). I believe the custom was initiated by the women themselves, as "a protection . . . and to preserve their own women's values" (Harding, 1971:69), and that it preserves "social ambidexterity" (Boulding, 1976:7), a concept that appeals greatly to me.

This brings us to the ultraradical feminist position that "equal rights in a man's world" are much less important than "a totally different reality, a different language, a different attitude toward power and authority" (Adler, 1986:343).

Chapter 1

Seclusion at Work

An anti-Taliban petition widely circulated online compared the fundamentalist Afghan government's "war" on its own women "to the treatment of Jews in pre-Holocaust Poland. Women must wear full burqa," the petition continues,

> the windows of their homes must be completely screened . . . they cannot work, they are forbidden to go out in public without a male relative. Women are banned from all professions. . . . Women cannot be seen by outsiders and they are not to be heard even in their homes, where they must wear silent shoes and obey and serve silently. (Quoted in Githango, 2001)

Many of the thousands in the West who signed this petition assumed such conditions existed in other places they associated with the word "seclusion." This probably included a spread both in space, to any place crosshatched for "Islam" on a world map, and in time, back to the darkest and most depraved of pasts: the fair white maid stretched helpless at the feet of the dark, foreign, evil enemy.

Now compare this vision to that discovered by an English lady at the turn of the twentieth century. "The term seclusion can be misleading," she wrote, if we think of quiet and peace when we hear the word. In contrast to the Taliban's enforced silence, the harem, or zenana in India, was "a crowded, noisy, even raucous place." During a dinner party in the harem of an Indian woman she attended,

> in addition to large numbers of women guests, there were about fifty servants and slaves all running around apparently at random. The mistress would direct them from wherever she was in a loud shrill voice. [The English lady] asked her Indian friend

A History of Women's Seclusion in the Middle East
Published by the Haworth Press, Inc., 2006. All rights reserved.
doi:10.1300/5666_02

"if Indian ladies generally had such loud voices and command-ing tones," and she laughed and said, "Well, if they have not to begin with they soon acquire them." . . . It takes a strong-minded woman, and one with no mean executive ability, to keep peace and harmony in an Eastern zenana. (Copper, 1915:176)

So which image is most accurate?

I was asked much the same question in Turkey concerning my tril-ogy of novels set in the Ottoman Empire of the sixteenth century: "At one point, you give the impression that entering the harem is a night-mare; 'the belly of the beast,' you call it—dark, evil, serpentine. In an-other place we see bright colors, the loud chirp of birds and the laugh-ter of women echoing off tile. Which is it?"

"But you see," I replied, "in one reference, we are in the point of view of someone for whom the harem is the antagonist to his goals. In the second, we are in the mind of a woman who has discovered the harem as the passage to her dreams of power."

How fiction reflects reality came home to me in the reactions of Turkish, mostly women, readers who said, tears of gratitude running down their faces: "You've captured just how it was. My grandmother told me, and this is just how it was." Other readers, men mostly, told me they threw the book in fury after just a few pages. "You got it all wrong," they fumed. "The Ottoman Empire was the time of our glory. It was a time of purity, not like the Western corruption of today. No Ottoman woman would behave as wantonly as you've portrayed her. She wouldn't have been allowed to live." (I may editorialize that if in-deed the Ottoman Empire were a time of such paradisiacal purity—control—as these gentlemen imagine, I fail to see the glory in it.)

There's the crux of the problem. If a person's mind runs to black and white, perfect good and perfect evil, whether living in the East or the West, and this person cannot hold the possible truth of two contra-dictory views at once, he or she is obliged to choose one view of the harem over the other. He or she chooses the Taliban's evil, since it's the simplest, the easiest, to compartmentalize and control, to sell something to. Whether you're a rabid feminist or a Muslim funda-mentalist, it is the same, and the two poles feed off each other. I've faced the same thing from Catholic fundamentalists when I've writ-ten about Joan of Arc, Jews when I took on King David, Protestants with Adam and Eve. Nobody has a corner on purists with causes to die for.

Since I assume the reader can find scores of books eager to paint the millennia-old institution of veils and grilles with the blackest brush possible, this will not be my purpose here. Decades of study of the history of the institution have led me to these conclusions:

1. Seclusion began as a counterweight to urban—yes, early capitalistic—culture with its greed for the exploitation of women's and children's lives, indeed their very souls.
2. Women were instrumental in both seclusion's rise and its maintenance over the centuries, not because they were benighted and suppressed but rather were attempting to maintain some control within ever-increasing patriarchy.
3. Seclusion's religious overtones are part and parcel of the institution as it stands in opposition to an increasingly materialized world. The religion of the institution's origins, uncomfortable as it may make proponents of "Islamic dress," is pre-Islamic, polytheistic, and goddess centered.
4. Human-caused ecological crises are enmeshed with both urbanization and straitening social institutions.

I hope to lay out my case in the chapters that follow. First, a word about my sources. For a society that says it is intent on breaking down barriers, scholarly disciplines in the West remain remarkably intent on keeping them up. Paradoxically, this study about maintaining and building barriers between men and women will skip through the literature of anthropology and archaeology, history and sociology, as well as times and places that may make the purist's hair curl. My excuse for this is the counterpoise of impression, of allegory, against the dead weight of our current scientific monolith.

Indeed, "my excuse for venturing across disciplines, continents and centuries," exactly echoes that of Marvin Harris (1974:vii): "The world extends across disciplines, continents and centuries. Nothing in nature is quite so separate"—no, not as the harem from the "real" world, but "as two mounds of expertise . . . such efforts must be made more responsive to issues of general and comparative scope."

Thus, for the present chapter, I have created a montage of vignettes, for the purist shocking in their range of time and place but more modern than early, that I hope may help to illustrate how the practice of seclusion works in women's lives. Understanding the mechanics will help clarify the purpose to which the edifice was built in the first place, not as a static prison, but as a social tool, a help to women, all different kinds of women, in their daily activities.

EXAMPLES

One story I particularly like is that told in the novel *Palace Walk* by Egyptian Nobel Prize winner Naguib Mahfouz (1990). The mother of the family in this story, Amina, hasn't been out of the house since she was married, but one day when her husband al-Sayyid Ahmad is out of town, her grown sons encourage her to visit the local shrine of a saint whom she reveres. She finds the outside world bewildering. Unable to maneuver well in it, she is hit by a car; her collarbone is broken. Her escapade now cannot be hidden from her husband, who acts as the law of honor requires and divorces her.

I tell this in support of seclusion? Wait; the story is not over yet. First, let me tell the story of a friend of mine, living in the United States, whom I'll call Teresa. She had been married for seven years and had two children when her husband "Bill" divorced her. He wanted to be a millionaire, and a wife and two kids were putting a drain on the resources. This, too, it seems to me, is a point of "honor" or prestige in our society, as marrying a younger, more attractive woman might be. Al-Sayyid Ahmad, the Egyptian husband, and Bill the American are both dealing in the ultimate currency of their respective male hierarchies of value. Both, we may editorialize, have equally silly reasons to break up a marriage.

In the American case, however, no one stands up and says so. Teresa, never one to sit around when she wasn't wanted, weaned on tales of independence, agreed to offer no contest to the divorce. She was busy helping the children adjust to this difficult time, busy trying to find a job, and so very willing to make the parting short and sweet that she didn't bother to hire legal counsel. Imagine her horror when, arriving in court at the appointed time, she found herself confronted by a battery of lawyers. It wasn't until later that she was able to realize the full impact of what hit her that day. Before, she had always left the financial details to Bill. She had no mind for it, and it was of such concern to him that he made himself good at it. To her grief, she learned the difference between having an ambitious, abrasive, hardheaded man fighting for herself and her own, and having that same ambition turned against her. Teresa had inherited quite a substantial sum from her grandparents and, while she and Bill were married, she had had no objection to Bill using that money to buy a boat and invest in a small rental duplex. Without thinking, and confused by the flood of legal jargon, she agreed in court that, since she had no interest in sailing nor in being a landlord, Bill might as well keep his little projects.

"Too late I realized I'd give my right arm to have half of that duplex for me and my children to live in," Teresa said after she'd been unable to keep up payments on their nice suburban home and she found herself living with her mother (also single) in a tiny apartment, trying between their two skimpy salaries to make ends meet and give her children some sort of future.

Now let us see what happens to Amina, the Egyptian woman. Plenty of Middle Eastern divorces end right where we left her. We are all acquainted with the sorrows of mothers bereft of their children who, of course, belong to their father's clan. However, at least at this point, Amina is in her father's house with her bride-price and gifts (which are traditionally hers to keep), and her children are with their father. The broken-up couple and their children have what Teresa and her children do not: financial security. For Amina, however, yet one more trump card exists. The final court in this case is not before a hoard of briefcases and pinstripe suits that jump to the same tune as her husband.

Enter Mrs. Shawkat, the neighborhood's rich widow. According to Shawkat's scales of justice, al-Sayyid Ahmad's actions are criminal. Cutting across lines of pride and class, widow Shawkat offers to have her son marry the family's daughter if al-Sayyid Ahmad will swallow his pride and take his wife back. How can he refuse? For honor he divorced; for honor he will take Amina back again. Of course, these situations don't always work out so nicely in real Middle Eastern life. Howver, the mechanisms are in place and can be resorted to by the people with greater or lesser success as fortune—not the pocketbook—wills.

"Provision for the consequences of divorce are particularly important in Muslim society," writes Nadia Youssef (1978:81-82) in a sociological study.

> The divorced woman's right to return to her parental home is undisputed. The legal codes relieve her of a considerable portion of child care responsibilities since religious family law assigns

> guardianship to either the maternal or the paternal grandparents,
> until such a time as the ex-husband uses his prerogative to claim
> custody rights over his children. . . . The acknowledgement of
> economic obligations for [the] care [of the divorcée and the
> widow] is considered an unquestionable duty

in return for which the duty to keep the family's moral strictures
seems reasonable enough. What seems unreasonable is the fact that,
though she realizes this fully, Youssef makes another statement: "It is
only when family responsibilities for the economic support of female
relatives begin to be questioned that the present structure of control
and the prerogative of male family members to impose restrictions on
their women will" be weakened (1978:77). "May it only happen
soon!" Youssef seems to say. She doesn't see that this weaked control
is the cause of feminized poverty in America.[1]

For our next example, consider the "intent, self-confident faces"
seen on a group of female activists in Iran early in this century: "It
would be hard to believe that these are women who have emerged
from centuries of purdah if we did not know that purdah involves an
active underlife" (Boulding, 1976:720).

A pivotal part of this underlife is the bathhouse. With its alternate
days for men and women to congregate, the bathhouse plays an important part in creating this unity and self-confidence. It plays such a
large part in traditional women's lives that the subjects of a film on
women in Morocco[2] insisted that the filmmakers (Western women)
come with them to the baths and film. The Western women carefully
took all the shots so you can't see individual faces, but no woman
came that day who didn't want to. Crowds showed up. The Moroccan
women knew their naked bodies would be seen all over the world, but
this weekly congregation of women was too vital in their minds for
prudery. It is in this light we can understand the statement, "The bathhouse alone probably fomented more than one revolution" (Boulding, 1976:720), including perhaps this one over whether Iran should
make peace with a belligerent Russia on its borders:

> Three hundred veiled women marched out from the harems of
> Teheran [sic] to the assembly . . . , tore aside their veils and con-
> fessed their decision to kill their own . . . sons if the deputies
> should waver. . . . Many of the women held pistols under their
> skirts or in the folds of their sleeves. (Boulding, 1976:721)

The feminine point carried this day.

The feminine point also carried the day in the story told by Farid al-Din Attar in his biography of the eighth Christian century Sufi Hasan of Basra. A woman comes to the saint with a complaint against her husband in such a desperate and witless state that she has forgotten to veil herself (Levy, 1957). Rather than being cause for locking the "poor" woman up, however, such a ploy never fails to touch the heart of the potentate.

It did so as early as the time of Muhammad's birth in North Yemen, whence comes the tale of Ruma, the wife of St. Arethas, as told in the letter of Simeon, bishop of Beit-Arsham. It was during the persecution of the Christians by the ruling Jews in Yemen that Ruma was brought before the persecuting king. As she pleaded for her people, she removed her veil in distress. At this all the courtiers were stupefied "because ever since she was a girl, no man had seen her face" (de Vaux, 1935:413).

The veil has often been used as concealment for male weaponry—sometimes in male causes, sometimes not. The old 1930s film *Algiers* records a historical incident of women helping to gun-run the French blockade of the Casbah. Many types of contraband, including banned literature, can be hidden in the harem, as the very popular book *Reading* Lolita *in Tehran* (Nafisi, 2003) testifies.

However, Ayatollah Khomeini's minions deluded themselves when they entered the home, the private rooms, of a woman teacher. This was not a return to the inviolable traditional harem. When they discovered banned books there—by Flaubert, Zola, Rousseau—for which discovery the teacher was hauled out and executed (Morgan, 1984), this was the harem invaded, violated, and forcibly drawn to the male power monolith, as in the greatest crimes of the West. The original harem would protect—indeed, encourage—such deviance. Upper-class Ottoman women were the first to read (in French) books banned from their country. None of the men making the rules, in true, earlier "tradition," would dare invade a woman's personal space to tell her what she might read.

Veils have escorted women safely out of the country when the authorities wanted them to remain in one place, as in the case of Halidé Edib Adivar, a Turkish nationalist at the turn of the century (Fernea and Bezirgan, 1977:167-192). Even men have even been known to hide successfully among their veiled female relatives when they suddenly became unpopular with the powers that be, or in "Arabian Nights" fashion with forbidden romance in mind.

Western men have claimed that the harem hid an infestation of lesbianism. Perhaps this did not exist in either the degrees or the beastliness that these men imagined, but why not? No male would charge a woman with anything if it was between consenting parties behind harem walls. Such a public parade would be too great a blow to his honor.

The best source of the concrete examples is often the anthropological literature, but this is unevenly fruitful. For this study, we demand, first of all, that the fieldworker have close, even intimate access to the lives of women in seclusion. Therefore, she must be a woman. There is "abundant evidence" among male fieldworkers "of an almost grotesque inability even to suspect what women do" (Illich, 1982:88). The same blindness appears pandemic in a world that has embraced men's values wholeheartedly—except, perhaps, to the wife and mother who, having given all her energy to "The Man" all day comes home to "women's work."

Even many female anthropologists from the West have failed to give seclusion a sympathetic eye, either because of androcentric prejudices they bring to the field with them—they often fail to see, for example, the difference "between a symmetric influence and hierarchic power distribution" (Illich, 1983:88)—or because they are not readily accepted into the confidence of the women they are trying to study because of their Western habits. Such habits, of course, usually smack of precisely the evils women in seclusion are taught to shun, for they are the habits of men.

One study that is particularly successful in avoiding these pitfalls is that of Susan Dorsky (1986) describing her time in North Yemen. Studiously, she adopted modest dress and avoided all public contact with men, including her husband, anywhere within the town of her research. She also allowed herself to become personally, sometimes actively, involved in these women's lives and did not try to be all things to all people. Such "tactics" (if one may use so calculating a term) paid off. One of the women gave Dorsky the supreme compliment of asking her to attend the birth of her child and then named the little girl Susan.

Dorsky relates one story of how a group of women forced their point of view upon an abusive husband in their lane. When his wife left him, instead of bringing in food as they normally would do to cover for any slack among their "sisters," they unanimously refused to do so. The man and the brother who lived with him were obliged to take their meals in the souk. Now, according to our Western monolith of values, it is quite respectable to be seen lunching out. If you can manage a fancy restaurant and perhaps a curvaceous blonde on your arm, so much the better. In Yemen, however, eating in the souk "is strongly stigmatized. . . . The food is thought to be dirty and inferior." More important, "it demonstrates social isolation"—the whole street was against them— "and a loss of independence" (Dorsky, 1986: 172). Such isolation seems to be counted a virtue among us, and the loss of that kind of "independence" is what the ad men on Madison Avenue are aiming for. Also, for such an alleywide boycott to work, access to resources must be dually allocated and so severely segregated that it is women and only women who know how to turn raw produce into a meal, although it is men and only men who shop for the groceries. If anyone is to eat with honor, then, it must be (although they do not always sit down together) as a unit of male and female.

As many vital activities as possible should likewise be bisected between the segregated sexes; otherwise, seclusion is, as Westerners see it, a prison. "For the weaker partner in a social structure, the ability to create and maintain . . . a sense of obligation in the stronger is a real exercise of power" (Friedl, 1967:108). Three main ways women do this in seclusion are (1) playing men against each other, (2) seeking alliances and support from other women, and (3) minimizing contact with husbands (Pehrson, 1966). Importantly, women in seclusion do not depend on men for their sense of self-esteem, for the governors and mentors of their lives are other women. Papanek (1971:523) found that Turkish women show much more self-esteem than American women in what are considered male occupations; they "are able to maintain a poised detachment when working with [men] because they are accustomed to a situation in which colleagues and companions are other women." They feel little pressure to measure up to men's standards; they are used to creating their own in a world where to be born female grants one immediate and unquestioned access. I have also found this in my personal experience.

Throughout this book, I will make much of the need for women to have access to independent images and values in their art forms. In North Yemen the male ethnographer may be told that men are intellectually and morally superior. Yemeni women, however, know no such tradition. Indeed, informal skits are often enacted in the harem "in which males and their activities are ridiculed to the hilarity of all present" (Dorsky, 1986:21). Ahmed (1982) recounts the similar products of her teaching playwriting to students in an all-girl school. Since the worlds of the two sexes are so separate, it is these sorts of influences that create a girl's self-image. It doesn't really matter what the men think, or what they tell anthropologists.

Arabic literature, too, has a "distinct literary genre called *nissaiyyat,* from the word *nissa,* or women" devoted to compilations of the lives and deeds of great women. Widely read and acted out in harems across the Arab world, these compilations include feminists not based on copies of Western lives but dating back to the Egyptian poetess Aisha Taymour who was born in 1840 (Mernissi, 1994:128-134).

As for the traditional Western view that the Middle Eastern man despises all children that are not sons, this, too, holds little water. All the usual incentives for boys are present in Yemen, of course: unlike daughters, they will remain in the household after marriage; if a woman is inclined to a life outside the harem (something not at all as popular as Westerners might think), she may indeed want to "live through her son"; so on. North Yemeni women's folklore, on the other hand, is filled with tales of divine retribution on those who don't appreciate the birth of daughters, such as families in which only the daughter turns out to be respectful and filial. Many songs and stories express similar sentiments.

Another insightful ethnography that deals entirely with the separate spheres of value protected by seclusion is Lila Abu-Lughod's *Veiled Sentiments* (1986). Abu-Lughod describes in detail the relationship between sentiments and experiences among the Awlad 'Ali (a Bedouin tribe) and the "two contradictory" forms of discourse that "express and inform" them. There is "a genre of oral lyric poetry of love and vulnerability on the one hand, and the ideology of honor in ordinary conversation and everyday behavior on the other" (p. 10). Women are custodians of the former, men of the latter.

How jealously protective women are of their genre is seen by this example: A woman of a neighboring camp sent her verses on to the home camp through the fieldworker, but, realizing the dubious nature of the bearer, she disguised the source under a pseudonym that only the women could decode. Also, when early in her study Abu-Lughod

(1986) happened to recite one of the poems she'd overheard from the women to her host, asking for an interpretation, her hostess severely scolded her for her "indiscretion" and told her "never to reveal any women's poems to men" (p. 26). These verses are described as being "like Japanese haiku in form but more like the American blues[3] in content and emotional tone. They usually described a sentiment and were perceived by others as personal statements about interpersonal situations" (p. 27) when such sentiments were not socially acceptable according to the male view of things (as perhaps it is not acceptable to worry about a sick child on the job in the West).

When, however, these verses either conspiratorially or by accident become known to those in power to do something about the heartaches expressed, these people never fail to recognize them as "the Truth" and do their best to act accordingly. "I never knew she felt that way about it!" exclaimed the guardian of a girl who hated the prospect for marriage he had been devising for her. He quickly called off the arrangement. Part of his willingness to do so, however, was that his ward had not been trumpeting her dismay all over the camp; he learned of it only by accident. If she had been open, his only course of honor would be to refuse her wishes. Since she displayed an outward face of obedience, he was pleased to grant her inner wishes—because, paradoxically, she kept them within.

In an ethnography describing the lives of the women of Jeddah, Saudi Arabia, Altorki writes that women's influence

> must derive from a different source of power than control of resources. I suggest that the women's eminent control of information . . . constitutes this source. The very nature of the women's exchange network gives them an almost exclusive access to information on which the decisions of their male relatives depend. By manipulating their knowledge to accommodate their own interests . . . , women actually manage to direct or impede the men's efforts. (1977:5)

Altorki limits this knowledge to information relating to possible marriage alliances, which, of course, loom much larger in life in Jeddah than they are allowed to in modern America.

Abu-Lughod comments that

> the structure of information flow between the men's and women's worlds was not symmetrical. Because of the pattern of hierarchy, men spoke to one another in the presence of women, but the reverse was not true. In addition, young and low-status men informed mothers, aunts, grandmothers and (for the latter) wives about men's affairs whereas no one brought news to the adult men. A conspiracy of silence excluded men from the women's world. (1986:23)

We can see two things from this: first, that seclusion is a very effective way to create a blackout if one so desires, and second, that modern America has put access to information in the same hands as those who control the resources. (Unless the data processors of the world [mostly women] should rebel . . .)

American society encourages women to share everything with their spouses. This is the way, we are told, to work out marital problems. Certainly when mobility or other social forces have conspired to give one few close friends outside of the marriage bond (for which one is encouraged to give up all else) there may be no one else to confide in. In my experience, however, this is not very effective; such sharing is likely to be perceived as "nagging" and become counterproductive. Still "morally problematic . . . even in this era of moral permissiveness" when a dozen greater sins are winked at, back-fence gossip may have been railed at from the pulpit and punished on the pillory like witchcraft for more than its ability to "promote friendship, . . . group cohesion . . . [and] self-esteem" (Goodman, 1994:3) among its (usually female) practitioners. The powerful elite fear gossip's power to instill the values of the weaker into a society where caring and emotion, like the speech that evokes them, are unwanted time wasters. The elite may have been too aware of gossip as a means to access the knowledge they dismiss as unimportant, but which is, in fact, vital. Women confiding grievances to one another—needing only to vent, not the immediate "fix" of male-influenced unisex discourse (Tannen, 1990)—sustains stronger marriages than the "honest relationship" strategy. "The distinctive feature of modern totalitarian regimes, as compared to traditional despotisms, is that they manage to invade even [gossip's] territory" (Goodman, 1994:5).

In today's world, we are encouraged to advertise ourselves to our friends (or to protect ourselves against their encroachment into precious territory) by glowing reports of our marriages, showing TV-commercial sides of our relationships except within those relationships alone, where the stress finally breaks us down. No wonder the world of the Awlad 'Ali, "a sociable world in which people hug and talk and shout and laugh without fear of losing one another" is so removed from our experiences. "There is no loneliness," the fieldworker writes wistfully as she contemplates her return to America, "always someone to sit with. I feel so much part of something here. I don't remember ever feeling that before" (Abu-Lughod, 1986:xiii).

Of course, for all the veils and grilles and separate parties, "there are many social situations [in the Middle East] in which men and women must contend with the simple fact of each other's existence" (Rosen, 1978:570), and negotiations between the two realities must take place. Although his account heavily favors the male side, naturally, Lawrence Rosen is not totally blind to the fact that the Moroccan woman's worldview is just about as likely to win in any given negotiation as the man's when she brings all her hidden knowledge, understanding of personal relationships, and kinship reinforcements into play. Can the same be said of an American woman's worldview? She is told to submit to "reason," "power," or the verdict of the bank statement. Because she is supposed to have the same "reasonable" values, she usually does. Moroccan men's worldview tends to blind them to personal relationships with an emphasis on stereotypes, such as "that's the way the world is" or "that's the way women are"—abstractions. So does Western men's worldview but, I submit, in the West it is *the* worldview that all must accept.

When she reads Rosen's description of one such Moroccan negotiating session, the Western reader's first impression is that obviously the poor woman has lost the war and is bowing humbly before the bluster of the man. "Well, I don't know," says the mother of a girl whose father has arranged a distasteful marriage for her. "Who knows what's what? I don't understand it. It's in God's hands."

"May Allah give her pain, that little bitch," says the male friend of the family, called in for consultation. "She makes for such unrest! She is absolutely consumed with passions, like all girls. But we will take care of everything. . . . When Si Abdelqader returns we'll take the groom to my house . . . , make a *fetha* and register the marriage. That will finish the matter once and for all. That will cool your daughter off."

"Well, sir," the mother goes on. "Maybe that's the way it is. I just don't know. Everything is in the hands of Allah . . . " (p. 573).

Rather than "simple assertions of weakness and fatalism," however, as your average fieldworker might have seen the mother's words, Rosen states that

> by her expression and her utterance . . . she was, in fact, implying that the men might think that they have a grasp of the situation but that control over the matter is not theirs alone. This does not mean that it is in the hands of God either. . . . The mother was able to imply that the women were not without additional resources of their own. The references to Allah, then, might be interpreted less as a literal statement of theology than as a cautionary phrase, a sort of conditional marker, an assertion that power is not always what or where it appears to be. (1978:578)

Oh, that Rosen had been a woman, so that he might have learned all that was going on behind the scenes, which he only suspected! That the contestants in this battle were very nearly matched, in spite of appearances, is shown by the fact that a year and a half later when Rosen returned to the scene, the men still had not had their instantaneous will, and the girl was still not married.

Some time ago, Steven Goldberg produced a book titled *The Inevitability of Patriarchy* (1973). As long as our present course in the West is in the direction of ever-increasing hierarchy and linearity, patriarchy is inevitable, and for reasons Goldberg makes clear: no matter what activity is given the prestige and power (or its tangible representative, money) in a society, men will gravitate toward it. Not only that, but they will frequently be better than women in the same field because, Goldberg says, of their biological propensity toward agonistic behavior—what might be called ambition; or aggression; or their ability to extract themselves much more readily from the demands of the next generation in the form of children or natural resources. This is what I call the case of the nutritious egg versus the sneaky cell and will speak of at more length: A woman who has a child has immediately put more of herself in this direction than the child's father and this woman is, therefore, at a greater disadvantage.

Many ambitious women, capable women, are willing to sacrifice much and may actually achieve more than many men. Nevertheless, still today men rise more easily to the top of any given monolith of power and prestige—unless it is a monolith of women, exclusively women.

Goldberg uses the medical profession as an example. When he wrote his book, the number of women in medical school in the United States was a single-digit percentage. The percentage is greater now; the majority of medical students are now female according to a recent Associated Press announcement (Emery, 2003). The reason, I believe, is because of the rapid socialization of medicine in our country. Medicine is no longer the materially and prestigiously rewarding profession it once was. In the former Soviet Union and in China, on the other hand, *doctor* was/is considered a female profession. Because of the socialist system, a doctor gets paid no more than the average worker. This does not mean that socialism is the great feminist utopia. On the contrary, Goldberg points out, when one considers the jobs of true power and prestige—those of officials in the Communist Party— one must sink four or five levels down before finding any women at all. Come to think of it, with the money and prestige incentive taken away, physician is a job fraught with long hours and unpleasant tasks, hardly better than nurse, hardly worth the years of training and toil unless one is truly a nurturing soul.

An opposite shift can be found in cyberspace. Computer programmers in the early years were women as often as they were men, perhaps because of the similarity of the work to traditionally female clerical jobs, perhaps on the wave of 1970s feminism. Today, while "nationwide women hold 11.2 percent of board seats in Fortune 500 companies . . . of the more than 504 available seats at [Silicon Valley companies], only about three percent are held by women" (Silverstein, 2000:2). "Women in technology (28 percent)," complains a recent article,

> are nearly twice as likely as women in other lines of work (15 percent) to believe that gender has been a significant barrier to advancement in their jobs or careers. Additionally, nearly 41 percent of women in technology assume they have to fit into a masculine workplace as a prerequisite for career advancement. (Ericksen, 2001)

As the digital sphere became the place to make (and lose) money, however, and as Silicon Valley became ever more cutthroat, women left in droves—to find something more compatible with family and real life. Medicine, perhaps?

Such conditioning begins at home, but attempts to solve this problem with coeducation seem not to be the answer. The National Association for Single-Sex Public Education (NASSPE) notes that "coeducational settings actually reinforce gender stereotypes. Girls in single-sex educational settings are more likely to take classes in math, science and information technology" (www.singlesexschools .org). In a discussion that included the failure of "separate but equal" education as a solution to black advancement, a female African-American educator mentioned to me how as a student "I always felt like a guest, like I had to be grateful to be allowed to attend" coeducational science classes. This was not because of her race, as minorities were well represented in her Chicago classrooms.

At the same time, boys, who in "smaller and smaller proportion are going on to college" (Conlin, 2003), are more "likely in single-sex schools . . . to pursue interests in art, music, drama and foreign language" (NASSPE) and to resist the distractions that lead to dropping out.

Let us revisit the Middle East. The medical profession was also chosen by Papanek (1971) for examination in her study of modern occupations for women in Pakistan, a country where the financial and prestigious rewards associated with medicine are quite substantial, probably surpassing those currently held in the United States. Here, the percentage of medical graduates that were female in 1961 was twice that of the American percentage and has been growing by leaps and bounds.[4] The reason for this is easy to see: Few women in purdah will allow themselves to be examined by a male doctor. As a matter of fact, in my hometown, the only female gynecologist for years and years (I hunted her down particularly) was a Pakistani. In 1978 in shahist Iran, more women sat for the entrance exams for the school of medicine than did men. In Morocco in the 1990s "one third of the doctors, lawyers and university professors . . . are women" (Mernissi, 1994:139).

Ahmed (1982) extends our doctor example to other callings. "The strict segregation of Islamic societies," she says,

> has meant in fact freedoms for women . . . to engage in activities that their Western sisters engaged in literally at the peril of their lives. For in segregated societies, all or almost all activities per-

formed in the world of men for men and by men must also be performed in the world of women for women and by women. The woman saint, the woman soothsayer, the witch, the seances held for women by women to exorcise or empower (practices for which women were destroyed in the West) are a common and accepted part of Middle Eastern folk life. (528-529)

If the rewards can remain high and equal for serving either a man or a woman, but only a woman can serve a woman, then more equity can reign and break "the inevitability of patriarchy."

Ironically, or so it seems to the Westerner who does not understand the practice and its purpose, many studies have shown that factors that might be thought to discourage veiling—greater political stability, increased contact with outsiders, and emancipation of slaves—may actually be fueling its increase (Pastner, 1972). Increased prosperity, rise to bureaucratic jobs, and rapid urbanization can be added to this list (see, e.g., Vreede-de Stuers, 1968; Pastner, 1974; Shaker, 1972). Clearly, Western tendencies "have not done well in meeting the Middle East's problems" (Keddie, 1980:530), not nearly so well as the older, more flexible answers.

I am not at all surprised to see that Pakistan and Turkey had female heads of state before the United States. Certainly Benazir Bhutto rode her father's coattails, as it were. Few American politicians do not have similar connections. We might have hoped from her (had power politics not interfered) a reign approaching those of medieval heiresses to their fathers' thrones, many of whom won the epithet "the Good." The gene pool is a more liberal dispenser of gentleness than the ballot box.

When a feminist as radical as Robin Morgan (1989) goes among Palestinian women, insisting on female interpreters, and interviewing not just those in bourgeois positions but "real" women, I'm not surprised that she finds women's resistance and rebellion. She will move with them, she declares, "together with all . . . women who have left 'the company of our fellow-men,' and with all the life forms who—like myself and those women—have always been invisible in the 'world of appearances'" (p. 345). The Palestinian women call this American woman—so radical in her feminism that the FBI watches her—"sister" and "the American woman with the Arab woman's heart," and hold out their trust to her. Morgan has never been more flattered in her life.

The article that appeared in 1982 in *Feminist Studies* titled "Western Ethnocentrism and Perceptions of the Harem" (Ahmed) was written by an Arab woman who, upon her first arrival in America, "knew" like every American "knows" that women in the Middle East are hopelessly exploited and suppressed, and who came to *know* after living here for a while that Arab women have much to teach us. The "fact" of Eastern women's suppression, she rightly tells us, was "manufactured in Western culture, by the same men who have also littered the culture with 'facts' about Western women and how inferior and irrational *they* are" (Ahmed, 1982:523).

Do those who follow Islam believe women have no souls? Ahmed finds no indication of this—except among writers who are influenced by Christian theology on the same subject. It is Western men who are down on the harem because of the lechery *they* imagine goes on there—what *they* would do with the (imagined) opportunity. Otherwise they are against it because they fear it, because it "enables women to have frequent and easy access to other women in their community, vertically, across class lines" (p. 524), class lines they are working so hard to solidify.

Is the veil an unbearably oppressive item of clothing? "It is not experienced as such by women who habitually wear it" (p. 523). She gives the example of Lady Mary Wortley Montagu who in the eighteenth century traveled with her diplomat husband to Turkey. While visiting with women in their bath, she had removed her stays and caused a sensation. "See how cruelly the poor English ladies are used by their husbands!" the Turkish women cried. "You need boast indeed of the superior liberties allowed you, when they lock you thus up in a box!" (quoted in Ahmed, 1982:525). Much the same may be said of our modern high heels, or any fashions we use in desperate attempts to ingratiate ourselves to male society rather than mark ourselves off from it.

"Saudi society," Ahmed writes:

> gives individual men control over individual women, nevertheless, the *shape* of that society allows men considerably less control over how women think, how they see and discuss themselves, and how they see and discuss men. Saudi society would seem to offer men less control than Western society, where women live dispersed and isolated among men. (p. 528)

All of this suggests to Ahmed, as it long ago did to me and set me to writing this book, "that it was women who were doing the forbidding, excluding men from their society, and that it was therefore women who developed the model of strict segregation in the first place" (p. 529). Those with direct experience of harem life may exclaim along with England's Lady Craven, who traveled in the late eighteenth century, "I think I never saw a country where women may enjoy so much liberty, and free from all reproach, as in Turkey" (Garnett, 1890-1891:I:440).

"Men and women are different." Virginia Woolf stated the obvious, which is becoming not so obvious in America today (quoted in Pearson, 1992:231). "What needs to be made equal," Woolf went on, "is the value placed on those differences."

A RETURN TO THE TALIBAN

I do not mean to justify the Taliban's horrors—not in the least. But hold up the mirror for a moment.

Pre-Taliban Afghanistan, too, had female graduates of medical school beginning in 1963 as well as female graduates in jurisprudence appointed to courts. Fifty percent of the civil servants, 40 percent of the doctors, and half of the students at Kabul University were women (Armstrong, 2002:2, 55). Afghanistan was the first country "to accede to the Convention on the Political Rights of Women in 1966" (p. 134)—until the same civilization that brought us Stalin and Hitler discovered that this neglected people sat on the "largest untapped oil reserves in the world" (p. 43).

So the United States armed and supported a group of mountain warlords, uneducated men who filtered "tradition" through such oil interests, as a deterrent to Soviet interests. While huge numbers of Afghan war widows were denied the means to go out of their homes to support themselves, "California-based Unocal,[5] a U.S. energy company, was the leader of a consortium to build an oil and gas pipeline . . . to Pakistan. The Taliban stood to gain $100 million a year" from the project (pp. 147-148). "Telephone Systems International signed a $240 million contract with the Taliban to build a cellular phone network in Afghanistan" (p. 148), while children were beaten for flying kites. The black-turbaned leaders would pay for this using money laundered from the sale of opium, of which they controlled 70 percent of the world's trade—destroying the social structure of women in inner cities in the United States and allowing al-Qaeda operatives even faster communication. Members of the Revolutionary Association of the Women of Afghanistan (founded in Kabul in 1977, long before the Taliban) "wrapped themselves in [their] burqas, concealed cameras and notebooks under their garments and went underground" (p. 141). Their version of tradition had taught them to do this, to undermine the oppression by recording—at risk of their lives—everything from beatings in the street to a stoning in Kabul's former sports stadium. Via the Internet, they cried out to women around the world to come to their support in the traditional ways—if such ways existed anymore.

All the while, the men who undermined the power of American unions by shipping the jobs to places beyond the organizers used the tricks of the various clandestine "-gates"—Watergate, Irangate, etc.—turning secrecy's power, covert operations, against women's networks. The Taliban have fallen, but U.S. occupation proves not to be the magic bullet. "Most of the women who have managed to find jobs" there now "are not being paid" (p. 200), and you may be quite certain that the moment oil starts flowing in proper amounts, it will be placed in the hands of men who even now scowl at the unburqaed Afghan woman as she goes about her business. If a modern rogue state, impoverished and war-torn by Western imprecations dating back at least to the colonization efforts of Britain's Great Game, worked with the traditional tools at its hand to emulate the power, the outrages of its Stalinist, Nazi predecessors, should we be surprised? Europe and the United States teach the world to be "modern"—or think they do.

During the Middle Ages in Europe, differences between lordly, political rivals clanked themselves out on the battlefield while peasants toiled away undisturbed in the next field. The rise of the modern nation-state brought with it the efforts of those grown-up political powers to control the laborer as well, to invade individual space in order to put purified personal belief behind the power, first with the witch hunt, then with ethnic cleansing. Any totalitarian regime's first task—and megalithic totalitarianism is the gig in the name of self-defense, the euphemistic homeland security—is to "blur the boundaries between the personal and the political, thereby destroying both" (Nafisi,

2003:273). The Taliban, having seen Western invasion into sanctified spaces of all sorts, having felt the invasion of Western powers seeking to take their wealth as their own, certainly dared.

Another regime, the one that prides itself on being the world's educator, also wants its women to be fantasy objects. "To censor all narratives but its own" (Atwood, 2003:7), it strips underage girls to the bare midriff. What is the Western man's view of Eastern seclusion and why? Why does he stereotype these walls, insist they need to be breached? (He taught the Taliban to breach them, all in the name of political purity, safety.) Why does he complain about the veil? A very thick veil it must be, to keep Lolita from the grasp of the fantasy, as the regime effects the "confiscation of one individual's life by another" (Nafisi, 2003).

I hope these examples have helped to focus and breathe life into the framework of historical seclusion that we will build in the chapters to come. For, merely to have demonstrated historical survival of a custom "is almost a confession of defeat before the challenge to find a contemporary sense" of the practice (Pitt-Rivers, 1977:vii). It is, after all, an explanation of the survival of seclusion that we are seeking; the mere maliciousness of mankind and the passivity, nay, stupidity of womankind not being satisfactory answers.

Chapter 2

Ancient Veiling

ARTISTIC REPRESENTATION

The most obvious proofs for the topic of this discussion are admittedly in short supply. I know of no archaeologist who has uncovered a female corpse with the shreds of her veil about her, nor is this likely. In addition, artistic representations are rare, for the simple fact that the usual reason for such attempts—portrayal of the individual and her beauty—stands contrary to the veil's purpose. Nonetheless, such depictions are not completely lacking, and I offer five of them here with brief comments calling attention to aspects of the execution that help us understand the less tangible aspects of the practice better.

Çatal Hüyük, a Neolithic village (ca. 6300-5700 BCE) in Anatolia, and its ongoing excavation have justifiably attracted much attention from feminists, although it is less clear than formerly that the major divinity is the goddess (Hodder, 1998).[1] Two reliefs on the walls of buildings are of particular interest to us here. Although Hodder is correct that the lack of breasts may cause doubt as to the sex of the figures, or even as to their humanity, the swollen belly has suggested pregnancy to many viewers. One relief is positioned between two red-painted posts and above a red panel, which made the excavator comment that she had "the appearance of coming through a door to show herself to the worshippers" (Mellaart, 1967:114), i.e., from some place hidden beyond their mundane (male) view.

A second relief is from the same level. In this manifestation the goddess "had been clothed in a gaudily painted dress with patterns in red, black and orange and the dress extended *like a veil* behind her between the upturned arms and legs" (pp. 113-114, italics mine).

A History of Women's Seclusion in the Middle East
Published by the Haworth Press, Inc., 2006. All rights reserved.
doi:10.1300/5666_03

Above the final relief are "two holes in the plaster on either side of a slight knob [which] indicate perhaps the former existence of a headdress or, equally possible, they were used to fix a hanging over the sacred figure of the divinity" (p. 115). Before we leave Çatal Hüyük, I should mention a little alabaster figurine, definitely female this time, was also supplied with an indentation to affix something—perhaps a headdress; or, like the pattern that covers our second relief example, a veil?

Often accompanying the obviously feminine figurines are the felines that continue to attend Near Eastern goddesses well into historical times. As Mellaart suggested, "a continuity in religion can be demonstrated from Çatal Hüyük to Haçilar and so on till the great 'Mother-Goddesses' of archaic and classical times, the shadowy figures known as Cybele, Artemis and Aphrodite" (Ibid., p. 25).

Such shadowy figures of women also cling to purdah. One is tempted to see the veiled goddess of Çatal Hüyük, revealing herself to her worshipers in the sacred place where life and death meet. I believe there is a connection, at least of symbols in the ancient feminine mind, between the practice of seclusion and the ancient form of social life as found at Çatal Hüyük. The most important aspects of this social life, which seclusion attempted to perpetuate, were

> a mode of community control in which women and men lived more interdependently, with more sharing of power . . . which enabled women not necessarily to control the society but to express their own values and experiences in it. . . . They created the community's religion . . . devoted to the conservation of life in all forms, devoted to the mysteries of birth and nourishment and life after death. (Barstow, 1978:9, 15)[2]

The great age of such phenomena, near the beginnings of agriculture and in a very early urban setting, would lend what was to come more reverence.

Figure 2.1 comes much separated in time from our first examples, but from no more than 300 miles away. A bas-relief discovered on the Temple of Bel in Palmyra, Syria, from the first Christian century shows the procession of the sacred camel and litter. Known among nominally Muslim desert Arabs as recently as a hundred years ago (Musil, 1928), this is the *'atfa* or *qubbah*. The latter is the same word that is used in the Hebrew Bible—translated in the King James ver-

FIGURE 2.1. Palmyrene bas-relief; veiled women following sacred camel litter. *Source:* Seyrig (1934), Plate XIX.

sion deceptively as merely "tent" in Numbers 25:6-8—to indicate the holy of holies in the "tabernacle of the congregation" during the Israelites' desert wandering. The tale concerning "wickedness" committed with a Midianite woman in this place (which Aaron punishes with a javelin and God with a plague) offers all sorts of interesting parallels to the Bedouin and earlier Palmyrene practice suggested by this image. A young woman, sometimes stripped to the waist, would climb into this litter to go before her tribe as a rallying point in war. Although we can't see the young woman in this case, the artist did provide us with veiled women accompanying her.

We are certain of three things in this case: (1) These veils are pre-Islamic, (2) they are connected with the sacred, and (3) although the tendency is to see the veil as more urban than a product of the desert, here this is not the case. Tertullian (1956) chides Christian women for being so free when the very desert barbarians cover themselves. Intensifying first in the cities, as we shall see, over history, the practice goes in waves out to the hinterland as people are pushed there—and then comes back on backwashes of prudery.

Hints of veiling come to Greece and Rome from Chalcedonia and points east along with Dionysius and his wine skins (Jeremias, 1931). An example is Athena Skiras. Contrary to first impression, this is the aspect of the goddess connected with (1) a woman-only festival in Athens and (2) the vintage and Dionysius, which encourage women to behave in violent and ecstatic ways (the Bacchae) when worship includes cross-dressing and boundaries are broken.[3]

Final mention should be made of numerous examples, in spite of Islamic prohibitions against representation, of the Prophet Muhammad in Turkish and Persian miniatures. One sixteenth-century manuscript in the Topkapi Museum in Istanbul reproduced in Stewart (1967, p. 29) depicts two veiled figures at the death of the Prophet: one is his mourning daughter Fatima and the one on his deathbed—not a woman at all, but the Messenger of God himself. Being so holy, Muhammad's face is never painted. Instead, he does not hesitate to take portions of this aspect of feminine holiness to himself—as Moses did in Exodus 34:33 to protect average mortals from the glow of speaking to divinity face-to-face still upon him.

WRITTEN EVIDENCE

The next most solid form of evidence is written evidence, which does not appear until long after seclusion had been practiced for millennia. Some time between 1500 and 1450 years before the Christian era, a Middle Assyrian potentate erected a large stone on which were carved his decrees dealing with women's concerns—rape, marriage, and so on. Two paragraphs of this stele read as follows:

> #40. Neither wives nor widows nor Assyrian women who go out on the street may have their heads uncovered. Their daughters, whether in street costume or in garments of the house, must be veiled; they must not have their heads uncovered. . . . A concubine . . . who goes with her mistress in the public streets, must be veiled. A hierodule, whom a husband has married, must be veiled in the public streets; but one whom a husband has not married must have her head uncovered in a public street; she shall not be veiled. A prostitute shall not be veiled; her head must be uncovered. He who sees a veiled prostitute must arrest her; he shall produce free men as witnesses and bring her to the

entrance of the Residency.[4] Her jewelry shall not be taken from her, but the man who has arrested her shall take her clothing; she shall be beaten 50 stripes with rods, and pitch shall be poured on her head. Or, if a man has seen a veiled prostitute and has let her go and has not brought her to the entrance of the residency, that man shall be beaten 50 stripes with rods; the informer against him shall take his clothing; his ears shall be pierced and a cord shall be passed through them and be tied behind him; he shall do labor for the king for 1 full month. Slave-girls shall not be veiled, and he who sees a veiled slave-girl shall arrest her and bring her to the entrance of the Residency; her ears shall be cut off, and the man who has arrested her shall take her clothes. If a man has seen a veiled slave-girl and has let her go and has not arrested her and brought her to the entrance of the Residency, and the charge and proof have been brought against him, he shall be beaten 50 stripes with rods; his ears shall be pierced and a cord shall be passed through them and tied behind him; the informer against him shall take his clothes; he shall do labor for the king 1 full month.

#41. If a man will veil his concubine, he shall summon 5 or 6 of his neighbors to be present and veil her before them and shall speak, saying: "She is my wife"; she thus becomes his wife. A concubine who has not been veiled before the men and whose husband has not spoken, saying: "She is my wife," is not a wife but still a concubine.[5]

No one with knowledge of this passage can doubt that the "evil of Islam," as some have called the practice of veiling, existed two millennia before Muhammad was born.

Yet there remain very important differences in interpretation[6] of these passages that can color our entire view of seclusion. Gerda Lerner (1986) is the most impassioned and "conservatively" feminist—if that be not a contradiction in terms.[7] Lerner certainly has her insights, particularly when she labels these laws as a prime attempt of the state to invade the power of the family. However, as she finds veiling a major ingredient in the "creation of patriarchy," and as I hold the opposite view, namely that it is a tool, nay, a weapon indeed, in the preservation of "matriarchy," my comments will be mostly, if unfairly, aimed in her direction.

First of all, the stele on which these laws are preserved is but one of five. The other four are lost or fragmentary; by merest chance, it is the one dealing with women that remains. Then again, these five steles are but one set of laws written by one ruler in one place during one year out of the thousands of years of Mesopotamian cultural evolution. This accident leaves the false impression that Mesopotamians were obsessed with regulating women's behavior. Laws have been promulgated for purposes of propaganda or frivolous reasons before the present.

Even in the most despotic of societies, the declaration of a law cannot mean instant and universal obedience. Consider the modern American speed limit. To expect obedience in Assyria, in a state where almost everyone (particularly the women) was illiterate and where no mass media existed is surely foolish. Certainly we cannot claim that the promulgation of a law by some petty king of Assyria—at that time still a rather backward, northern state, although not without ambition to join the bigger flow of civilization—was the start of such a deeply rooted and widespread custom. (Although I will admit to stranger sources of customs on occasion, some in my own family.) The two sources of behavior—law and custom—are indeed usually at odds.

With her "conservative feminist" outlook, Lerner finds it difficult to understand why upper-class married women would go along with this "new" (she assumes it is new) scheme. Great forces of coercion must have been at play, forces that to this day still tend to divide classes of women from one another and subsume them to the male power hierarchy. Actually, if we notice, this upper class of women is the one group for which the lawgiver found no need to devise a punishment. If it were a newly devised law, wouldn't he have said something like: "Any woman seen without her veil will be given 50 stripes"? Obviously, the wearing of veils was so entrenched among the native, prosperous, more powerful group that no one—not the lawgiver, not the women themselves—could imagine life any other way—or even, desired it any other way.

Should there still be doubts about the customary nature of these coverings for upper-class women already at this date, another Middle Assyrian document clinches the point. This is a medical text in which prescriptions for a woman in difficult labor are given. The woman is in such pain and difficulty, the text reads, that "Her breast is not [covered], her locks are scattered, She wears not veil and has no shame" (W. G. Lambert, 1969:32). So entrenched is the custom that it is a figure that can be used for literary emphasis.

The veil, besides being the mark of a well-to-do woman, was also and at the same time, perhaps primarily, the mark of a sacred prostitute. Mesopotamia provides us with some indications of this,[8] but perhaps the most complete evidence of usage of the veil to denote women's divinity comes from the Bible, Genesis 38, the story of Tamar and her father-in-law Judah.[9]

Briefly told, the story runs like this: Tamar[10] was the wife of Judah's firstborn son. Upon the son's death, being childless, Tamar was passed in fine leviratic fashion from brother to brother. By none of these did she get any children. One day "at the sheepshearing," while sitting around "a widow in Judah's house," waiting for the youngest son to grow up and marry her in his turn, Tamar seemed to have grown bored. She threw a veil over her face and went out "to play the harlot" by the side of the road. Lo and behold, who should come by and snatch up the bargain but (the lately widowed, we are assured) Judah, by whom our veiled heroine conceives—twins, no less! She is prudent enough to demand certain "tokens" of her paramour before they part so that when her state is discovered she can legitimize herself, escape the death sentence for adultery, and be declared by Judah himself as being "more righteous than I."

Here are conundrums galore, not the least of which is how Judah's sons thought they'd be able to follow in their father's footsteps and become patriarchs if they kept practicing coitus interruptus. We are certainly shocked to learn that the reason Tamar never conceived was not her barrenness, as is the usual verdict passed against childless biblical matriarchs, but the fact that her husbands, these virile, pro-life types, kept "spilling" their "seed on the ground." Another surprise is the mode of execution Judah devises for his daughter-in-law when he first learns she is with child: "Let her be burnt." Any Sunday School student knows that this is not the usual punishment for adultery. Doesn't Jesus save the day for another adulteress by saying: "He that is without sin among you, let him cast the first stone at her" (John 8:7)? What is this about burning? In the normal run of things, Tamar should be stoned. Can this be the normal run of things?

Let us consider, then: If fire is not the customary means of disposing of an adulteress, what sorts of things *are* burned? Sacrifices come first to mind. Burnt offerings to the Lord. *Herem,* things off limits for everyday use—because they are holy. We recollect that the conquering Israelites put everything they won from the Canaanites, everything in the cities the Lord claimed for himself, through the purification of the fire. Only that which survived could they keep for their own use—i.e., gold, silver, weapon blades.

Searching elsewhere in the neighborhood for parallels, we find that Old Babylonian practice, with which biblical law has much in common, prescribed death by the flame to a particular class of women, the *nadītu,*[11] the sacred prostitute. This was particularly true if they were found to be with child when "wisdom" alone should "live in their wombs." As human beings devoted to the gods, even for the most flagrant crimes against their station, they could not be executed in the same manner as ordinary criminals. Theirs was the same ritual slaughter as holy sacrifice. It seems clear. Tamar must have been a *naditu,* perhaps the daughter of a local Canaanite lord, married into the patriarchal clan for the powerful connection (not for the children, obviously). The connection seems to have been so powerful that the budding young monotheists did not dare to thwart her customs, even if they had wanted to, which is not at all a given at this stage of the Yahweh cult.

Now everything falls into place. The Israelites compiling the tale many centuries later would have found "a woman's unwillingness to have children . . . inconceivable" (pun intended?), and so they shifted "the responsibility for Tamar's artificial sterility to her husband," whereas now we can see that "the initiative of contraceptive technique would . . . have originated from her, in agreement with her status" (Astour, 1966:192). There is even some indication that the reason Judah hesitated to give her to his youngest son was because the Lord had slain his older sons, i.e., Tamar's power was seen to be such that one did not invite her into one's bed lightly.

"Commentators have paid little attention" to another detail which now stands out as all-important:

> The thing happened during shearing the sheep (Gen. 38:12-13), and this was a major feast in the tribe of Judah and with the neighboring clans of the Negeb. It is known that feasts of the pre-exilic period were accompanied by ritual fornication with

the magic intention of securing rich crops and increase of herds. Judah's visit to a hierodule at that time of the year was a predictable, ritually prescribed act (pp. 192-193),

as was Tamar's part in the festival. Her veil makes perfect, ritual sense.[12] Indeed, we would have been surprised if she hadn't been veiled and perhaps would have assumed it was deleted by later compilers who had to struggle with the story this way and that to make the patriarchs and the ancestress of the clan of David—of Jesus himself—"more righteous than I."

This biography of seclusion in the Bible shows us clearly the origins of the millions of witch burnings this world has witnessed since. "Thou shalt not suffer a witch to live," and, because she is the priestess of a pagan religion, burning is the prescribed method of disposing of her. Paganism is allowed that concession at least, the burning of what is *herem*.

At this point, let us gloss that patriarchy in and of itself is not the bane of women. Women had found a defense against this in their veils, in seclusion. It is biblical patriarchy in its later interpretations, patriarchy without matriarchy, a patriarchy which disallows any parallel power structure, that is the real menace, not only to women and their children, but to anything outside the patriarchal hierarchy.

Now let us return to the Middle Assyrian law. The women who are in danger of breaking the law are those who would like to wear the veil when they (in the view of the lawgiver) would be better without, namely harlots and slave girls. I cannot believe that what we have here is merely a sumptuary law, something to keep the poor from ostentatiously adopting the fashions of the rich. I could be argued into the view that your common variety of pimp-mongered harlot was putting on airs, even committing blasphemy, when she put on a veil. However, as Lerner herself points out, ancient Mesopotamia saw a radical difference (one we can hardly appreciate) between turning tricks for commercial gain and serving the divine feminine in this most sacred of obligations. Indeed, the presence of the veil adds to our understanding of the meaning of the hierodule: A man was to come to her not because she wore short skirts and heavy makeup and he was lured by her particular, *individual* beauty, but because in her facelessness, the sacred prostitute represented all women, or the

Woman. Union with her was not for personal gratification, but for the general welfare, fertility of the land, etc.

We can imagine that the ancient lawgiver did not like the freedom sacred prostitutes enjoyed and wanted to control this subversive element by requiring them to marry before they could be allowed to be "respectable." That takes care of one group of culpable women on this stele. Notice now what we have left: it is precisely the two women *most* under male thumbs, i.e., the slave girl and the common harlot, who would be most likely to try *to escape to the freedom veil* and need definite threats to keep them from doing so. The ancient lawgiver might have assumed he would have male complicity in carrying out this edict. No doubt he—and his soldier thugs—were frustrated that the prize booty of their campaigns kept disappearing into the anonymity of drapery around him. But the majority of men (let's say, everyone but the whoremongers, the unwed military men, and the slave merchants) also needed a good thrashing over their heads to encourage compliance. It seems to me what this law is calling on men to do is to spy into their own harems and report publicly on the private behavior of their womenfolk: Who is it that's welcoming suppressed women into their midst, putting veils on them and making them disappear? This spying would be a severe breach of the customary power and autonomy of the harem. It is a written, male law trying desperately to take traditional female power into its own hands.

Fortunately, I can say with confidence that this attempt to control women's lives by decree failed. Three thousand years later, the great-great granddaughters of this ancient despot were using the same ancient ploys to thwart his great-great grandson. In my mind, it is a law doomed to failure from the start because it is basically unenforceable, regardless of whether it is carved in stone. Although small children are adept at picking their mothers out of a room of veiled figures, adult males in the Middle East are notoriously ignorant of the proximity even of one of their own. Few "bother" to learn the fabric of their female's street coverings, new veils are always forthcoming, particularly among the well-to-do, and, among the poor, a quick switch with a friend provides entertainment—and a ready disguise. The question remains: How on earth was the average man to know if this veiled figure he happened to see (and it is customary for men not to "see" the shadowy figures that flit by the edges of their world at all) was a slave or a lowly harlot? (Or even another man, for that matter?)

I submit that this regulation by the state of sexual mores, as Lerner would see it, was about as enforceable as those laws on the books in some parts of the United States where the sexual positions of consenting adults are regulated.[13]

Chapter 3

Domestic Architecture

Unlike other writers on the subject of seclusion (de Vaux, 1935; Lerner, 1986), I do not see the ancient limit of our study bounded by the explicit and rather harsh regulation of veiling in the Middle Assyrian laws. Our task in the next two chapters will be to demonstrate the existence of separate living spaces for the sexes in Middle Eastern living arrangements as early as the prehistoric era. This is important for three reasons: First, to dispel any notion that, if it wasn't the Assyrian potentate who decreed these living arrangements to women, it must have been another man at another time. The evidence predates any written law, certainly, and predates the time many students point to as the "rise of patriarchy." Second, it provides an idea of what it might be like to live in such spaces and how the physical use of space can be used to arrange and regulate relations between the sexes, their various accesses to power, resources, etc. Finally, Chapter 4 deals with sacred space for the sexes in the ancient Middle East, for it is a point to be proven that, although Islam did not originate seclusion, seclusion is definitely connected with the sacred.

Domestic architecture has suffered from the gross neglect of the archaeologist's spade. Who can blame an excavator for throwing his limited time and funds at the ruins of a palace or a temple, where he is more likely to uncover documents or gold and ivory artifacts to garnish his sponsor's museum? Nevertheless, this is a perfect example of limited resources going lineally to the powers that be. Neglect of domestic architecture is, in fact, analogous to neglect of women's history.

On top of a specific neglect of vernacular architecture has been the general theoretical neglect of the importance in gendered societies of gendered space.[1] As the following descriptive history is read, the details it uncovers should always be compared to the modern apartment,

A History of Women's Seclusion in the Middle East
Published by the Haworth Press, Inc., 2006. All rights reserved.
doi:10.1300/5666_04

which has been aptly likened to the modern garage, both of which "are rationally and economically built for the overnight storage of a productive resource. . . . To the degree that they become more productive economically, both men and women become homeless" (Illich, 1982:119, 122). Even as she chooses wallpaper and curtains, the modern woman must feel somewhat uneasy that it is not really *her* home. It was built by men with profit as their motive; ditto the appliances, furniture, even that same wallpaper and curtains which she may not buy unless they have the sanction of the latest glossy "women's" magazine—which runs under the same motive. "Unisex architecture is necessarily male-sexist, as is the unisex ticking of watches. Such designs place women, in their flesh and rhythms, in double jeopardy" (Illich, 1982:122). Opposed to the modern state of affairs, we have the evolution of domestic space we find in the Middle East.

Although all traditional cultures make some segregation of male and female space, as early as the Paleolithic period, there seems to be evidence that hunting and gathering in the Near East commanded more severe sexual divisions than those created in other environments. In "the arid highlands of Mesoamerica," for example, archaeological discoveries from the "late food-gathering era," 8000-5000 BCE, indicate

> two types of settlements: "macroband" camps, occupied for most of a season by 15-20 persons, and "microband" camps, occupied by 2-5 individuals for anything from a day or two to most of a season. Since even microband camps contain both men's and women's tools, . . . [they may be attributed] to the kinds of "family collecting groups" recorded . . . for the Indians of the arid Great Basin of the western United States. Presumably, therefore, the "macroband" camps resulted from the periodic coalescence of numerous scattered families (who normally foraged by themselves) during times of high food resource availability in certain areas. (Flannery, 1972:25-26)

During the rest of the year, subsistence was based on widely distributed yet stable resources, which each family gathered and stored on their own, as a separate unit.

In contrast, subsistence in the Near East in "the later part of the 'food-gathering' era—20,000-10,000 B.C." (Flannery, 1972:24) centered on herds of large land mammals. Labor-intensive when they appeared, they often had to be hunted for days and at a great distance from base camp. Here the domestic remains suggest that small bands of men only, or men accompanied by but one or two women, made tools with a heavy hunting cast to them and camped for short periods in small rock shelters or in the open. Elsewhere is base camp, with vestiges of a much larger, mixed population and more general, maintenance tasks. There is even a particular women's tool kit which appears alongside the male hunting assemblage from one end of the Mousterian deposits to the other and which shows a different evolutionary pattern. Added insight is gained by the fact that "expedient use" of stone found close to the home base is made in this tool kit. The model the excavators present to us "is that of women carrying out restricted tasks close to the site, making use of local flint sources, and making tools by slightly different techniques than did the men" (Binford and Binford, 1966:283). It seems to be the case in the Middle East at this time that "concepts of descent and territoriality [were] very weakly developed, and *division of labour [was] along the lines of sex rather than families*" (Binford and Binford, 1966:283, italics mine). Therefore, some ecological basis exists for greater task specialization and the division between male and female work groups characteristic of later village life already in the Near East of the late hunting-gathering period.

The next items in our chronology do not elucidate segregation or seclusion much, but they are useful because they point to means domestic architecture used to secure the resources of the family or clan. The growing implication of such means in Mesopotamia points to an increased shortage of such resources and of growing social constraints as to who had access to such resources and through which channels.

Once sedentarization was accomplished—or forced upon populations—the next great change in the physical surroundings of the domestic scene is the change from circular to rectilinear houses. Good examples date to 7000-6500 BCE and come from Beidha in southern Jordan (Kirkbride, 1967:7). I cannot resist the comment that this indicates a switch away from "a non-rectangular, curvilinear mentality" (G. Wright, 1985: 127).

More practically than this, dwellers in rectangular houses were "more selective" in their sharing of resources than those of circular compounds (Flannery, 1972) where anyone, even the soul who hadn't done his "fair share" of the work, could dip in as needed. "Opportunities for intensification greatly increase" (Flannery, 1972:48). Here is incredible power to extract more and more work from everyone for a bit of the wealth the headman may (or may not, since it is hidden) have.

The same purpose may be seen behind the enclosure.

> Now, the idea of enclosure seems to us so simple that we are inclined to assume that it might have originated independently in many places. If we study the material, however, we see that many early settlements are without any enclosing wall. No traces of such walls are reported, for instance, for the primitive settlements in . . . [Egypt]. . . . The same is true of Europe; none of the many villages of the Stone Age around the Federsee in southern Germany had any enclosing wall, which feature appeared here first in the later Bronze Age. (Müller, 1940:170)

The earliest examples of enclosures seem to come from Mesopotamia. Mesopotamia also originated another kink in rectangular living. Figure 3.1, from Jarmo, Kurdistan, dates somewhere between 6750-6000 BCE. Someone standing in the central corridor of the early rectilinear houses in Jordan would have a pretty good view of every little alcove. Now put that same person in the first room she would enter in the Jarmo house, labeled "living or sleeping." She has two turns she could make, two discrete living areas. If the visitor were a visiting man ushered quickly to the room at the top of the figure, the women's areas to the left of the figure, complete with oven and grinding stones, are completely beyond his ken.

There seems nothing wrong in accepting the belief that the Mesopotamian central-court house type, which will become so important later on, did evolve from the enclosure we find at Jarmo.[2] Accepting this is nothing against the idea that Egyptians and Europeans could have invented the idea themselves when they needed it. I believe their culture simply did not need it as soon as the Mesopotamian. It has been suggested that Mesopotamians liked this type because it "gave them such good protection against the marauding bedouin" (Müller, 1940:170). If that is so, why didn't the people at Beidha, there at the edge of the desert near the Dead Sea, find similar practicality? Why wouldn't a communal kraal such as the Europeans preferred for mil-

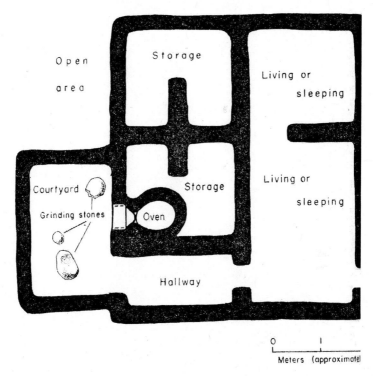

FIGURE 3.1. Jarmo, Kurdistan (Iraq), prehistoric house. *Source:* K. Flannery (1972), 42. Used by permission of Gerald Duckworth & Co. Ltd.

lennia suffice just as well, if it were only "strangers" that caused concern? It seems more likely to me that the private enclosure began as an effective barrier against one's immediate neighbors. "Some early Near Eastern rectangular houses have courtyards which are walled off from the rest of the village; . . . even work space was not . . . shared" (K. Flannery, 1972:39).

Let us investigate more floor plans from Mesopotamia. From the village of Tell Hassuna dated c. 5500 BC and located twenty-two miles due south of modern Mosul we have the excavated home illustrated in Figures 3.2 and 3.3. Here the space which theoretically began as an enclosure for herds and other valuable possessions is unequivocally a court. It is the "primary element of design" here, around which rooms are grouped almost as secondary considerations. This is

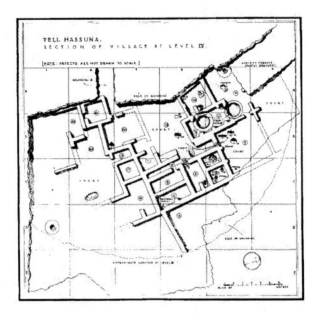

FIGURE 3.2. Tell Hassuna floor plan. *Source:* Lloyd and Safar (1945). "Tell Hassuna Excavations by the Iraq Government Directorate General of Antiquities in 1943 and 1944." *Journal of Near Eastern Studies* 4:4, pp. 255-289. Copyright The University of Chicago Press. Used with permission.

something detailed study (G. Wright, 1985:498) failed to find in South Syrian and Palestinian architecture, even when courts, under influence from the East, became fashionable.

In fact, this prehistoric house is so similar in plan "to houses occupied by Arab fellahin in the modern village of Hassuna" (Lloyd and Safar, 1945:274) that the excavators had very little difficulty with their reconstruction. It might almost be the house visited by Gavin Young (1980):

> Like all the houses here . . . the Haji's house is delightfully simple—a courtyard leading to a few ground floor rooms with . . . floors covered with rugs and mats; storerooms behind . . . The courtyard, which you duck into through a door in a high all-embracing wall, has . . . a garden with fruit trees, flowers and a wooden frame that supports a grapevine. The house, inside and out, is spotless. . . .

At mealtimes, in the dutiful Arab tradition, [the sons] trotted briskly and cheerfully back and forth to the kitchen fetching and carrying the various dishes—lamb stew, rice, bread, vegetables, herbs, yoghourt, and then tea. In the evening, with the same smiling grace, they carried in mattresses to lay on the floor and blankets and pillows, and a jug of cold clear drinking-water from the well, and glasses which they arranged on a small table. (p. 89)

Room 1 in Figure 3.2 is what Young has called "the living room." He has nothing to say, however, about rooms 2, 3, 4, 5, 6, and 15 except to refer to them vaguely as "the kitchen." As a male stranger, of course, he would not be permitted a glimpse of these rooms, even in

FIGURE 3.3. Tell Hassuna, reconstruction. *Source:* Lloyd and Safar (1945). "Tell Hassuna Excavations by the Iraq Government Directorate General of Antiquities in 1943 and 1944." *Journal of Near Eastern Studies* 4:4, pp. 255-289. Copyright The University of Chicago Press. Used with permission.

the interest of "science." His place as honored guest in the north-facing, around-the-corner room served very well to keep him perfectly ignorant of the comings and goings of any of the womenfolk. In fact, as long as he sat there, the women could even carry their lives out into the court (with the sons to run quickly and give warning should the guest make a move to leave) as if the stranger and his world did not exist at all. We may assume that the women who lived in Tell Hassuna seven-and-a-half thousand years ago enjoyed the same kind of freedom from scrutiny.

The next house plan, Figure 3.4, shows a house excavated at Khafajah in the Diyala River plain in the northern part of southern Mesopotamia. It dates to about 3500 BCE and is separated from the jumble of its neighbors in this crowded section of town by dark shading. Note that it has two entrances from the street (three actually, but room 33 may have been a shop): one from street 32 and another from the back

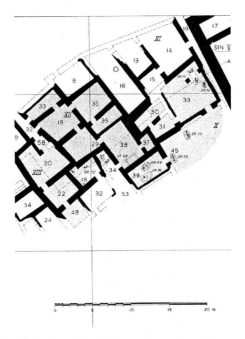

FIGURE 3.4. Khafajah, Iraq, Early Dynastic house with separate entrances. *Source:* Delougaz, Hill, and Lloyd (1967). *Private Houses and Graves in the Diyala Region.* Chicago: The University of Chicago Press. Copyright 1967 by The University of Chicago. All rights reserved. Used with permission.

alley numbered 34. Two sections of the house are created, which communicate only through the doorway near number 29. Perhaps no more is at work here than the front and back doors common in many an American suburban home today. Nonetheless, dual entrances are still used in the Middle East present to keep the comings and goings of one part of the house out of sight and out of mind of the other.

The archetypical Mesopotamian home from perhaps 1,000 years later is shown in the plan drawn on the tablet reproduced in Figure 3.5. It is from the nearby site of Tell Asmar, identified by other tablets found there as the ancient Eshunna. It shows a main room surrounded on all four sides by smaller rooms. Such a house is what all home owners would try—and were mostly still able—to emulate at the earliest levels. However, as urban land values increased, as homes were divided by inheritance, as rebuilding had to take place in what little nooks and crannies were available, concessions to the dream home

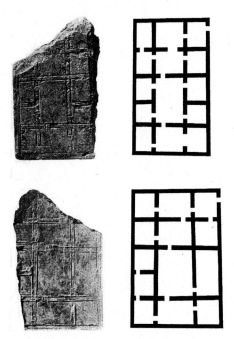

FIGURE 3.5. Tablet house. *Source:* Delougaz, Hill, and Lloyd (1967). *Private Houses and Graves in the Diyala Region.* Chicago: The University of Chicago Press. Copyright 1967 by the University of Chicago. All rights reserved. Used with permission.

had to be made. Granted, two or three thousand years after the dream has been lost, the practical effect for the present generation is the same. Originally, however, when the gulf between rich and poor was not quite so abysmal, this plan was held in common. Although she is totally unaware of the fact, when any modern Middle Eastern woman longs for seclusion, it is a longing to return to a previous common value—now a luxury—for the Middle Eastern city dweller.

Hence the harem this plan provides was neither a late development nor an emulation of the idle rich in the spirit of conspicuous consumerism, as some have suggested. This should allow us to discard the Western thesaurus's synonym for harem as something like a private brothel for an oversexed Eastern potentate. I certainly mean to use the term consistently as this separate, women's "forbidden" part of even modest homes.

Let us look more closely at the version of this archetypical plan represented in Figures 3.6 and 3.7, dubbed the Arch House by the excavators because its fine state of preservation allowed several full arched doorways to be uncovered. At this level it has usurped a block of four rooms from the northeast; but discount those for the moment and remove the main entrance to room 41 instead, and you have the

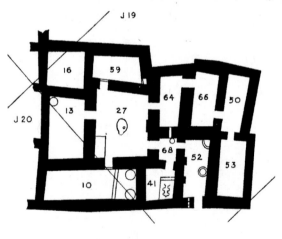

Stratum Ⅴ b

FIGURE 3.6. The Arch House. *Source:* Delougaz, Hill, and Lloyd (1967). *Private Houses and Graves in the Diyala Region.* Chicago: The University of Chicago Press. Copyright 1967 by the University of Chicago. All rights reserved. Used with permission.

FIGURE 3.7. The Arch House window. *Source:* Delougaz, Hill, and Lloyd (1967). *Private Houses and Graves in the Diyala Region.* Chicago: The University of Chicago Press. Copyright 1967 by the University of Chicago. All rights reserved. Used with permission.

typical floor plan. In this plan, as in every case—even the most poverty-stricken—"the entrance from the street is through one of the small rooms at the front and never, as might often have been convenient, directly into the main room" (Hill, 1967:147).* Here is usually placed the bread oven, which, assuming women did the bread baking, would limit their seclusion. However, if we accept the hypothesis that the main rooms were covered at Eshunna because of the heavy winter rains, any other position would make the heat from baking intolerable when summer came.

---

*Excerpts from Delougaz, Hill, and Lloyd (1967), *Private Houses and Graves in the Diyala Region,* The University of Chicago, Oriental Institute Publications, Vol. LXXXVIII. Chicago, IL, copyright 1967 by the University of Chicago. All rights reserved. Used with permission.

"No uniform orientation of our plan, with the larger element [the male reception or living room] and the entrance to the north, exists; but consistent orientation would not be possible in a block of dwellings" (p. 146). "More significant" than orientation of the [male] guest room

> is the avoidance of having the outer and inner doorways on the same axis. Whenever possible, the entrance is so placed as to afford privacy for the small rooms [at the rear] rather than to provide ventilation. . . . It is evident that doorways to all rooms are consistently placed toward the corners and almost never at the centers of walls and that in the case of a long room the doorway is wherever possible at one end of a long side. (p. 146)

> Throughout the plans the arrangement of doorways, frequently with intervening anterooms, was apparently intended to increase the privacy of the inner house. . . . The entrance was always through the front unit, which thus became a vestibule intervening between the public street and the private living room within. Some of the larger houses [even] seem to show a division between public and private parts. This division is best exemplified in the Arch House . . . where the two large units of which the house is composed are connected by only one doorway, at one corner of the . . . main room

between rooms 27, the main room, and 64. "It is possible that the inner part of the house could be shut off from the anterooms, as suggested by . . . a pivot stone in the main room at the northwest jamb of the doorway to . . . 68" (p. 157).

Because the ruins were preserved to such a height in our Stratum Vb we have one final remarkable discovery. The little white gap in the plan between rooms 64 and 68 in Figure 3.6 represents the little window shown in the photograph in Figure 3.7. The window was "set about 1.70 m above the floor . . . [and] may have been intended to ventilate room . . . 64" (p. 157). Or perhaps it allowed the women to check on the baking without actually having to enter the vestibule area. In my view, the window's most important purpose was to allow "visitors to be inspected before they were permitted to enter the more private part of the house" (p. 157.) and to allow the women to observe men without being observed themselves.[3] Every indication in the rubble at the foot of the wall showed that this window had once been fitted with some sort of grille of baked clay or wood. It is a very vital part of the system of seclusion that the women are allowed to see what goes on in the men's part of the house—if they care to. The ability to see and not be seen—practical omniscience—is a form of knowledge that gives power.

And so we have the physical domestic backdrop against which millennia of seclusion have developed and been played out. It should not surprise us, then, to discover that in Mesopotamian artistic representations of men and women in public, they are shown spatially separated; as far as art portrays their spheres of influence, these, too, are firmly segregated from as early as the third millennium BC.[4] We find variations of the theme of courtyard, public and private sections of the houses in the inner city of Babylon consistently throughout history beginning in the last quarter of the second millennium BCE, through the New Babylonian and Seleucid periods. Houses still standing today in Baghdad, from the simple (Figure 3.8) to those fit for a king (Figure 3.9), reveal enduring features.

This may seem merely coincidental until these plans are compared with houses from Tell Masos (Palestine, early first millennium BC), the traditional "Palestinian three-room-house" (often appearing in the four-room variety). Clearly, Palestinian homes were more open and

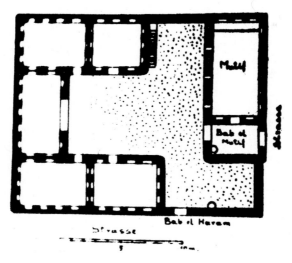

FIGURE 3.8. Recent house in Baghdad. *Source:* Reuther (1910).

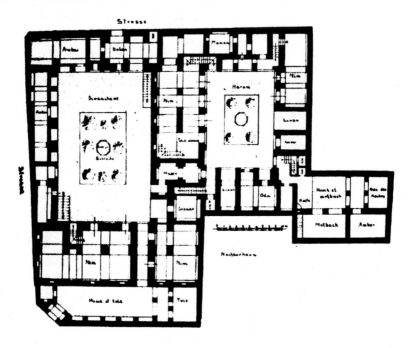

FIGURE 3.9. Recent, palatial home in Baghdad. *Source:* Reuther (1910).

airy using pillars, posts, and columns to support flat roofs (G. Wright, 1985). Indeed the pillar (and its airiness) are proverbial for the house in the Bible: "Wisdom hath builded her house; she hath hewn out her seven pillars" (Proverbs 9:1). This may be a reflection of a more pleasant climate,[5] certainly as far as a more pleasant climate is reflected in more equable social customs.

As the "benefits" of Mesopotamian civilization spread westward across the world, however, so did the benefits of seclusion. By the late Bronze Age, c. 1100-1000 BCE, we begin to find houses that we might mistakenly place in Babylon not in Mesopotamia but in Palestinian Megiddo among the upper classes, for example (G. Wright, 1985).[6] The home plans Alexander and his army discovered in Babylon, portrayed in the Seleucid period, they carried back to Europe with them as the height of civilized behavior. Figure 3.10 shows even wider distribution of the separate-spheres house plan by the first

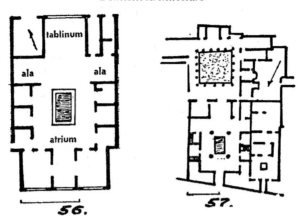

FIGURE 3.10. Houses in Pompeii. *Source:* Graham (1966), "Origins and Interrelations of the Greek House and the Roman House." Copyright *Phoenix,* Journal of the Classical Association of Canada. Published by University of Toronto Press. Used with permission.

Christian century in Pompeii. In that figure's 56 we have the House of Sallust, built along traditional Roman lines with the open atrium in the center. Compare this with the somewhat later House of the Silver Wedding (57), which incorporates the atrium but also adds a women's court at the rear of the house.

A house plan that allows for purdah does not necessarily mean that its inhabitants are obliged to live by that law. Nor does a house plan that portrays no physical sign preclude seclusion in practice. Of this there is ample testimony in lands that have adopted the practice with the spread of Islam. Figure 3.11, for example, is the compound of an extended Muslim family in Nigeria. Were an archaeological excavation to uncover this plan, or, as is more likely, a part of this plan, it would be very difficult to see that it is in any way different from the compounds of many other folk in Africa: even a pair of circular huts, the oldest structures on the site, remain. It takes some modern ethnographic fieldwork to learn that the visits of strange men are restricted to the little enclosure in the bottom left-hand corner, allowing the women to keep their tasks and their seclusion in the rest of the area (Schwerdtfeger, 1972).

Another brief example to warn us from putting too much faith in the evidence of floor plans alone is described in a study of Muslims in

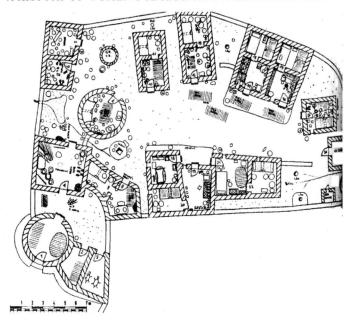

FIGURE 3.11. Compound of a Muslim polygamous family in Nigeria. *Source:* Schwerdtfeger (1972), "Urban Settlement Patterns in Northern Nigeria." In Ucko, Tringham, and Dimbleby, *Man, Settlement and Urbanism.* Proceedings of a meeting of the Research Seminar in Archaeology and Related Subjects held at the Institute of Archaeology, London University. London: Duckworth. Used with permission.

an Indian city (Vreede-de Stuers, 1968). Since the partition of India from Pakistan, these people have found themselves in an increasingly unenviable position as lower-class citizens. Their living quarters are old abandoned palaces where whole families, even extended families, are relegated to a pair of rooms or even a single room. Even when a single room is the home, the women contrive some seclusion with the use of curtains. For hundreds of women in such conditions, purdah means that their faces never see the light of day—but they cling to the practice as their last shred of respectability. The excavator of such an old palace might find the remains of dual courts that indicate how seclusion was practiced in the olden days of glory, but next to nothing would remain to show him or her how it is carried out at this present time.

On the other hand, the plan of a modern Bedouin Arab tent (Figure 3.12) shows just how basic and ancient the physical division of the sexes is to domestic life in the Middle East. The physical division came, as did Abraham, from the cities and their clay walls to the hull of life and worsted curtains in the desert.

It has been said that "the social uses to which buildings are put seem to have much more influence on the style of building adopted than do the building materials used" (Hodges, 1972:523). Some of the examples presented in this chapter are prehistoric, a number pre-class. These hint that the practice was not originally—although certainly it has in many cases become—a means of flaunting wealth and power. The aspirations of the poor to be "respectable" in this manner have more the flavor of a Paradise Lost when seen in this light. Prehistoric Middle Eastern women—as long as the memory of such

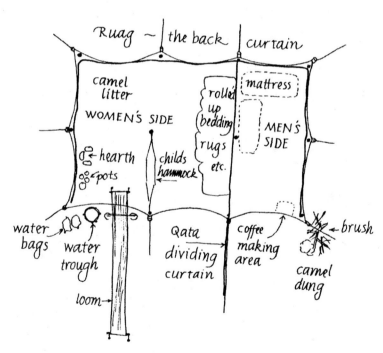

FIGURE 3.12. Organization of a modern Bedouin tent. *Source:* From *Tents: Architecture of the Nomads* by Torvald Faegre, p. 24, copyright © 1979 by Torvald Faegre. Used by permission of Doubleday, a division of Random House, Inc.

things held—may have longed for a time when their separate lives had been relatively more unencumbered by the scrutiny of men. The wealthy could still afford it, along with their secluded courtyards and gardens. The poor, in their cramped quarters and with the demand for outside income to support those quarters, could not. The modern American woman, tending her little pot of chives in an apartment window, may similarly long for fresh garden vegetables, even only in the form of her mother's memories (or the enticements of glossy magazines). More and more, such things, once taken for granted and even grumbled about, are becoming luxuries only for the well-to-do.

The ruins we explore in the next chapter will add the spiritual dimension to the domestic arrangements uncovered in this one.

Chapter 4

Architecture: The Sacred

Missing from the last chapter was any evidence that the sacred nature of women's compounds descended to the modern harem. This chapter hopes to rectify that lack physically as far as possible because it is this aspect of spirit, so hard to pin down, so elusive to the outsider, that makes the difference between the enclosure as a prison and the enclosure as a holy of holies. The rest of our study will be dealing with the spiritual manifestations of this religious practice.

By the time we have written records to help us, ambitious patrilinear individuals trying to escape the religious compulsion of hearth and home had coalesced in that great symbol of state religion, the temple. This was centralization indeed. However, the power of the mothers was too strong to cut the apron strings yet.

Entrances to temples worked similarly to those in private homes. The worshipper approached the god at the top of the great ziggurat in a straight line, whereas the goddess Ishtar is approached in her holy of holies in a crooked path—the same entrances common women claimed for themselves (Martiny, 1966).

IN THE SACRED STOREHOUSE

Matriarchy followed patriarchy to the temple. It was easy enough. The temple was supposed to be the god's house. Naturally, it would have to have a harem. The *giparus* or *gagûms* (women's sections) of ancient Mesopotamian temple complexes are easier to see, both physically when excavated and in their effects in society, as recorded on clay tablets of the time (Weadock, 1975; R. Harris, 1963).

The "lady of the *gagûm*" listed on several accountants' records from the Uruk II level (c. 2400-2300 BCE) was the *nin·dingir,* the

A History of Women's Seclusion in the Middle East
Published by the Haworth Press, Inc., 2006. All rights reserved.
doi:10.1300/5666_05

"lady who is a god," the high priestess, the incarnation of the goddess Inanna herself. Sinkasid of Uruk is known to have built a special section of the temple called an *e·gi·par·ku* (house of the *gipar* foundation) for his daughter Nisi·inisu, the *nin·dingir* (Renger, 1969). Another name for the priestess who made this compound her home is *entu, en* having "the basic meaning of successful economic management; it implies the possession of a power to make things thrive, to produce abundance and prosperity" (Weadock, 1975:102). We know the names of many of these women, most famous among them Enheduanna, daughter of Sargon of Akkad. They were chosen through omens, but usually a close relative of the king, such as his sister or daughter—never a wife—who could be expected to be more faithful to her own kin.

In Ur, the *giparu* was part of the temple compound, a particularly holy part of the "sacred city," "the walled area reserved for gods and kings which occupied most of the northern half of the town" (Roux, 1980:156). "Cloister" and "close" are all translations that this Akkadian word *gagûm* has received. It is itself probably a borrowing from the Sumerian gá.gi₄.a, literally "locked house" (R. Harris, 1963:108) or "storehouse," where produce was stored (Weadock, 1975). "In vocabularies, it is equated with *É nakmītu* and *E kilûtu,* 'a place of hiding' or 'detention' respectively" (R. Harris, 1975:304). It "was a wall-surrounded close in which . . . women lived with only limited direct contact with the outside world" (p. 302).

From as early as 2900-2300 BCE Ur comes the palace excavated in the 1920s, identified as the *gagûm* (Figure 4.1), and it is the earliest we know of on the site only because the excavators dug no lower. Weadock points to two entrances to the maze of rooms, at C1 and A1, both leading to main rooms, C7 and A6 only by circuitous ways, and indeed A5 offering drains for purification before approaching what seem to have been the *entu*'s private rooms. Nearby, in the warren labeled B14-26, were the tombs of her predecessors, who were invited to dine with the living in the elegant B12, serviced by the kitchen in C32. "Offerings were made to the dead *entus* ['the resting ones'] in the hope that [their] power would continue to be exercised for the good of the community" (Weadock, 1975:103). The rooms south and east of these rooms are basically the temple, with the *cella* at C7. Behind it, in C28, were uncovered the remains of a bedstead. This was the *kumma*—"Shamash enters his *kumma;* may the great gods of

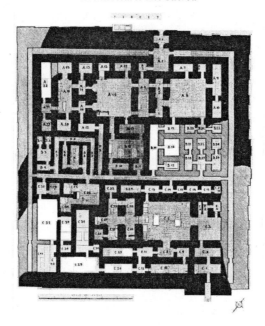

FIGURE 4.1. The *gipar* in Ur. *Source:* Weadock (1975), Plate XXVI. © 1975 by the British School of Archaelogy in Iraq. Reprinted with permission.

night . . . take (their) places" (Weadock, 1975:117)—where the otherwise sharply segregated worlds of the *entu* and the king or priest who represented the God united to cycle the world and bring fertility in the *hieros gamos*. The sacred marriage, celebrating the end of a successful harvest, culminated in the center of the storehouse. The hymn accompanying the rite exults: "At the lapis-lazuli door which stands in the *giparu* she (Inanna) met the *enu*-priest." This would mean so much less if segregation were not the rule the rest of the year.

The Sumerian word for cloister gá.gi$_4$.a is remarkably close to the word for "daughter-in-law," é.gi$_4$.a. "The many pious phrases found in their letters testify to the close attachment which the *naditus* felt toward their 'father-in-law' [the God Shamash] and even more toward their 'mother-in-law'" (R. Harris, 1975:308), his consort, the goddess Aja. The "lady of the cloister," be she originally daughter of the high priest or king or some other authority figure, was first and foremost the daughter-in-law of the god or goddess of the temple to which she was attached. This relationship was consummated, quite literally, in the annual Sacred Marriage. As such, although she might retain her original claims upon her secular or mortal kin, this kin could, in fact, be ignored or overridden when her divine kin so indicated. She lived in a sacred, secure place close to the temple. If magical pegs (see the following section) were not security enough, if age caused walls to sag and expose the sacred to the profane, the *en*-priest or the *lugal* (king) might gain great honor to himself by undertaking the construction of more physical security in the form of massive clay walls; in Old Babylonian times some kings took the names of their years of reign from just such deeds.

Ruined archives of *gagûms* show that "ladies of the cloister" owned vast estates and that they, not their kinsmen, had control over how these resources were used, putting them into fallow and bringing them out again.

Let me indulge in my vision of the cultural organization of the Sumerian cloister. To this haven, to claim a part of these resources, would flock women and their children for whom the slings and arrows of snowballing linear power were overwhelming. They were orphans and widows to male ambition, victims of physical abuse when the stress of others' ambition weighed too heavily on their kinsmen's shoulders, slaves to less noticeable, but no less devastating, economic abuse. They knew they would find refuge in the shadow of the pegged walls. The "lady of the cloister" would put them to work. That was all right. They were used to work. Even if they couldn't function to capacity through illness or pregnancy, with the demands of children at their heels, they knew they would still have a portion of the gods' generosity. Their children would not starve. Indeed, there was honor in the place. These women emphasized the honor by speaking their own, separate dialect of Sumerian (see Chapter 18), by composing lyrics that emphasized their own values as opposed to those of the vicious outside world they had fled.

No doubt "the lady of the cloister," as became her station, was also mistress of women and their children taken captive in the king's latest foray. In light of this, the conflict expressed in the Middle Assyrian laws (Chapter 2) is clarified. It is not impossible to think that the lady of the cloister was overseer of the "women's house," the temple workshops where fine fabrics, the staple of Sumer's lifeline of trade, were woven. After all, women were the ones who understood the mysteries of this bit of capitalism and, although it would be an early target for male ambition, it would take a while for the separation of expertise from control to take place. So, the lady of the cloister would have control of this vast economic resource to benefit her women—even the slaves. As she was not to marry or have children, there would be little use in her selfish ambition. Religion, the religion of her mothers, gave her a vital interest in the welfare of all women.

A much worse life may be imagined than what these slave women found at the end of their road of tears. For those with other skills, the looms were not the only outlets. The cloister needed judges, scribes, cooks. For these women, too, here was security for themselves and their children.

The *gagûm* probably oversaw yet one other feminine profession, the "oldest" of them all. Under *gagûm* surroundings, even those chosen for sacred prostitution could not have found their lot too hard. They suffered from few of the modern ills of that institution. No social stigma was attached: indeed, the mistress of them all participated in the act in the guise of a goddess once a year. Efforts may have been made to prevent conception (see, e.g., Astour, 1966) but the children of such a union were also without stigma, being the children of the god, and they were assured support. Religious taboos would keep clients from demanding acts detrimental to the women's health or committing rape. As for the lack of love present—well, it was millennia before that became something anybody thought was necessary before sex, or even before sexual enjoyment.

Such was the *gagûm* in Ur. The existence of other *gagûms* is known from the texts of Kish, Nippur, Ischiali, and Elam, suggested by the excavations of foundations from Khafajah where one of our private homes is found. Such was the direct ancestress, I believe, of today's harem.

SACRED PEGS

In the Old Babylonian period, i.e., early second millennium BCE, and in the northern town of Sippar, contemporaneously with the great lawgiver Hammurabi, we get the best view of this women's world bustling with activity. The women of this cloister buy, rent, and sell fields and houses, hire laborers, demand payment, incur debts, and come before the judges again and again to unravel the difficulties such activity cannot help but produce—all with a freedom and a self-confidence that is gratifying to the modern feminist.

And yet, all is not well in this Amazonian Eden. At the very beginning of the period, the head official of this complex is a *naditu*[1] "priestess" herself. The *gagûm* has its own (female) scribes who serve as witnesses to the transactions they record. However, these prerogatives quickly disappear. The overseer becomes invariably male, male witnesses are required, and the temple's male *sanga* "priest" tightens his grip on the ladies and their economic activities. There is one record of the *gagûm* demanding—and getting—a judge of their own to hear a case. Once this might have been a guarantee that the women's interests would not be bulldozed under, but this fellow seems to have been drawn from the city's regular judicial body. Although he is called to be the *gagûm*'s judge for this particular case, his fortune and interest must clearly lie elsewhere. This case is of interest because it shows that the *naditu* women expected the prerogative of their own judges and demanded them when much was at stake, when they felt they couldn't get a fair trial from the male hierarchy. Unfortunately, the institution had crumbled. As the city of Sippar herself has become absorbed into the Babylonian empire, the *gagûm*, too, has been sucked into the male hierarchy.

So our trail continues with the reign of Aššurballit I (ca. 1392-1327 BCE), the Assyrian king who laid down the rule for his *gagûm*, which had become a private harem through evolution, we can imagine from the previous paragraphs. Aššurballit's rules say that any handyman undertaking repairs within the palace who happened to pass by certain marking spikes without the knowledge and permission of the "Palace Inspector . . . makes . . . himself due for punishment" (Weidner, 1954-1956:268). Such cones or "spikes" are found by the bucket load in most excavations of Mesopotamian palaces and temples.[2] Cones are found from the Early Dynastic Period (ca. 3000 BCE) until Middle and even Neo-Assyrian times when, although the shape of the pegs was much changed, the basic idea seems to have been the same. Usually made of clay, these pegs must have been of little practical value, for they would shatter if actually nailed into anything. See Figure 4.2 for a particularly elaborate example, of a God maintaining such a peg with his might (from a stele in Elam).

Yet King Hammurabi (1792-1750 BCE) wrote to his underling Samaš-hasir: "I am sending you herewith Sin-magir, the overseer of

FIGURE 4.2. A God claims sacred territory with a peg. *Source:* Ellis (1968), *Foundation Deposits in Ancient Mesopotamia.* New Haven, CT: Yale University Press, Figure 16. © Yale University Press. Used with permission.

the metalworkers; in his presence, drive the peg into the field that you have marked out for the metalworkers, and show all the metalworkers their peg" (quoted in Ellis, 1968:173-174).

Throughout ancient Mesopotamia, it seems, pegs were used, as in this letter, to show ownership of a field, or they were placed in the walls of houses that were mortgaged, etc. They were also used in sacred contexts, in which they seem to have had the same basic intention: "to designate the 'nailed' property as reserved for a certain person . . . The basic idea of the peg in business transactions was that of fixation, hence of reservation" (Ellis, 1968:87).[3] In sacred texts specifically, they marked "the temple area as sacred ground for the service of the god" (p. 90).

More elaborate metal spikes often accompanied by engraved tablets form part of foundation deposits marking the corners of the temple holy of holies, in "a little chamber behind the Ninhursag Temple [in Mari]—a vestibule giving access to the esplanade of the temple to Dagan" (p. 60) (the *kumma?*), or "in pairs, flanking doorways, passages, and stairways" (p. 62). "They were placed in the upper part of walls, horizontally, with their heads either protruding from the wall-face or completely covered" (p. 84). They appear in buildings erected as late as the time of Ashurbanipal (ca. 668-631 BCE), when they were set in a new configuration: "point upwards, in little holes dug in the floor along the wall of the naos in the temple sanctuary" (p. 83).

"Let him lay out the temple correctly," an Old Babylonian hymn exhorts (p. 82): "Let him place the pegs." The "Hymn to Enlil" contains these lines:

> Enlil, when you marked off holy settlements
>   on earth,
> You built Nippur as your very own city. . .
> The Abzu, the holy shrine, so befitting for
>   you,
> The deep mountain, the holy cella, the place
>   where you refresh yourself . . . (Pritchard, 1969:574)

A personage called the *rabi sikkatum* is found in the records, probably "master of the spikes." This was not at all a mean position, as officials of this title are frequently listed first among witnesses in documents. The task of keeping all within these glorified businessman's spikes pure in the cultic sense must have been a powerful and full-time job—like that of the harem's head eunuch under the Turkish sultans? A *rabi sikkatum* of old Assyrian Kül-tepe is mentioned (M. David, 1933:218) as the recipient of a quantity of copper, so it is likely he had charge of the manufacture of these spikes as well.

By the time of the Middle Assyrian laws, holy pegs begin to appear in the palaces. Because the temples themselves were now mere tools of male interests, the holy of holies had retreated to hearth and home again. Here it maintained not only the outward trappings of cult but the sacred function as well. This is substantiated by the etymology of the word "harem" itself.

"HRM"

The root *hrm* is common to all Semitic languages. Its first occurrence is in Akkadian. *Harāmu* means "to separate." Among things which may be separated, we have *harmu,* said of Tammuz and Apsu, meaning a (male) lover. This seems to be derived from *harīmtu,*[4] which we have translated to "harlot" in the Middle Assyrian laws.[5] "Harlot," however, fails to convey religious aspects in English, which it certainly has in Akkadian. From other related meanings, *harimtu* must mean "sacred woman," the two aspects "sacred" and "woman" spinning off in various but connected directions over time.

Interestingly enough, the Kuwaiti dialect of Arabic still has a related term meaning "prostitutes": *banat al haram* (Dickson, 1949:245). It means something similar to "daughters of that which is forbidden." The same Kuwaiti who disparages the morals of such women of the night will use words from the same root to refer, most circumspectly, to his own highly guarded womenfolk. In Baghdad in recent times, certain pieces of ground were by law withdrawn from use, their owners being able to make a profit from them by either cultivation or building. Called *harim,* this usage maintains some of the sense of being preserved from exploitation that I ascribe to a harem of women.[6]

This confusion of the sacred and the forbidden, that dedicated to the divine and the unclean, is remarked upon often in anthropological studies.[7] Biblical usage of *hrm* also underlines this. Old Testament religion seems to prefer *qdš* (related to *qadištu,* the other term for Mesopotamian sacred prostitute) for "holy." I myself have excavated many clay pot handles from an Israelite city at the time of the dual monarchy. On each one was scratched, crudely but definitely, the three letters *qdš,* indicating that the oil or grain in that jar was destined for the temple and was "holy to the Lord." *Hrm,* however, does appear in Hebrew, most frequently as a given name preferred among priestly houses for their male children—maybe even firstborn males, those the Lord demanded.[8] Then there are the passages in Leviticus 27:28f and Joshua 6:17-19 and 7:1-15. These speak of a person or thing devoted to the exclusive service of God (Steinmueller and Sullivan, 1959), viz:

> Notwithstanding, no *devoted thing (herem),* that a man shall devote unto the Lord of all that he hath, both of man and beast, and of the field of his possession, shall be sold or redeemed: every *devoted thing* is most holy unto the Lord. None devoted, which shall be devoted of men, shall be redeemed; but shall surely be put to death. (Leviticus 27:28-29)

Remember Tamar the Hierodule?

Even when we come to the tale of Esther[9] and Vashti (Vashti is identified by Re'emi [1985] as the wife of Artaxerxes II [404-358 BCE]) where it is quite clear that what we have is a harem, the biblical term is "house of women," pure and simple. *Harem* in the sense that we are used to—for the secluded part of the house or, euphemistically, for that section's inhabitants collectively, "women"—seems to be quite a late development indeed.

The *Mu'allaqat,* a collection of pre-Islamic Arabic poems, contains the root twice, referring to fighting and feuding, which were "forbidden" *(hrm)* during the Holy Month, ancestor of what is now Ramadan. Another occurrence does deal with women in a very interesting fashion. The rakish poet 'Antara sang:

> Forbidden *[hrm]* to me is my beloved,
> [i.e., by her vigilant kinsmen]
> Would that it were not so! (Abel, 1891:63)

Although this is not quite the modern sense of harem, we can see how the meaning might have developed. Derivations of the root *hrm* appear over eighty times in the Qur'an, including "Have we not established for them a *sanctuary?*" (28:57), "Turn thy face towards the *Holy Mosque*" (2:144), and "bidding them to honour and *forbidding* them dishonour" (7:157) (Kassis, 1983:544-546, my emphases). The ninth-century CE Hudailian poems contain five related words: *hurmatun,* "god's commandments"; *haramun,* meaning an "inviolable area"; the related adjective; *hirmiyun,* meaning an inhabitant of the *haram* of Mekka; and *harma,* "desiring the male, [said] of a she-camel," i.e., in heat.

By pre-Islamic times, pegs are no longer used to mark this holy, inviolable section of the palace or private home. However, other signs existed, even if only in the hearts and minds of seclusion's practitioners. That all was not always immaterial is shown by Figure 4.3, which was excavated from second century CE Dura Europas, a prosperous caravan station on the route across the Syrian desert. This building has gained much attention because it contains some of the earliest evidences of Christianity in the region in the form of a baptistery decorated with outstanding murals. Of major interest to us here, however, is the fact that the building started life as a private home before being transformed into a church. How the transformation was

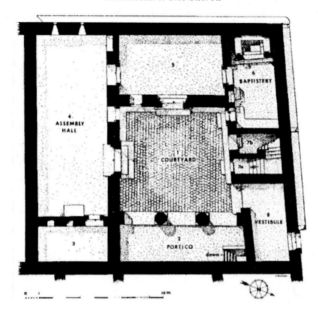

FIGURE 4.3. The Christian building at Dura Europas. *Source:* Kraeling (1967), *The Christian Building.* New Haven: Dura Europas Publications. Used with permission.

made is relevant: the men's sitting room (properly on the southern side of the building facing north) became the general assembly hall into which all were invited; the harem transformed itself into the baptistery and anteroom where the greatest mysteries were explained only to the fasting, repentant neophyte.

Did these ancient Christians realize that a blue faience saucer had been set over the lintel of the door to their holy of holies by the original builders of the house (between rooms 4 and 5)? It was discovered there by the excavators. Such objects help ward off evil spirits. Its place between the harem and the world is a very telling bit of magic, probably repeated over and over again throughout the ages, but it is only rarely that we have a lintel preserved. I suspect the Christians wouldn't have minded it there at all. They must have felt that something very harem-like happened to the soul who chose to join himself to Christ, and evil spirits ought to be left at the door behind him. Remember the lapis lazuli (blue) door at which Inanna met her consort, where the two worlds joined to make the whole?

It seems clear that our present meaning for *harem* is the descendant, not the ancestor, of the *haram* of Mecca and Medina, i.e., the sacred, inviolable center of these shrines. It is probable that the meaning was carried to the safe haven of the home when enough time had passed between the destruction of pagan harems so that the connection was not immediately obvious. Note that there is never any sense, as clings to our Western use of the word, of prison. It is sanctuary, holy, inviolable, not crushed and dominated. It is no coincidence that within living memory the shrines of the holy cities, like the harems of great households, were guarded by eunuchs. At one time a temple sanctuary and a separate place for women were one and the same thing.

Chapter 5

Balance in the Paleolithic:
Sacred Time, Space, and Persons

The connection of the domestic harem with the sacred should immediately sound the alarm and alert us that all is not as it appears on the surface. Whenever we find something categorized by Western scholars as "religious," it is usually some practice that stands against the shortsighted logic of personal gain in favor of the long-term survival of the whole group and the ecosystem. The archaeologist presumes that many remains are religious merely "because they are not utilitarian in our own society" (Piggott, 1972:951). Paradoxically, however, interest in practical living and not mere metaphysics produces these "primitive" beliefs. Most "primitive" peoples are not as certain as we are about where the division between church and state lies.

As a matter of fact, "primitive" peoples "know" what modern folks all too often forget (because the knowing does not suit our definition of what can be known). They "know" that if anything is to survive the onslaught of rational (two dollars plus two dollars equals four) power, it must be subsumed and protected by the opposite of rationality, namely under a coalition of religion and the arts.

There can be no doubt that linear, purposeful thought, the ability to determine goals in the abstract and then go after them, is one of the major things that sets humankind apart from—and at odds with—the rest of our kindred species. What a boon it must have been to naked, clawless, fangless early men to be able to say to one another, "If you go there, and we go here, we can drive this woolly mammoth over that cliff!" However, this intelligence is often in danger of breaking "up social cohesion at certain points" (Bergson, 1977:119), to say nothing of driving mammoths to extinction.

A History of Women's Seclusion in the Middle East
Published by the Haworth Press, Inc., 2006. All rights reserved.
doi:10.1300/5666_06

Assuming . . . society is to go on there must be a counterpoise, at these points, to intelligence. If this counterpoise cannot be instinct itself, for the very reason that its place has been taken by intelligence [in humankind], the same effect must be produced by a virtuality of instinct. . . . It cannot exercise direct action, but, since intelligence works on representations, it will call up "imaginary" ones, which will hold their own against the representation of reality and will succeed, through the agency of intelligence itself, in counteracting the work of intelligence. (Bergson, 1977:119)

Every taboo created by any primitive society must have originated as

a prohibition in which [that] society had a well-defined interest. Irrational from the point of view of the individual, since it suddenly checked intelligent activity without resorting to intelligence, it was rational inasmuch as it was in the interests of the society and the species. (Bergson, 1977:128)

It is thereby that Nature sets "up intelligence against intelligence" (p. 129).

"It is precisely in the place of an instinct that these phantasmic images"—myths, fictions, and cultural symbolism—"arise in the mind" (p. 110). Investing women and their tasks with an aura of "honor," I contend, serves this purpose of ancient taboo, of pitting intelligence against intelligence with the myths and fictions of cultural symbolism.

That this response was relegated to the sphere of the ancient religions in the Middle East should not surprise us. Muslim apologists today who insist that there is nothing "religious" about the practice (hence it should be amputated from their "modern" religion) are deluded. Perhaps Muhammad did not mean to include seclusion in the rational, abstract dogma he was creating. Perhaps it did creep in as dross left over from the "Time of Ignorance," as some apologists suggest. That is beside the point. The point is not to include rational, abstract dogma under the "banner" of religion we are talking about.

Religion, in fact, is "society's defense against the 'dissolving power' of the human mind" (Bergson quoted by Rappaport, 1978a:67). "It is by no means certain," it is further suggested, that scientific representations of nature are more adaptive than the images of worlds inhabited by spirits and unknowable forces that guide the actions of men in some "primitive" societies. Indeed, our "more accurate" . . . models may be less adaptive than the "less accurate". . . models of some "primitives." To invest nature with the supernatural is to provide her with some protection against human parochialism, greed and destructiveness. On the other hand, parochialism, greed and destructiveness may be encouraged or at least not strongly discouraged by a rational naturalistic view of nature. (Rappaport, 1978b:85)

To be complete, enduring, and flexible, particularly in relationship to the environment, cultures or their religions "must find some ultimate way of affirming" (M. Douglas, 1966:164) anything that the intelligence in its pursuit of resources has chosen to brand "useless."

The completest religions . . . seem to be those in which the pessimistic elements are best developed . . . cults which invite their initiates to turn round and confront the categories on which their whole surrounding culture has been built up and to recognize them for the fictive, man-made, arbitrary creations that they are. (pp. 165-169)

Primitive societies almost without exception manage to incorporate rites that do just this. One example Douglas gives is of the African Lele, who for most of the year observe a rigid ritual that seems to fill every corner of their daily life. In particular, they avoid all contact with the pangolin (similar to an anteater), because its anomalous character defies all their laws and ideas of how the world should be.

Then comes the inner cult of all their ritual life. [Here,] initiates of the pangolin, immune to dangers that would kill uninitiated men, approach, hold, kill and eat the animal which in its own existence combines all the elements which Lele culture keeps apart. (Douglas, 1966:170)

In a similar fashion, ancient Egyptians were forbidden pig flesh save on one day a year when, in connection with worship of the goddess, it was ritually consumed (Herodotus II:47). That modern Middle Easterners almost without exception are forbidden this food at all times, while at ancient Eshunna pig bones make up a certain proportion of the kitchen remains, is a cultural conundrum that Marvin Harris (1974, 1985) brilliantly links to the diminishing of resources in the region. Harris does not favor Douglas's more philosophical explanation at all, but I think here we have room to dovetail the theories to this degree: the more limited resources become, the less we are allowed the luxury of even annual anomaly.

Like in a garden, "if all the weeds are removed, the soil is impoverished. . . . The special kind of treatment which some religions accord to anomalies and abominations to make them powerful for good is like turning weeds and lawn cuttings into compost" (M. Douglas, 1966:163). Traditional religions provide rituals which mix up and compost polluting things, rituals which provide "the basis of 'more complete religion'" (p. 165). Traditional systems of symbols cannot have survived the generations if they did not provide this to their people. Unfortunately, philosophies more desperate for resources come to value efficiency too much to stop for composting.

Some more examples of the ways in which "primitive" cultures use religion, rite, and art to protect people and the environment in their variations may include the taboo protection of certain areas, such as "game preserves" where plants and animals may find refuge to repopulate. Seasons, species (as with totem avoidance), or portions of the harvest are dedicated to the divine. Some religious counterbalances to individual intelligence might also be classified as the ritual control of population at levels easily sustained by the environment. Such rituals may include mutilation of the genitals (both male and female), tolerance or even prescription of homosexuality, age at marriage, postbirth taboos, death or nonremarriage of widows, polygyny,[1] ritual abstention periods, and some ritual diets imposed on women in particular. Feuding and "social-ceremonial" warfare[2] ("occasions closer to a contemporary football match than war as conceived in our present civilization" [Forge, 1972:370]), which amount to ritualization (see, e.g., Rappaport, 1968) of the male aggression found in animals, did their part. The reader who doubts the efficacy of anything more "primitive" than pill and condom should investigate accounts of the Gahuku-Gama tribe in Papua New Guinea, whose families averaged only one child per couple (their environment was very strained) (M. Harris, 1989:314-315), or the rural Japanese of the last century who, as a general rule, not only managed to have the perfect number of children per family, but managed "first a girl, then a boy," so the older sister could help raise the son and heir (p. 218).

Hunters and gatherers maintain their populations at desirable levels under carrying capacity also by ritually providing for non-food-producing persons and activities. Non-food-producing persons constitute up to 41 percent of their groups, and those who work do so only three to five hours a day. These nonworking persons may be the elderly whom ritual imbues with reverence so they are not abandoned; the young; and then, members of the population who are able-bodied but on whom religious duty falls more heavily than the duty of gathering food. This last description may include women during their times of "uncleanliness,"[3] shamans, or other religious leaders. At times, this may be all adult members of a community, or a great portion of them, for days, even months of the year when religion calls for their energies to be spent elsewhere, such as on making masks and ritual implements; preparing for rituals; memorizing myths and liturgy; preparing musical, dance, or poetic performances, magic paintings, carvings, elaborate and ritual meals; and even drug or alcohol preparation and consumption. In short, included are any of the artistic, right-brained activities we know and love. I believe that a human craving for these activities is a biological need, not just frivolous "diversion" and "relaxation" (words our left-brained society tends to place under the "evil" flag), and that like any other trait it developed in response to ecological pressures. Those primeval groups who felt they couldn't spend the time to develop these traits overpopulated, destroyed their environment, and left fewer descendants.

Do you remember the story Solzhenitsyn (1975) told? A group of prison camp inmates survived the terrible conditions in Siberia not by each carrying an equal part of the burden, but by pooling their meager food rations to support an old woman among them who did not work but who used her strength to weave them strange new stories each night. In spite of less food and more work per individual, this group lost none to the rigors of camp life, while in other groups, inmates died like flies.

I find most compelling this example from Bali. The ancient ritual life of Bali includes intricate ceremonies to be performed at the hundreds of different temples on the island according to a very precise schedule throughout the year, but no two temples are on the same schedule.[4] It is a strict schedule that requires the population to take time off from their everyday labors of rice-growing to erect elaborate offerings of fruits and flowers and to perform weeklong dances and musical events. All planting labors in the paddies must be forestalled while these activities take place. At one point, well-meaning agents from the "developed"[5] nations suggested to the Balinese that if they ignored the old schedule they might get three crops of rice from their fields in a year, not just the customary two. The climate was favorable to such an expanse in the economic base, and foreign-aid funds were available. The old rituals might even be humored for those who still had faith (modern nations believe in freedom of religion, after all) and, incidentally, for those entrepreneurs who wished to attract the tourist trade. The only requirement was that they should no longer be allowed to interrupt the pursuit of gain and all of its benefits.

Well, the agricultural specialists forgot to take into consideration one small detail, and that was that Bali does not have enough rainfall flowing down the mountain streams to water all of the island at once. When the modern scheme was put into effect, it immediately became evident that if all Balinese were to share the water equally, they would have to take turns flooding their rice paddies. They would have to set up some sort of schedule to regulate the water flow to the various parts of the island. It would need to be a schedule very like—almost to the day—that of the temple ritual schedule already in effect, with one part of the island waiting the month or two it takes to put on a festival in order to allow other parts of the island to have their turns.

The wonderful intricacy of this ecological system became even more apparent when it was discovered (another oversight on the part of the experts) that during these fallow periods, the Balinese traditionally send their flocks of ducks out to the paddies, where they ate the pests and fertilized the soil. Without these periods of fallow, the Balinese would be forced to import fertilizer and pesticides and would be without one of their major sources of animal protein. The developers' plan would not lead to greater prosperity but rather to greater dependency, with damaging effects on the whole population.

It did not take the Balinese long to discover the evil of the developers' plot. They were aided in this discovery by the eruption of one of the island's major volcanoes, a disaster which caused the destruction of villages and the deaths and suffering of many people. Although we may smile cynically and try to refuse this natural phenomenon as a sign of the gods' anger, the intricacy and perfection of the Balinese temple schedule in a culture for all intents and purposes preliterate cannot help but amaze us. I would submit: If this is not miraculous—and, yes, divine—what in this world is?

Some further understanding of these time-consuming rituals can be gained by considering the vestiges that still cling to some of our major holidays. Interestingly enough, it is mostly women who still occupy themselves with these rituals, although middle- and upper-class women alone are allowed the luxury of them these days. Holiday foods differ from everyday fare—and this is true throughout the world—mostly in the time it takes to prepare them. A time-consuming recipe one's mother always made and intricate decorations "it just wouldn't be Christmas without" are hard work, but it is work diverted from mechanical, efficient feeding of mouths to the feeding of souls and community. The guilt one feels when one's tiny urban apartment and pullman kitchen cannot support the traditional "and all the trimmings" effect of a snowed-in farmhouse testifies to the power of the religion that made these rituals.

Suffice it to say that each culture worked with combinations of rituals at various levels of intensity to achieve the necessary balance between intelligence and the environment (in spite of their seeming permanence in the individual's life they were sensible and flexible to shifts in the environment). The hunter-and-gatherer environment protected the arts and religion, and arts and religion returned the favor in a coevolutionary relationship, protecting approximately 80 percent of the environment above carrying capacity as sacred and inviolable.

Any number of other reasons may exist for why a given traditional practice was adopted and why one culture should choose one over another. Not all cultural practices, when closely investigated, are immediately geared to maintenance of life on Earth. But once the flag of religion has been raised, it should signal us to move carefully before we dismiss it as "detrimental" or even "useless."

John Honigmann (1957:161) would have us believe that "purdah [is] neither more nor less suited to survival than certain other culture patterns, like circumcision or the use of drugs." This chapter has shown that drug usage in many primitive societies (when they control both the labor and resources to create their own drugs) may be a way these societies have of siphoning off energy to keep their members from becoming too ambitious against their environment[6]—or anything else within the grasp of that culture that might be exploited to a dangerous degree.

I do believe, along with Honigmann (pp. 161-162), that "it is naïve to suppose that many men could enforce seclusion without the cooperation of their mothers, wives and daughters." Why, then, would women in the Middle East—the setting of some of humanity's greatest and earliest accomplishments that we call civilization—have accepted this "intolerable" oppression for thousands of years? Religions have come and gone in the region so often that surely sometime between the Stone Age and the present they might have been able to replace the harem as the women's Mousterian stone assemblage was replaced—unless the protection it provided against intelligence was something they craved.

Chapter 6

Evolution

Unlike most of the examples of protective religious practices cited in Chapter 5, seclusion was called forth to protect not the environment but something that "primitive" cultures could not imagine exploiting—persons within the culture itself. These persons specifically include women and children, but generally anyone who doesn't fit the optimum (for a culture seeking the most efficient[1] means of exploitation) healthy-twenty-to-thirty-year-old-male mold. It will be the task of the rest of this book to show (1) how this exploitation developed and grew and (2) how seclusion works to counteract it.

It should be obvious that any society which fails to protect its children to the utmost stands little chance of propagating itself very far in the future. Yet, in the United States, close to one-third of the children live below the poverty line, one out of ten children is born addicted to crack, and—well, you know the statistics. Somewhere, somehow, the obvious became not so obvious. To understand how this happened we must go back to our hominid origins.

You were probably given the impression somewhere along the line that human development is all dependent on the large brain; or perhaps at some point you got the prehensile-thumb theory as well. As a matter of fact, much evidence indicates that the first tools were made "by a hand that had still to undergo considerable modification in a human direction" (Woolfson, 1982:20). Bipedalism came shortly afterward; for, in order to carry those tools, free hands were needed. Bipedalism clearly "outstripped enlargement of the brain" (p. 19), so much so that some of our ancestors may have walked with more grace than we do (see Lovejoy, 1980), for an enlarging brain, when it did finally come, put stress on women's pelvises in the other direction. Most recent scholarship must confess that "from fairly early in human evolution the leading edge of its development was provided by

A History of Women's Seclusion in the Middle East
Published by the Haworth Press, Inc., 2006. All rights reserved.
doi:10.1300/5666_07

the first tentative *cultural innovations*" (Woolfson, 1982:21, my italics). These innovations were "underway well before organic development closed." Human beings must be seen as "not just the producer of culture, but in a specific biological sense, its product" (Woolfson, 1982:21).

In some respects the popularity of the large-brain, the prehensile-thumb, and the upright-gait theories of human evolution is understandable, coming from a culture that likes to emphasize the individual as much as ours does. These are traits of individuals, and no doubt stories of the lone Homo sapiens among the Neanderthals have won their permanent place in our mythology on just such grounds. There is nothing "lone" about our earliest development, however. That loneliness is a recent, probably even a historical, development.

"There can be no question that the most critical selective forces on any species are those which directly affect survivorship and reproductive rates" (Lovejoy, 1980:250). These are forces which are more critical, even, to females than to males. Certainly, they are most critical for children's survival. So what is it that gives humans their reproductive and survival edge?

Biologists distinguish between two poles of reproductive strategy. At one pole is the *r*-selective strategy. This is aimed for by fruit flies and oysters. Their idea is to have as many thousands of eggs as possible, investing very little time in each one. With an upbringing measured in milliseconds, a mother can afford to lose many (in fact, most) of her offspring and still rest assured that her genes will appear in sufficient quantities in the next generation. For an oyster, the production of 500 million eggs per year compensates for the fact that she is immobile and has very little intelligence and is therefore unable to care for the eggs at all. It is a successful adaptation for oysters and fruit flies.

K-selection is the other strategy. "I won't go so far as to say that *K produces* intelligence, but the two are certainly related" (Johanson and Edey, 1981:326). Evolution toward humankind favored those with more *K* to their strategy, that is, those who had more intelligence and who spent more time and energy on each of their infrequent offspring—"more brains, fewer eggs, more *K*," to put it simply. These writers propose that, considering the evidence of clutches of fossil dinosaur eggs, which contained no more than a dozen or two dozen eggs, if the ancient reptiles were no better parents than their modern reptilian kin, "you don't have to look for sunspots, climatic upheavals or any other weird explanation to account for the disappearance of dinosaurs."[2] They could no longer compete "in a world that was beginning to fill up with 'K'-oriented mammals that were better parents" (p. 323).

Be that as it may, the modern ape, which produces only one offspring every five years, may have

> pushed that strategy too far. . . . A chimpanzee mother will not become sexually receptive until her baby is about five years old, the practical reason being that she has her hands full with the first one and cannot cope with a second. The biological reason is that nursing and infant care actually inhibit the onset of estrus. (pp. 324-330)

The apes, we are told, run the risk of extinction in the very near future, with or without man's "help," simply because too much care is put into too few infants.

Of all the apish creatures that came out of the Miocene jungle then, it was our ancestors who found a way out of the *K*-oriented trap. Simply put, they did away with estrus. They gave up "some of these sexy visual signals, the swellings and the exciting odors that say, 'I'm in heat'" (Johanson and Edey, 1981:334). A hominid female is sexually receptive at all times.[3]

In fact, most of the differences between hominids and their closest relatives are of particular importance to the female of the species:

> longer gestation period; more difficult birth; neoteny, in that human infants are less well developed at birth; long period of infant dependency; absence of body hair [nothing for infants to cling to]; year-round sexual receptivity of females, resulting in the possibility of bearing a second infant while the first is still at the breast or still dependent; erect bipedalism; possession of a large and complex brain . . . food sharing; and finally, living in families. (Slocum, 1975:39-40)

What seems to have happened is that women (and, less directly, men) were called upon to put ever more into the next generation in order to make culture possible.

The biological cost of this prolongation of infancy . . . was high . . . Selection could only favor [it] if the advantages . . . were great. But they were. The added years supplied the time to learn the skills required by the new way of life, [the culture], and the wider territory. . . . Social skills take the same kind of repetition over the years that sports and technical skills do. (Washburn and Moore, 1974:147)

The prolongation of dependent childhood was only possible with the addition of a male to the mother-infant bond already known to apes. It matters not whether he was the brother, uncle, or husband of the female. What matters is that he freed her from some of the resource culling, defensive duties, and, yes, at times, child care responsibilities, so that dependency, instead of lasting a matter of seconds or up to a few months as among other species, could be protracted to the eight or nine years at which time human beings can first begin to fend for themselves.

So how is the male added to the mother-child bond? We are not an instinctive species. The female, it has been suggested, "begins to rely on some permanent features of her body—her hair, her skin, her shape" to attract the male at all hours and seasons. Lovejoy calls it "being in love" (1980:334). This pushes into the realm of romantic love, which, I believe and intend to show later, is a new and rather anti-female invention. Still, it has its point.

Certain paleologists' descriptions of sexual attraction can raise the hackles of a feminist. More than that, they actually contradict their own theory. It is just at pregnancy (and lactation), the time when the female may need the extra help the most, that the very individual attractions of hair, skin, and shape are lost—maybe forever—at least according to modern taste. Something more has got to be at play here than cultural perks that tell people to fall in love.

The greatest distinctions between early humans and their nearest anthropoid cousins are therefore, (1) that the females are always sexually receptive and (2) that this biological trait was backed up by culture. Our ancestors "did not feed as they ranged. . . . Fruits and plants gathered over a wide area [were] not individually consumed on the spot but [were] brought back to the group and shared out among its members"(Woolfson, 1982:23). Contrary to the forces of evolution on most other species, ours is so constituted that if a dominant australopithecine had taken all the food, the rest of the troop might have perished in hard times, and the dominant could not have survived alone, or have left more offspring. Selection at last began to give the edge to cooperation. The troops that shared . . . became those which flourished and continued. (Washburn and Moore, 1974:139)

"Carrying food, whether meat or vegetables," continues another author (Woolfson, 1982:23-24),

opens the way to storage, sharing, and division of labor. . . . Food sharing and the kinds of behaviour associated with it probably played an important part in the development of systems of reciprocal social obligations that characterize all human societies we know about . . . What is being discussed here is a form of exchange and orderly sharing that is unknown in the animal world.

Most telling, perhaps, is the "home base"[4] behavior pattern which was already "well established 1.8 million years ago at Olduvai" (Isaac, 1972:175).[5] This is the main trait some paleologists use to distinguish hominids from other primates, but it is really only one other indication (and one quite readily found in hominid archaeology) of the more elusive behavior pattern of food and task sharing. It is this sharing and the social skills that go along with it, rather than bipedalism or a large brain—attributes which may give an individual a natural edge or which he may develop with time and energy to his own personal aggrandizement—that can indeed be seen as the sine qua non of human life.

Taking care to remember that the !Kung of the Kalahari are no more "primitive" than we are, their hunting-and-gathering way of life helps us expound on that of our ancestors. We learn that "the key to the success of the !Kung way of life does not lie in the complexity of their tools but in their socially interconnected behaviour" (Isaac, 1972:175), an attribute they share with every apartment dweller in any modern city. "Their basic technology is relatively simple. What is genuinely complex is the shared knowledge of the environment" and the plant and animal species it contains.

We find further evidence as to the antiquity of such social arrangements in the testimony of the footprints from Laetoli in Tanzania.[6] Here, more than a million years ago, a variety of animals scurried as random individuals here and there across an expanse of rain-dampened volcanic ash, but the hominids walked as a pair. Naturally, footprints in "cement" cannot tell us the sex of the members of this pair but, although it is a leap of faith to see the smaller but deeper prints as those burdened by pregnancy or a clinging infant, it is not so farfetched to unite them in whatever was the early Pleistocene epoch's version of the bonds of matrimony.

Let me temper this assertion just a bit and hope that even the most dyed-in-the-wool of "traditional" feminists may then find it easier to swallow. Surely, almost from the start, hominids and then early humans did not see themselves merely as couples, but as couples as part of an extended kinship. The family, the reproducing couple, is now prepubescent boys and girls who must be indoctrinated in the proper ways to extend kin into the future, now the aged couple with aid and advice to offer, now joined to the reverend ancestors. Rather than insist on the symmetry of a couple (which most modern feminists, equal to their culture, can only see as asymmetry—asymmetry fostered in good part by the paring down of kinship by modern "rationalism" to nuclear pairs alone), let us expand it to include a mutually sharing extended family group. For, surely never was there a society before our own that expected a teenager to face a helpless, wailing infant without an older, experienced woman by her side, or the young hunter, no matter how keen his eye or powerful his arm, to face the dwindling waterholes and vanishing game without the wisdom gained in a previous lean year and hidden beneath gray locks and rheumy eyes.

"Family ties, vitalized by ideology," argues even a radical and feminist economist,

> bind together labouring and non-labouring individuals, and secure for the latter a share in the product of the former. . . . In precapitalist societies all the members of the family helped to produce the family subsistence which included support of the non-labouring members, and those whose *individual* productivity was insufficient to ensure their survival [the aged, the young, and women occupied with child rearing]. The surplus-labour involved in this support was appropriated by the family members themselves in the process of family production. (Humphries, 1977:28)

It is precisely at this point, in the competition for the surplus, that kinship comes in conflict with "rational" thinking exemplified by the marketplace and hence is being eroded by it.

Humankind, by having both the ability to produce faster (women do not experience estrus) *and* nurture their children for years, as previously discussed, became the most successful animal of all. But herein lies a very basic and dangerous paradox of our natures. Because the injection of male behavior into the infant-rearing cycle is culturally, not instinctively controlled, its responsibility can change as necessary from uncle to father as the culture finds it useful to become matrilineal or patrilineal. For the very same reason, however, humans can step back from these practices, compare them with other societies, and decide that no one needs to take responsibility for children today because other, more pressing problems exist. They can decide that their personal aggrandizement is better served by breaking traditional bonds of family responsibility. In fact, we can come up with a culture that institutionalizes this irresponsibility: If you cannot demonstrate that a present loss is not regained within five years, you cannot use it as a tax write-off (it takes longer than five years to raise a human child); children (or their proxies) are now the only group of citizens allowed no vote in national elections; we call our system of divorce "no-fault" and in it, one party gets responsibility for the children, the other the benefit of workplace experience and seniority, while material resources of the dissolving family are divided evenly down the middle as if the couple were only two equal individuals who are going their separate ways. It remains to be demonstrated if such a state of affairs can survive another generation. The prognosis is not good.

For millennia, this risk to the human child posed no real problem. No culture before ours wanted the benefits of demanding children and an oyster's irresponsibility as well. A great portion of the culture humans taught their children during this time was the various strategies that the daughters could use to avoid being duped, left alone, or forced to neglect their children, and, to the sons, values that would make them less likely to philander the next generation. Always and above all else was a terrific faithfulness to the group that must survive, even if individuals did not. We can be certain that in the endless years of slow development and experimentation in this direction, the time of dependency could extend no further than the ability of the culture to protect its children in ages to come. Seclusion for the women and honor for the men is a perfect example of such a cultural system, a system developed for the particular temptations an urban society would place before its members to lure them from the coop.

Chapter 7

Biology

It is in place of an instinct to protect the next generation and her own individuality from exploitation that the Middle Eastern woman is taught to seclude herself and to employ all of her intelligence in the very vital maintenance of the seclusion system. It is now necessary to understand why women instead of men were obliged to take on the burden of seclusion in order to see the society into the next generation, why women are inherently more exploitable than men. This is not a mere chance fall of the dice. If adults are going to intellectualize their way out of responsibility, women are not as free to do it as men. They do not "make oysters" as easily as men. This is not something culturally determined. We can not hope for better systems of child rearing to equalize things in the future. (How can we hope for better child rearing practices anyway, if all adults are going to become oysters and put all their energies into something else?)

Woman's closer connection to children and her ability to identify with all things exploitable is in the biology. As the past forty years of scholarship have struggled so valiantly against the "biology is destiny" ideology, I know I utter heresy here. However, to fail to accept this, as I'm afraid much feminist scholarship does, is to open women up to greater exploitation than ever, if only in the form of greater risk of medical malpractice as attempts are made to make female chemistry male.

In *The Selfish Gene* (1976) biologist Richard Dawkins creates an interesting scenario of the evolution of the two sexes that is of particular importance to our topic. He theorizes that originally a type of "sexual" reproduction existed in which all sex cells were the same. (He is speaking, of course, of matters long before humans appeared on the scene.) "Maleness and femaleness [did] not occur [and] anybody [could] mate with anybody else." This state of affairs still exists

A History of Women's Seclusion in the Middle East
Published by the Haworth Press, Inc., 2006. All rights reserved.
doi:10.1300/5666_08

today among "certain primitive organisms, for instance, some fungi" (p. 152).

By the natural variation of biology, however, some cells were bigger than others and obviously these bigger ones had an evolutionary edge; they provided more energy and nutrition to get their offspring off to a good start. These Dawkins dubs the "honest" cells, for they no sooner had established themselves when other cells found that by making themselves tiny yet fast-moving, they could mate with more of the big, more stationary cells in the same amount of time. They could also spend their energy producing more cells. Both strategies made them very biologically successful vis-à-vis the bigger cells. Dawkins calls these cells "sneaky."

In this scenario, the only losers in the long, evolutionary sense were those cells in the middle. They did not supply enough energy to make their offspring successful, nor were they fast enough to get to the large cells before the little ones.

> The sneaky ones would have evolved smaller and smaller size and faster mobility. The honest ones would have evolved larger and larger size, to compensate for the ever-smaller investment contributed by the sneaky ones. . . . Each honest one would "prefer" to fuse with another honest one. . . . The sneaky ones had more to lose and they therefore won the evolutionary battle. The honest ones became eggs, and the sneaky ones became sperms. (Dawkins, 1976:154)

In all the thousands of plant and animal species that today reproduce bisexually, this is the one criterion biologists use to tell male from female (so much variation exists that any other criterion is impossible): "One group of individuals has large sex cells. . . . The other group . . . has small sex cells" (Dawkins, 1976:151)

Under this system,

> if one parent can get away with investing less than his or her fair share of costly resources in each child, . . . he will be better off, since he will have more to spend on other children[1] by other sexual partners, and so propagate more of his genes. Each partner can therefore be thought of as trying to exploit the other, trying to force the other one to invest more. . . . Since she starts by investing more than the male, in the form of her large, food-rich egg, a

mother . . . stands to lose more if the child dies than the father does. More to the point, she would have to invest more than the father *in the future* in order to bring a new substitute child up to the same level of development. . . . Therefore . . . if any abandoning is going to be done, it is likely to be the father who abandons the mother rather than the other way around. . . . The female sex is exploited, and the fundamental evolutionary basis for the exploitation is the fact that eggs are larger than sperms. (Dawkins, 1976: 151, 157-158)

That's the biology. We're stuck with it, and all the culture in the world cannot change but only attempt to work with or somewhat alleviate its harshness. Any more altruistic system "is inherently unstable" (p. 126). If we want our children to be otherwise, we must teach them to be so, "for we cannot expect it to be part of their biological nature" (p. 150).

Humans, unlike birds of paradise or elephant seals, cannot be expected to develop either restraint or coyness, or another suggested defense, that of being able to see through the philanderers, by instinct. "As a species," Marvin Harris (1979:62) remarks, "we have been selected for our ability to acquire elaborate repertoires of socially learned responses, rather than for species-specific drives and instincts." In our case, therefore, it is cultural indoctrination that must give the woman the protection she needs—and if the culture is really seeking stability, it must provide for her, too, in the off chance that even its collective wisdom is duped.[2] What could be more coy and reserved than a woman behind her grille in the harem?

It would need no more than this sinking of more of ourselves into the next generation from the instant of conception in our biology to make exploitation a danger. However, a feminist who is first of all a woman and is not trying to be a man realizes that other factors of her biology are bowled over in the modern press for "equality." To her, it is obvious that men are different from women. When she notes findings that the corpus callosum, which facillitates communication between the brain's two hemispheres, is wider in female brains, implying a greater ease and frequency of cerebral communication in females than in males (Morgan, 1989), she doesn't cry "We need more study!" This has been her intuition all along. When she sees "the growing number of studies linking formative testosterone (in utero), as well as that circulating post-puberty, with aggression and with 'homicidal violence, whether spontaneous and outlawed or organized and sanctioned for military purposes'" (p. 336), she does not say, "Come out in the parking lot and prove it, buddy," nor does she sign up for the closest assertiveness training class nor investigate testosterone therapy for herself. She only wonders what convulsions of irrationality have led to the present impasse where compartmentalization and aggression are seen as virtues for everyone, for anyone, never mind just for the male minority of human beings. She toys with the idea of "conceiving a society wise enough to compensate for biological difference" (p. 336), rather than trying to cram one through the (male) courts that will ignore both scientific evidence and her own intuition.

"We are not the same as men!" she cries. "It's an insult to say so. The 'same' is a standard defined *by* men—and is as aberrant as any standard defined by only a part declaiming itself to be the entity."

If she dabbles in history (or prehistory, which, as a woman, is more her provenance), she will soon become aware that most human societies—before our own—did indeed make such compensation. In many instances these compensations are just the "inequalities" that her feminist sisters—and perhaps she herself—have been misunderstanding and railing against for so long.

And then she understands the "honest cell/sneaky cell syndrome," and other issues become clear to her.

A female psychiatrist observes that the loss or even threatened disruption of relationships is perceived by women "not just as a loss of a relationship but as something closer to a total loss of self " (J. Miller, 1986:83). Men, on the other hand, are observed to feel that relationships are an "impediment" or a danger, secondary to their self-image and something a man "can afford *only* after he had fulfilled the primary requirements of manhood" (J. Miller, 1986:69). The feminist doesn't then blame outmoded child-rearing practices for the female neurosis; she blames biology—biology she can do nothing about but try and arrange those child-rearing practices (which is hardly a one-woman job) so that part of a man's manhood *must be* connected to how well he maintains lasting, helping relationships, particularly with women.

The feminist sees why, in a "free" society in which one is encouraged to be as sneaky as one can be, she can initiate moves for civil rights or sound ecology, only to have the power of these movements taken over by men with male objectives. Race and clean air affect men as well as women.[3] But once these same men are comfortable, do you think these sneaky cells, freed to total sneakiness, are going to come and join her when she tries to get child care or maternity benefits, little Band-Aids, really, for the total worldwide crisis of honest cells facing us? Once his belly's full, do you think that sneaky cell's going to get up off the couch (where he's being congratulated by male-valued fare on the tube) to change the baby or help with the dishes? "Fat chance," says the feminist, for all her appeals to morality (he calls it "nagging").

The feminist begins to fear that nagging may be the only weapon she has left (guns and knives being the weapons of the other side) to try and change the sneaky cell into an honest one when she is struggling against her nature to be both as well. Why should he? He is, after all, sneaky. The kind of morality she is appealing to has been tossed out with the bathwater, leaving nothing but a soap-film future. No wonder today women perform two-thirds of the world's work, earn one-tenth as much, and own one-hundredth of the property men do (Morgan, 1984)!

"The man's simpleminded," the woman despairs, whether she's thinking of that bum on the couch or that other man she doesn't know personally, that corporate head, who just dumped her water supply full of the deadliest substance known to man. "He's an idiot. He's blind [to the interconnectedness of us all]." Then she sees that society doesn't think so, and continues to heap on him its greatest rewards. Our society gives her man no help in bridging the gap between his brain spheres. In our society, the race is to the swift, the aggressive, the brazen, the compartmentalized, the selfish; or, failing these virtues, the sneaky.

Rather than justifying a subservient role for women, however, I think these facts of biology lead to quite the opposite conclusion. To deny these facts, as most feminists do, is to beg for even greater exploitation. It is certainly to misunderstand seclusion.

What have other cultures done? the feminist asks. What about seclusion?

Chapter 8

The Clan

Seclusion carries some of the benefits of tribal support into an urban environment. To understand exactly what this means, we must first understand that, speaking generally, as they evolve, societies adapt different forms of social relations as suits their relation to the resources. Hunters and gatherers (as a general rule—and when their lands and resources are not being severely encroached upon by more "advanced" societies on the outside) maintain societies in which kin are bilaterally recognized and elders and headmen either don't exist or have very limited jurisdiction and tenure if they do exist.

> In most band and village societies before the evolution of the state, the average human being enjoyed economic and political freedoms which only a privileged minority enjoy today. . . . Women . . . generally set up their own daily schedules and paced themselves on an individual basis . . . No executives, foremen, or bosses stood apart, measuring and counting. . . . A woman might decide to look for grubs, collect firewood, plait a basket, or visit her mother. . . . Moreover, . . . logs for the grubs, fiber for the basket—all were there for everyone to take . . . (M. Harris, 1977:101)

The egalitarian lifestyle of hunters-gatherers breaks down as a population increases following Neolithic settlement. Settling down, particularly with agriculture, means that more and more labor is put into the smaller and smaller bit of land a single group has in the form of cleared fields, fences, terraces or ditches. It also seems clear that this, as Marx and Engels (1964) suspected, was at the root of the distinction that was first made between "ours" and "theirs"—a great developmental step in the distinction of private property. Marvin

A History of Women's Seclusion in the Middle East
Published by the Haworth Press, Inc., 2006. All rights reserved.
doi:10.1300/5666_09

Harris[1] (1979) following Harner (1970) is probably correct in seeing this as the stage during which unilineal—either matrilineal or, more commonly, patrilineal—clan systems come to the fore as opposed to the more general bilateral systems (in which kin on both sides are equally acknowledged) prevalent in simpler societies.

> Such groups constitute a systematic attempt . . . of the close kinsmen of . . . big men to a share in the permanent forms of property and wealth they have helped to create. While not yet private property—since land is held in common by the kin group—lineage . . . patrimonies nonetheless constitute a definite step toward the development of marked inequalities in access to strategic resources. (M. Harris, 1979:95)

Observing the sedentarization of the !Kung led Patricia Draper (1975) to note that when more time and effort had been put into a home, tools, and other possessions in a marriage, the pressure on a couple to stay together, no matter what their incompatibilities, greatly increased. In the domestic brawls that often ensued, it is not surprising that men often triumphed over their women, who—yes, even in that most physical of lifestyles—tended to be smaller and not as strong.

In fact, all types of interpersonal conflict seem to be diminished by a society that can still allow great freedom of movement. The Hadza of East Africa move on an average of every fortnight; ecological factors alone cannot be the explanation. Although the Hadza recognize witchcraft as occurring among their more sedentary neighbors, they themselves do not suffer from its ill effects.[2] With no deep, vested interest in property, hunter-gatherers can "segregate themselves from each other with . . . ease" (Woodburn, 1972:193-206, 295). The movement and loose society that has been called "confused and disorderly" by anthropologists (Lee, 1972:178) is really a means by which an individual's "social ties may be manipulated without strain" (Woodburn, 1972).

> In contrast to agricultural and urban peoples, hunters have a great deal of latitude to vote with their feet, to walk out of an unpleasant situation. And they do, not when the food supply is exhausted, but well before that point when only their patience is exhausted. (Lee, 1972:182)

Therefore, with the rise of agriculture, culture must become more stringent to regulate the possible conflicts that may arise and from which one cannot simply walk away.

Nonetheless, one must dig deeper in order to say that agriculture and the clan systems it grows like poppies in the wheat fields are so terribly detrimental to women: a woman from a poor clan shares the misfortunes of the accident of birth equally with her brothers and husband, after all. When one's birthright is the hunter-gatherer's traditional lore of how to deal with an open, wild, pristine environment, one's major limit is that environment: God alone, as it were. The labor of one's own hands makes possessions. Such possessions are meager in some eyes, perhaps, but they can generally be sufficient, especially if the clan accepts your children as a benefit to them and is willing to help.

When one stands to inherit more, however, namely the cumulated labor of generations in the form of "improved" fields, dug wells, canals, stone houses, one's duty to the clan becomes a factor that overrides individual preference. The spirits of the forefathers the fruit of whose labor you enjoy stand over your shoulder at all times. Your cousin and his sons also have a say in these benefits, for the grandfather you and he share built that dike.

For a woman, here is the rub: at marriage she will leave the clan. Her position vis-à-vis the clan is equivocal. Is she to be trusted to work for the best interest of her father's clan or her husband's? And what of her children? Clearly, prudent clansmen will move cautiously and listen with a grain of salt when women express their concerns.

Societies have come up with many ways to deal with this problem. Some clans divide up this world's goods into "female" goods and "male" goods (see, e.g., Friedberg, 1977). At marriage and other crucial events, the woman's side of the family must provide, for example, pigs and blankets, the man's yams and timber. Both sides remain important, for one cannot live without pigs and blankets *or* yams and timber.

In some societies, if the clan is powerful enough, it can make provisions whereby it need never give its women to anyone in marriage. Medieval European convents, with lavish gifts of property, often served as depositories of "unmarriageable" women as did the "convents" of ancient Mesopotamia.[3] The clan's women can then remain powerful figures. The clan can educate its female children and then have the benefit of their knowledge and labor without running the risk of that knowledge and labor going to help someone else. Or a system of very tight endogamy whereby clanswomen are only given to clansmen in marriage can be in force. This plan, however, seems to be very difficult to maintain in all but the most isolated of communities and, almost by definition, agricultural communities are rarely isolated for long.

Matrilineality is the favorite system of feminists in dealing with the equivocality of women among clans. It is true that a man under this system is more likely to consult with his sister. Her children are members of the same clan. She does not suffer divided interest. The jubilation of feminists in this small proportion of unilineal societies must be contradicted, however: the men are still in charge (M. Harris, 1979). Matrilineality simply serves the male clan members' interest best in groups in which men are often absent trading, warring, or hunting. Under this system, a man can leave the hard-won farmland in the care of a woman he can trust—a mother or a sister (a sister's son, rather), not a strange woman from another clan, his wife—while he is away. In practice, it is the men associated with these women who remain in charge. Matrilineality, seen in this light, may simply be an intensifying step on the unavoidable slide toward state building, as men's ambitions lead them on trajectories out of the clan's renewable cycle.

Matrilineality is a topic of very interesting implications, but we will deal no more with it here. Patrilineality is, of course, much more common in societies at the agricultural clan stage, and it is almost universal in the Middle East, the area that holds our interest. Where endogamy is preferred for marriages, a man would be a fool to invest as much in his daughter as his son. Resources are scarce and she will leave him after a mere thirteen or fourteen years to marry a stranger anyway. However, somewhere in the middle of genesis (Pitt-Rivers, 1977) men decided they would prefer not to marry a stranger at all. One's own sister would seem to be the marriage partner with interests closest to one's own, but as incest laws make this impossible, the next best bet is a girl of one's own clan; the closer the relation, the better. One's first cousin, a father's brother's daughter, seems safest. Even with such precautions, can a man trust his wife? Won't she favor his father-in-law's interests instead of his own? Certainly. It might be best to make her slave at the command of even the lowest of the "true" clan members for years and years until she has so much time and labor invested in the clan that she, too, might be humored as a "true" member. At the very least, the new bride cannot be trusted until she has provided a son to the clan. Then she *might* be presumed to have the future of that son, hence the future of the son's clan, at heart. But it might be most prudent of all to simply wait until that son is grown (infants do suffer high mortality, after all) and let *him* be responsible for deciding whether to trust his mother.

To the reader who finds nothing new in this, who finds that it confirms all of her worst assumptions of patriarchs and their primitive clans, let me only offer this caution. Patrilineality is not the worst thing that can happen and, indeed, it has some important advantages over what is to come. The clan still has a vested interest in women. It is interested in its future existence as a clan, which means children, which means women. The economy has many tasks relegated to women, tasks men cannot do, tasks that, even though they are given little status, cannot be farmed out to others. Therefore, although harsh conditions may make the clanswoman's lot unenviable—as unenviable as that of the clansmen—no clan, if it is to survive, will make her a complete nonentity; it will protect and make concessions to her whenever it can. It is to demand such concessions in the face of the next stage of cultural development that women seclude themselves and expect honor from their men.

In traditional Middle Eastern society, there is no doubt as to where custody and responsibility for the children belongs in case of divorce or the death of a parent. Unlike the United States, this is not a society of such intense monolithic power that nonetheless gives women (usually *a* woman on her own, with no kin network to support her) such great responsibility for the future generation while at the same time denying her important access to resources. The traditional Middle Eastern patriarchal clan has access to resources. It is only just—and prudent—that the patriarchal clan maintain both control of and responsibility for the children.

Middle Eastern society does not neglect the necessary role of maternal care in a child's upbringing. Traditionally, children of divorcing parents remain with the mother until age seven or so, when they unequivocally return to the father. The brutality we in the West read in the often-cited cases in which a woman may never see her children again after this age are, in my mind, outweighed by the cases in this country in which a child may never see either his father or his father's support again after this age or even earlier. The brutalizing to-and-fro tugs for affection and responsibility that are behind the majority of missing-child cases as well as the psychological stress found in the United States are also done away with in the East. Few court battles, few unsupported kids. Although I sympathize with women who find themselves in this situation, bereft of their children and—what is worse—knowing that these children are being raised in a society they've come to hate, I cannot help but think that this unpleasant solution to an always unpleasant problem is superior to one that accepts the priority of mother love—and then condemns mother and children to poverty while the father is never seen again.

Furthermore, we must consider that the horror stories we get are always from the point of view of the Western woman—a lone individual—who entered this relationship in what would be seen in the Middle East as very anomalous circumstances. Unlike a Middle Eastern woman, the Western bride does not bring her entire kin group to the East with her and, at the first sign of difficulty, she finds herself totally without support. No doubt there wasn't even a bride-price exchanged with the vows in Tulsa or Duluth—a bride-price which, unlike its often perceived function of turning women into chattel, actually provides divorce insurance. The Sinai Bedouin woman wears her bride-price in jangling coins sewn onto her veil. The symbolic connection could not be closer.

Many literal marriages between Western women and Eastern men end badly for the woman, no matter how prepared she thinks she is for seclusion when she views it with that demon romance fresh in her eyes. Here is the start of the fatal flaw: the couple relies on the Western system of family-less romance to create the match and follows it by immersion in the Eastern system afterward. Usually this is not a marriage of which the groom's family totally approves. Although they may allow him his whim for a while, they cannot support it wholeheartedly in the long run, as it brings no important allies along with it.

Finally, the point has already been made that the preferred form of marriage in the Middle East is very close kin, preferably patrilineal kin, kin in degrees so close that we in the West consider it incest. Although she may be divorced or widowed, then, and be forced to give up responsibility for the raising of her children to others, those "others" are likely to be her aunts and grandmother, or other similar close relations. It is not like she is returning halfway around the world to face a cold solitary life without offspring in Duluth. She may see her children every day. Certainly she is invited to all important family festivities and is even consulted on such matters. Because the clan is close, she can always pour her maternal affections onto her brothers' children—children that will remain with *her* patriliny and as such are much more *hers*. When her children, particularly her sons (although plenty of folk tales give daughters more credit for such behavior), are grown—in less than a decade from when she first gave them up—they are likely to seek her out, and none prove better at expressing filial devotion than children raised with Middle Eastern mores.

Chapter 9

Environment for Seclusion

Cultural phenomena do not exist in vacuums. They are the play of our basic biological tendencies with the environment. Only after having exhausted these physical explanations may we then resort to explanations such as, "Culture is the play of a vivid imagination with nothing better to do." Fortunately, with the case of seclusion, we do not have to look far. Ancient Mesopotamia was the perfect place for urban capitalism—and a defense against urban capitalism, seclusion—to arise. Consider the ecology of this part of the world.

The Neolithic farmers in Anatolia and northern Mesopotamia who first resorted to agriculture—the system that broke all mesolithic taboos at the end of the Ice Age and dipped deeper into what had been a primeval sacred 80 percent of resources—soon felt the instability of their new subsistence system. The fertility of their soil ran out or they experienced a drought for a few years, and the increase in their population used up more than 100 percent of their resources. The easiest thing to do in this circumstance is for some or all of the afflicted community to move on. So they did, taking their unstable subsistence strategy with them, for it was all they knew.

Those who pioneered westward into Europe faced little difficulty. Certainly, natives, peoples "still" living in the Mesolithic, were there, but they were no competition for agriculturalists. Even if their basic stone-weapon arsenal was the same, more intensive exploitation can support greater numbers of people than can less intensive strategies. It would be thousands of years before these farmers had slashed and burned their way to the Atlantic, before they found themselves compressed enough to find ways to explode across that natural barrier and find whole new continents of "virgin, empty"[1] territory to lay their axes and their plows to.[2] Indeed, it is only within the past fifty years or so that United States citizens can begin to get an inkling of what

A History of Women's Seclusion in the Middle East
Published by the Haworth Press, Inc., 2006. All rights reserved.
doi:10.1300/5666_10

was in store for those who, when instability struck, made the choice of following the Euphrates and Tigris rivers southward. Southern Mesopotamia turned out to be neither more nor less for the Neolithic farmer than a cul-de-sac,[3] and a rather unpleasant one at that.

Actually, no self-respecting Neolithic farmer, given the choice, would ever have settled in southern Mesopotamia. For thousands of years it was nonexistent, and then it had a rather tenuous existence as a fever-infested swamp. Heaven does you no favors there. It doesn't even bring rain with any consistency. Although the twin rivers have sufficient water for growing crops, you have to get the water to the fields yourself, "with your foot," as the Bible describes it. A difference also exists between the sort of irrigation possible in Egypt and that in southern Mesopotamia. "The Gift of the Nile" is a

> cheap and easy "basin type" of irrigation . . . where the [river] . . . freely inundates the valley for a time and then withdraws. . . . The . . . flood periods of the Tigris and Euphrates occur between April and June, too late for winter crops and too early for summer crops. (Roux, 1980:24)

Instead of washing nicely all over the land as fertilizer, the "sediment carried by the rivers will quickly choke canal systems" if not constantly cleaned out (R. Fernea, 1970:26). Floods threaten yearly to wash out seed already sown and "the southern Euphrates . . . is . . . capable of shifts of course which may suddenly leave previously prosperous areas of land without . . . water" (p. 27). Not all of this is nature's fault. Partially, it is "the product of human activity," that very activity which was bought most dearly: "Whatever man achieved in ancient Iraq, he did at the price of a constant struggle against nature and other men" (Roux, 1980:33).

Estimates as to what the shift in this intensive type of agriculture meant in man-hours run as high as "an increase from 1,000 hours of work annually per family to something like five times that figure" (P. Smith, 1972:412). Heaven help the family that fell short of hands! So the population must increase, and this burden is added to women's new quotas. Less time for art and recreation; less time to develop culture's gray areas and the rich deviations of individuals.

It seems clear that the first settlers in southern Mesopotamia cannot have been given a choice. It was probably the weaker tribes, "the depressed and the oppressed, the disgruntled and dissatisfied" (Allan,

1972:222) that were forced down from the preferred rain-watered regions into the desolate, sometimes swampy region between the two rivers only just building alluvial soil out of a shallow bay. No doubt many of the first arrivals tried and failed to make that land work for them, and just a few managed to live, as the Marsh Arabs today do, on their catches from the river supplemented by a few goats and a little hand-watered cropping here and there.

Now, when we consider potentialities for cultivation, we must remember that all soils are not created equal

> in their natural capacity to sustain cultivation. Some lose their fertility when cultivated for a year or two and regain it only after a long rest under regenerating vegetation.[4] Others can be maintained in fertility at acceptable yield levels under systems of alternate crop and fallow periods of short duration. The most fertile and durable soils of all, a very small fraction of the earth's mantle, can be cultivated at relatively high yield levels for long periods, or even indefinitely, with little or no break. (Allan, 1972:213)

Making or remaking good soils is possible only at a cost, i.e., with fertilizer. The modern farmer takes this for granted and works it into the (frequently bankrupting) budget. Fertilization amounts to the actual importation of fertility from elsewhere packaged in bags of Ortho. What, then, about elsewhere's fertility, or its suitability for any sort of life if the chemical plant leaks? For the ancient farmer, long before the development of wide-ranging trade systems, if the flocks' dung and kitchen scraps were not enough to replenish the soil, fallow—that is, taking no crop for shorter or longer periods as necessary—was the only other alternative.

Now "the alluvial soils of the great river basins . . . are among the most persistently fertile and naturally productive soils in the world"—when they have water—because "they have an almost inexhaustible supply of plant nutrients brought down from the upperlands drained by the rivers" (Allan, 1972:223)—handy and cheap Neolithic Ortho bags, those rivers. No doubt this is part of the cause of the rise of great early civilizations on the banks of such rivers—Indus, Ganges-Brahmaputra, Chang (Yangtze), Nile, Tigris-Euphrates. The traditional site of Paradise was between the Tigris and the Euphrates. But that was, we must remember, a paradise lost.

Although northern Mesopotamia's erosion loss was Sumer's gain, we have already seen that the floods in Sumer are ill-timed to the growing season and were not an unmitigated blessing. In addition, no amount of lush silt can do any good if it is salinated. The waters of the Tigris and Euphrates are markedly salty, and the waters underground are even more so (Butz, 1978-1979, 1984). Irrigation in alluvial soils and the artificial rise in the water table that it causes tend to bring salts to the surface, where they settle in a thin crust on the top of the soil.

Salination is a problem not appreciated as the first bumper crops come in from irrigated land. Indeed, American farmers in the West are only just coming to realize what a menace it can be. Making "the desert bloom" does not necessarily lead to an unequivocal and eternal rose, poetic as descriptions of the salination phenomenon are. Examples of these descriptions include "glistening" and "forming patches and traceries like half-melted snow on the brown earth" (R. Fernea, 1970:6). The ancient Sumerians were familiar with the use of fallow, leaching, drainage canals—everything modern farmers use to counteract salination. Think of the increase in man- (and woman-) hours needed then! In spite of all their best efforts, over the millennia, as the population still rose, the effects of salination were inescapable. A graphic recounting of the decline of productivity as represented in the archaeological record of Mesopotamia can be given:

> Counts of grain impressions in excavated pottery from sites in southern Iraq of about 3500 BC . . . suggest that at the time the proportions of wheat and barley were nearly equal. A little more than 1000 years later . . . the less-salt-tolerant wheat accounted for only one-sixth of the crop. By about 2100 BC wheat had slipped still further, and it accounted for less than 2 percent of the crop. . . . By 1700 BC, the cultivation of wheat had been abandoned completely in the southern part of the alluvium . . .
>
> Concurrent with the shift to barley cultivation was a serious decline in fertility. . . . At about 2400 BC . . . a number of field records give an average yield of 2537 liters per hectare—highly respectable even by modern United States and Canadian standards. This figure had declined to 1460 liters per hectare by 2100 BC and by about 1700 BC the recorded yield had shrunk to an average of only 897 liters per hectare. (Jacobsen and Adams, 1958:1252)

Contemplate the effect this must have had on the inhabitants of the area's cities: they appear "never to have recovered fully from the disastrous general decline which accompanied the salination process" (Jacobsen and Adams, 1958:1252). In fact, as part of a team hired by the Iraqi government to see what could be done to revitalize their agricultural lands, modern scholars had to throw up their hands and declare that even with a glut of oil dollars and a forced "fallow" of millennia, the invention of irrigation had done its worst and the abandoned fields must stay abandoned. However, the eventual abandonment of Sumer is beyond the scope of this section. Let us leave the setting as it was in preliterate times: for all the intensification of their labor—100 percent of the people working nearly 100 percent of the time—the Sumerians still began to feel a pinch.

Yet this was the beginning of civilization, a phenomenon which

> all my study of the past persuades me . . . is a most abnormal and unpredictable event of unique circumstances in a restricted area of western Asia some 5,000 years ago. . . . "The wonder is that such things occurred at all." . . . It is, I would rather suggest, the non-civilized societies of antiquity that were the norm. (Piggott, 1965:20)

Civilization is rather like a Van Gogh: for all its genius and blessing to the world, it is the product of very troubled times, very troubled minds, capable of doing horrible violence even upon their own members. It is evident that from the first, people pressed by overpopulation and ecological stress into this Mesopotamia—first inhospitable, then made to wear the cloak of hospitality, finally unmasking its true face in deadly inhospitality—had their linear thinking capabilities taxed to the utmost. But a muscle well exercised becomes strong.

What options were open to Neolithic farmers in southern Mesopotamia when their system showed its instability? Moving on? The archaeological record (see T. Young, 1972) shows this was still the preferred solution in the Diyala plain—that is the northern part of southern Mesopotamia—until much, much later. But this was no longer an option in Sumer. To the south was the Persian Gulf, to the west, desert.[5] North and east were the stronger farmers, well entrenched in their lands, who had pushed the Sumerians[6] down there in the first place. Ancient Mesopotamia had no resources to speak of. "Earth, water, reeds, date-palm logs" completes the inventory (T. Young,

1972:837). The bitumen that welled to the surface in places (perhaps deteriorating the fertility of fields even more) was used to water-seal boats and building foundations, but could not have been imagined in the Neolithic as a possibility for massive (but temporary) exploitation as it is in the oil rigs of today.

Improving one's technology may be the answer preferred by modern American entrepreneurs. Indeed, irrigation may be seen as such an improvement, but I have my doubts. Really intensive irrigation, more than what is accomplished by the members of a clan with a few hoes and a "simple" understanding of the lay of the land, does not appear in Mesopotamia until later. Indeed, a convincing argument has been made[7] that the great public works witnessed in mile-long canals as big as natural waterways and intricate networks of ditches are the results of cities, not vice versa. They are, at least, the result of new and intensified redistribution systems.

To solve their dilemma, the Sumerians perfected, if they did not actually invent, cities, and the cultural values to sustain them.

During the Jemdet Nasr period (c. 3200-3100 BC)

> a "balling" or concentration of population into the larger urban centres appears to take place at the expense of the countryside. Down to the end of Early Dynastic times [ca. 2500 BC] this sort of urban development results in a steady decline of the number of occupied sites in the area, with abandonment of whole districts previously occupied and under cultivation. (T. Young, 1972:832-833)

It is suggested that clans displaced by salination or drought were welcomed by those clans in more favored zones, forming conglomerations of people that became cities. The power of the Sumerian temple has been interpreted (Postgate, 1972) as emblematic of the role it played as a "support of the indigent, and of those for whose support the family structure of the time made insufficient provision," a stronghold of charitable feelings. This may have been part of a priestess's calling. We might postulate that those clans whose doctrine let them break the old limits of clannishness and open their arms to more and more of the displaced were able to field more men on the battlefield and take more and more of the good land away from those clans who weren't so charitable.[8] Hospitality overwhelming to the Westerner is still a facet of Middle Eastern culture, after all.

However, this open-arms scenario neglects something important in this description of the "balling" settlement pattern of the Jemdet Nasr period.

> The evidence of simultaneous, widespread abandonment of small settlements in [the] hinterland leaves little doubt that this extraordinary growth was essentially an implosive process, transferring rural population into a new, urban setting in response to some combination of internal tendencies toward the consolidation of political leadership and external . . . threats. (Adams, 1972:739)

I think it is important that the salination of the soil is not mentioned at this juncture. Evidence from near Nippur shows that "a formerly important channel of the Euphrates in the vicinity fell permanently into disuse at about this time" (Adams, 1972:740)—arguably not because the land it served went sour but because nobody cared any longer to keep the channel open. The suggestion is that not all the lands deserted were completely unproductive. To some degree we may have here not real (although in many regions it was real enough, as I have already explained) but "*effective* land scarcity" (Friedman and Rowlands, 1977:234), effected by changes in the social system. Certainly, at the very moment when food was in such demand, this abandonment of possible sources of food is a paradox. But there is something more to this compulsive attraction of the Sumerian city.

Indeed, if an unbounded charity to all comers is the main cultural ingredient required to create civilization, then what place is there for women's seclusion? Surely, in a world of utopian hospitality to all, women may go about as freely as men. There is more to this sudden and massive concentration of population than first meets the eye.

Chapter 10

Trade

Trade, as it has been ever since, was ancient Mesopotamia's answer to the difficult environment it had been dealt.

Many attempts to understand the role of trade in early Mesopotamia—or in the modern world, for that matter—conceive of trade as "symbiotic," that is, as exchange between equals who stand to profit equally because each is a member of an ecological zone which has "its own distinctive range of products." A little evenhanded bartering, and all can be happy. Self-sufficient communities certainly change, but they have no need to develop.

Traditional wisdom has it that ancient Mesopotamia was more than self-sufficient in the basic necessity of grain; indeed, that the development of a storage economy based on grain facilitated the glorious rise of the Sumerians' massive international and "mutually" beneficial trading operation. Grain can be given to workers as wages. Research (Butz, 1978-1979, 1984) indicates, however, that Ur at least, perhaps because of a particularly high water table in the region, was not self-sufficient in grain, and imported quantities from Lagash in exchange for the dung and produce of their more numerous flocks. Even if we accept the traditional version that grain remained plentiful in the region from prehistory to Alexander the Great, we have already called as witness the fact that Mesopotamia had nothing else—not the metal to make their weapons, not the wood to make their doors. This, if it has urban, superpower ambitions, is an economy of scarcity. Scarcity in the mentality begins to justify giving some less than others, some less than they need. Unless steps are taken to protect them, what is to keep that "some" from being the next generation?

"Symbiosis alone is not enough to explain the observed trade pattern" in rising civilizations or what we may call "superpowers" (Bray,

A History of Women's Seclusion in the Middle East
Published by the Haworth Press, Inc., 2006. All rights reserved.
doi:10.1300/5666_11

1972:920). The conclusions are valid for ancient Mesopotamia—and for modern "superpowers."

> Superpowers have outgrown their sustaining areas and are no longer self-sufficient in basic necessities. In a situation where colonization or emigration are not feasible, the deficit must be made good from the outside, either by extortion or trade, and it is no accident (Bray, 1972:920)

that "history began" in the difficult ecological niche that is Sumer. Where "communities are self-sufficient there is little opportunity for local or regional trade to develop and for specialized merchant groups to emerge" (D. Harris, 1972:257). Self-sufficient farming communities were no more the origins of civilization than was evenhanded trade.

Faced with ecological difficulties, a culture may expand its subsistence base in two ways: It may intensify "local productivity" and/or it may capture "resources from somebody else."

> Increased craft production, even if not on an industrial scale, represents an expansion of local production, but when the surplus is used for foreign trade it also plays a part in the "capturing" of resources from elsewhere. . . . Legitimate trade [can readily] merge with extortion. Trade and tribute-extortion can . . . be regarded as two faces of the same coin. . . . They are both means of capturing resources from someone else. (Bray, 1977:388)

That this was the tactic appealed to by ancient Mesopotamian cities could be demonstrated no more vividly than by the image of the great mounds of resources that are their ruins lying in the midst of the leeched-out, bone-dry countryside. Granted, most of the mass of these ruins is now only dried clay, but even the human resources and the food to feed them represented in the simple movement of that amount of dirt is awesome. In our own day, we may contemplate the resources removed from other countries into our own by the tons of broken bamboo screens, banana peels, coffee grounds, and plastic bags (made from petroleum products) in our landfills.

When the trading partners belong to cultures that are based on the close, personal relationships of clans, traders coming to them with "rational" views of exchange find it very easy to make a profit. In "primitive" societies, exchange means much more than just the search for a profit. It

> is not based on a precise evaluation of the worth of any of the commodities that are involved. Obligations are definitely created, but they are of an unspecified kind: "while there is a general expectation of some future return, its exact nature is definitely not stipulated in advance. . . . Since there is no way to assure an appropriate return for a favour, social exchange requires trusting others to discharge their obligations. (Layton, 1972:378-379, quoting Blau, 1964:93-94)

"Primitive" cultures also often have traditions that teach it is rude not to give the stranger anything he asks for, and so on. It should not surprise us, then, that Manhattan Island could, in a very open gesture, be "sold" to white men for twenty-four strings of beads or that similar tales should be repeated from one end of the globe to the other. This does not prove that the "primitives" are "stupid," much less that their "stupidity" makes them deserving of exploitation. But the traders' credo is to make a killing, and make it he does, every chance he gets, abroad and, then, at home.

> Purely commercial city states become totally dependent on their trade networks to survive. . . . The formation of . . . empires is linked to the attempt by individual states to establish a more secure basis for their own reproduction by converting trade relations into tribute relations. This need is itself a product of the increasing material dependence of individual political units on wider productive regions for their survival. . . . Dependence upon external exchange, in order to maintain a given complex of social and economic activities becomes almost absolute. (Friedman and Rowlands, 1977:233, 238-239)

It is no wonder that the urban version of the farmers' slash and burn eventually leads to "a conscious attempt to destroy all forms of local autonomy." This is clearly what happened in Akkadian Mesopotamia, "where local aristocrats are usually replaced by appointed officials and where former states are reduced to administrative provinces of the larger state" (Friedman and Rowlands, 1977:240).

Of course, once the military conquest was finished, good, honest trade could resume—the terms of trade for the conquered province being only what those reluctant to join in capital enterprise deserve. What happened in the ancient Middle East in the eighth century BCE, when Sargon II set up the stele after he had subdued Egypt, is a good demonstration of this. He had done what no king before had done, he said, although many had tried. He had finally made Pharaoh realize the benefits of trading his gold and his produce for the goods of Assyria (Gadd, 1954:179).

Mesopotamian traders "lived in a special 'harbour' district in a manner which suggests that the society as a whole perceived a significant cleavage between the activities of the merchants and those of the city proper." In the Aztec empire, too, "long-distance traders had a similar, somewhat culturally anomalous relationship to their society" (Trigger, 1972:586). People whose function is so important to the existence of the state must be allowed to get away with murder. They do not have to live by the rules of the average citizen because even the sovereign owes them his existence. The urban capitalist state must embrace Ayn Rand's vision: the "moochers and the leachers" (children, the women who care for them, the next generation, the aging generation, etc.) must make way for the "movers and the shakers," and their values, priorities, and needs.

A brief look at the types of articles traded further exposes the predatory nature of trade. Textiles and clothing products were Mesopotamia's favored trade items and continue to be a major means of exploitation, inducing trade and thereby securing somebody else's resources today. Here I mean to conjure the whole web of Malaysian sweatshops and teenaged fashion jeans at your local mall. Weapons of the latest technology are a wonderful inducement, particularly if you are hammering on the potential trading partner's gates with them. Other time-honored items of trade are any form of luxury item (such as incense that the later Roman empire became ritually dependent upon), tourism (witness Mecca in barren Arabia, Nippur as a holy city in ancient Sumer, and the various ploys of modern tourism councils[1]). Notice that it helps to have a state religion addicted to such items. Perhaps the best means, at least from the merchants' point of view, is to get one or the other or both of the trading partners physically addicted to the trade substance. The British tea–Chinese opium trade was the foundation of an empire (Hobhouse, 1986). Today corporations give free samples of baby formula to third-world mothers in the hospital and tell them it's the modern way to feed: a deadly dependence is created when the mother's breast milk is gone and so are the free samples. Drug dealing is another good example. Rather than being the antithesis of capitalism, it is its epitome. It's not drugs the drug lords kill one another over—it's money.

This chapter has given many examples of the ancient Near Eastern compulsion to trade. There still lingers a belief, founded by nineteenth-century Orientalism (if not by the Crusaders) that Islam, the last scion of the Middle Eastern house, "lacked . . . necessary condition[s] for capitalist development," to quote Marx. At this the following refutation may be thrown:

> Islam was primarily urban, commercial and literate. Mecca was strategically placed on the trade routes between the Mediterranean and the Indian Ocean; Muhammad's own tribe, the Quraysh, had achieved a dominant political position based on their commercial strength in the region. The Prophet himself had been employed on the caravans which brought Byzantine commodities to the Meccan market. The Koran itself is steeped in a commercial terminology. There has been a continuous conflict in Islam between the dominant urban piety and the values of the desert, but this conflict was also economic. Desert tribes threatened the trade routes and extracted taxation from merchants. Islam provided a culture which was capable of uniting Bedouins and urban merchants within a single community. Islam was thus as much a triumph of town over desert as Arab over Persian and Christian. (B. Turner, 1984:36)

That it should be the ambition of every hand on a Persian Gulf dhow to buy "a tiny shop in the *suq* of his home town" (Villiers, 1970:163) with the profits of his minor trading and smuggling is ambition that is millennia old. Our stereotypical Middle Eastern image—luxury-laden camel caravan, plodding across a bleak, denuded wasteland—is no mirage, but from time immemorial represents a vital artery.

Chapter 11

Capital and Land

We have seen that trade was very important for the rise of civilization in ancient Mesopotamia. We also have seen some indication of what its effect was on the trading partners. Now we must investigate what an economy based on trade does to the culture at home, for this is where women will begin to be secluded; this is what interests us most.

The "landscape of settlement" upon which urbanization and seclusion was "rapidly imposed" in Mesopotamia 5,000 years ago started out as "an intensely rural adaptation in which the recognized social units were prevailingly small and highly localized" (Adams, 1972: 742)—clannish, in other words. When a society is clan-based, "land and resources will be controlled by localized, kin-oriented, self-sufficient social units with rights of access distributed more or less equally among members" (Bray, 1977:381). The most important cultural change that must be effected before a society can move into full-swing capitalistic, urban trading is that the power of the traditional clans must be broken.

What does this mean for women? Briefly, capital must become the focus of the society instead of the clan.

Traditional clan elders, although male, consider the perpetuation of a way of life with room for all members of the community in their every deliberation. They give consideration to the land and resources on which that life is based. On the other hand, the capitalist's major interest is to plumb every possible resource in order to create and extract surplus for himself as quickly as possible. No one else is accounted for.

The first need of a trading expedition[1] is to devise some means of raising the capital to outfit the caravan. Certainly, one hopes for a return larger than one invests, but the means must be found to liquify

A History of Women's Seclusion in the Middle East
Published by the Haworth Press, Inc., 2006. All rights reserved.
doi:10.1300/5666_12

those assets one does have, and to put them solely into the hands of the man or men who are going to do the trading. At this crucial point in time, capital (still not money in our sense of the word) became a tool and a "means of exercising economic pressure" (particularly on women, children, and other weaker members of the population) "by making it a commodity to be rented and paid for" (A. L. Oppenheim, 1964:89). I believe an "interest" economy works toward linear interests and against women. It certainly tends to emphasize one hierarchy of value at the expense of all others. Everything gets a price tag and anything that can't be bought or sold is rendered valueless. The capitalist trader seeks the means whereby the only true wealth—land and the means to grow food—is turned into something basically intangible (capital, good only on paper) that he can carry with him on his journeys.

West (1972) gives a brief history of how this happened in Great Britain within the past 800 years or so. He is a lawyer; his tone is that of pride in what the lawyers have accomplished. I will correct that tone in my direction afterward.

> Between the thirteenth and fifteenth centuries it was the ordinary course of events for landowners to entail their land [to their heirs]. This led to a considerable amount of sterilization of realty. . . . In the fifteenth century the lawyers managed to produce a legal device which enabled entails to be barred and thus the owner for the time being could dispose of the estate. . . . The industrialization of the country in the eighteenth and nineteenth centuries made the problem of land availability an acute one. . . . Changed economic conditions made it urgent that land should be available for economic exploitation and of course for recharging with capital. The practice arose for private Acts of Parliament to be promoted to curtail individual settlements but the expense of this was prodigious. A Public General Act was clearly the only solution, and the first of these was passed in 1856. . . . This enabled tenants for life to dispose of the whole fee simple. (West, 1972:480)

In order for the capitalist to function, land must be made "a purchasable commodity" (Friedman and Rowlands, 1977:240). For those of us born and raised in a society where land is bought and sold every day and few of us (fewer and fewer each generation) inherit anything of production value except our bodies and our minds, this hardly seems to need comment. However, the fact is that most traditional societies perceive their lands as something inalienable to the clan—for all future generations. What is to protect children as yet unborn from the greed or desperation of a single moment, the ambition of an individual, if the land, the very means of subsistence, can conceivably be traded away? Some harvests are better than others, true, but welltended, one hopes they might stretch somewhere close to eternity. What sort of price, in reality, can be placed on season after season after season of harvests? "The interests of subsequent beneficiaries," West the lawyer promises us, are protected under this modern system "by having their interests attached to the proceeds of the sale" (p. 480). He assumes they will have the foresight to get themselves a damn good lawyer. As a matter of fact, of course, it is the person who wants to sell the hereditary land who bothers to think about lawyers.

It seems more realistic to think that

> as a ranked society evolves into a stratified society, private ownership (with the right to transfer from person to person) will become more widespread. By clever manipulation, particularly in the redistribution of vacant land, a minority . . . can become large landowners, forming the nucleus of an upper class. . . . If "improved" land (e.g., irrigated land, which represents an investment of labour) is involved, the emergent aristocracy is likely to control most of this. (Bray, 1977:381)

I've chosen to focus on the liquidation of land from women and children for trading purposes. The permanent environmental destruction of land for all future use in the search for immediate gain is a related and easily conceived notion.

THE BRITISH PARALLEL: ENCLOSURE

It was the enclosures of Britain (c. 1450-1850 CE) that first alerted Marx to the straitjacket of capitalism. This well-documented part of history can give us some insights.

During the medieval period, communities in Britain held their lands under what is called the open field system. These fields must have been laid out originally when England was first settled by farmers, when large distances existed between claims. This was usually "done with careful consideration of the lie of the land, so that some simple scheme of land drainage could be followed" (Tate, 1967:37)— considerations that the enclosures' hedgerows and walls rudely cut across. In addition, in medieval England, comparatively large areas of what was called "waste"—fens, moors, marginal land—were held in common. Some vestige of this was ultimately transported to the colonies in the form of the New England Commons, a public square of sorts where, originally at least, even the poorest member of the community could graze a cow or two. In its medieval incarnation, this system was much more extensive and included meadows as well as forests where anyone could gather firewood, nuts, berries, mushrooms, and herbs, and perhaps hunt a little. Such lands served all members of the community as a safety net in case of agricultural failure. However, it was actually possible for a soul in reduced circumstances to live on this common land every year, to glean[2] a little from the neighbors, and also to support children. This gives added insight into the word *commoner* and speaks of a general "right to a decorous, a customary existence, the right of every villager, of every member of the crowd to make survival the supreme rule of *common* behavior, not the isolated right of an individual" (Illich, 1982:111). Such an orientation bespeaks "an attitude . . . that protects the weakest from ruin" (p. 111).

The rights to these resources were not written down in any law book, but were fiercely ingrained in the people's minds, and their protection was a major element in so-called quaint folk customs. For instance, in many places in Britain it was a custom for all of the menfolk of a parish to make a joint circuit of their territory once a year. The fact that this procession was accompanied by song and drink dulled the urban Victorian mind to what was actually being accomplished here, but it was of such importance to peasant life that little lads were stood on their heads in pits they themselves had dug, or they were made to eat sweet, then bitter, foods at crucial points so they would not forget the contours of their land. This was a nonliterate, pre-map society, remember. Should any walls or fences prohibiting any man's (or woman's) access to these lands be discovered during the circuit, it was a sacred obligation of the parade to tear them down and perhaps to seek out the culprit (builder) and punish him.

"It will be found that the customs which are customs of the entire poor class are based with a sure instinct on the indeterminate aspect of property," Karl Marx was able to comment even so late as the middle of the nineteenth century (quoted in Bushaway, 1982:213). John Stuart Mill said:

> Competition, in fact, has only become in any considerable degree the governing principle of contracts at a comparatively modern period. The farther we look back in history, the more we see all transaction and engagements under the influence of fixed customs. . . . Custom is the most powerful protector of the weak against the strong. . . . Custom is a barrier which, even in the most oppressed condition of mankind tyranny is forced in some degree to respect. (quoted in Bushaway, 1982:8-9)

"The enslaved are the fittest to be governed by laws," said John of Antioch, "and free men by custom" (quoted in Bushaway, 1982:27). The Victorian Oliver Goldsmith wrote that "fixing a conquest must be done by giving laws, which may every moment serve to remind the people enslaved of their conquerors; nothing being more dangerous than to trust a late subdued people with old customs" (quoted in Bushaway, 1982:27).

But who is this great tyrant that took over "Merry Olde England" at this time when custom changed to law? We understand this period to be one during which the monarchy was finally reduced to figurehead form and the flower of democracy finally burst into full bloom. Basically, it was a new view of society, a new view of the world.

> Within "customary society" . . . the relationship between social groups was understood to be reciprocal. The structurally superior (farmers, landowners, parish clergy, lord of the manor) accepted certain duties and responsibilities for the structurally inferior (tenants, smallholders, cottagers and squatters, wage laborers, the poor), and in return received due recognition of their structural status; and compliance or co-operation with their enterprises and decisions. This contractual relationship was not based upon deference; nor was it perceived as such by contemporaries. (Bushaway, 1982:22)

Under customary law, the upper classes realized and gave ritual expression to the fact that if the lower classes did not help them cut their wheat or make their hay, it would not get done. To make the scenario particularly apply to women, the men in charge were forced to admit, publicly and to themselves, that if they did not have women not only to bear children but to mend their socks and bake their bread, the next generation would not come. Under the customary regime, it was the task of a woman to stand up for the household in opposition to what budding universal law was attempting to take hold. For example, if she claimed to be alone in the house, the tax collector could not enter; a higher law than the state exchequer was recognized. When women said nothing while they served beer and pretzels to the men it was not because they were subservient, but because that was not the time and place to use what they learned from such sanctioned eavesdropping. To do so would be to weaken the power of their gossip in its proper time and place.

The witch hunts of the early modern period were another very effective attack on the power of custom, as we shall see in a later chapter.

Thus we see that during the centuries of enclosure, "custom and ceremony became a battleground in the struggle between the labouring poor and the increasingly wealthy landowners and proprietors." It was a battle "over the defence of popular rights and the protection of . . . the idea of the community as a single unit . . . rather than [as divided] in accord with [the ruling] class's changing value system" (Bushaway, 1982:21-22, 151). Enclosure represented

> an overall transition from . . . customary society . . . where there was a balance between the claims and rights of the lesser members of the community . . . and the duties and responsibilities of the leading members . . . to a new form of social order, in which the prime importance was placed upon contract, the cash nexus and where responsiveness to market forces played the major role. (p. 231)

Seclusion and veiling in the Middle East are customs; customs, I submit, of similar import and purpose to English traditional Rogation Day parades. Women maintained and strengthened seclusion in the face of what was a similar loss of communal and clannish lands and access to resources as ancient Mesopotamia lumbered toward a capitalistic, trading economy. I have depended on English enclosure to provide a parallel because it is more heavily studied and documented. The evidence that this indeed occurred in the land between the rivers more than 5,000 years ago is of a technical nature and so will be consigned to a note.[3] However, one a study from modern Mesopotamia elucidates its continuing effect on general clan access to resources, and I will address this now.

Empires have come and empires have gone between the Tigris and Euphrates, defeated always in their linear quest by the cyclical nature of the land. Oil fields brought urbanizing, capitalizing forces to work once more.[4] "The traditional system of land tenure and use" in Mesopotamia "was . . . well suited to traditional methods of extensive cultivation; indeed, the two aspects of agriculture must have evolved together" (R. Fernea, 1970:54) and were probably in place in some form in prehistoric times. This includes keeping any field fallow every other year because of the intense risk of salination. "Some areas . . . recover in a year of rest while other soils . . . 'weaken' even if this system is followed"(R. Fernea, 1970:54). Obviously, this "year of fallow" rule is a convention, ultimately linear in its own way. But it serves as a customary shorthand, easy for the simplest farmer to remember without test tubes, litmus papers, chemicals, and so on, and somehow manage to keep some life in his soil.

The usual adage that it takes cities and strong central governments to make irrigation is called into question by this fact. Mesopotamia has been irrigated at this level for thousands of years and "lapses" (relaxes) back to this subsistence whenever empire building will leave it alone. It did so when the Tatars sacked Baghdad in 1258 CE and put an end to Abbasid rule. What causes more intensification, then, is a centralized government craving the harvest for itself. This has happened in recent years, first under the Ottomans, then the British Mandate, then the Iraqi monarchy, then Saddam Hussein, all of which are, in ultimate effect, gluttonous empires. It is, in part, I maintain, the power of seclusion and honor that has kept a skeletal tribal system intact for society to revert to when the blandishments of empire crumble.

Now, under the tribal system, "individual tribesmen cultivated parts of the tribal domain by virtue of their good standing in the tribe" (R. Fernea, 1970:31). It remains unstated, but seems nonetheless clear, that chronic abuse of a tribeswoman or any weaker individual in pursuit of the harvest of one's allotted land, beyond certain conventional latitude, would constitute untribesmanly behavior and threaten the abuser with loss of his land. Village elders periodically reallot land in keeping with crop rotation. This system prevents the same person from permanently cultivating the same piece of land (R. Fernea, 1970),

These successive Iraqi governments, however, have one after the other made moves to have all the land registered by owner—a single owner; the better to enter in their record books, the better to allocate technological assistance, the better to control the resources and exploit them to their benefit, in other words. Turkish officials typically sold rights to townsmen or friendly tribal leaders (R. Fernea, 1970). The British and Iraqis, although perhaps not quite so blatantly corrupt, still insisted that the land be registered under the name of a single individual. Tribal names won't do. Neither will the name of a wife, mother, or sister appear unless she owns it in her own right, which almost never happens without the umbrella of the tribe. Coworkmanship counts for nothing in the legal books.

Effectively, these policies

> resulted in the widespread . . . registration of tribal lands in the name of the incumbent shaykh. Where this happened, tribesmen have frequently left their ancestral lands or have been reduced to the status of share croppers, while the shaykhs . . . have become absentee landlords . . . (R. Fernea, 1970:12)

> With the registration of land, holdings are fixed and owners must do the best they can with land they inherit or are able to purchase. (R. Fernea, 1970:43)

Not unlike the case during the British enclosures, registration in Iraq has led to a situation in which

> the small farm owners clearly have the most unfavorable ratio of wasteland to farmland. (R. Fernea, 1970:45)
>
> Because his own property is insufficient as a resource, the independent farmer cultivates an average of six mesharas a year as a sharecropper, in addition to his own land. Furthermore he must yearly cultivate 30 percent of the land which, according to the traditional system here, should be left fallow. (R. Fernea, 1970: 45-46)

Thus what little good land he does have is deteriorating at a faster rate than that of the large farm owner who can afford the luxury of longer fallows. Also, he and his land cannot benefit from herding animals on the fallow, as the large landowner can.

In conclusion:

> This calls into serious question both the desirability of year-round high water supplies, made possible through the techniques and capital utilized by the central government, and the long-term wisdom of conventional agrarian reform as a solution to the political and social ills of this region. (R. Fernea, 1970: 152).

Young Iraqis—more every day—flocked in disinherited droves to oil cities and to Baghdad. "Extensive cultivation requires a flexible relationship between land and people, a situation in which land may be used for a time and abandoned, as its fertility declines, to the natural processes of recovery" (R. Fernea, 1970:54).

> Contemporary study suggests that extensive patterns of decentralized irrigation agriculture as practiced by the tribes may actually have been better suited to the physical environment of southern Iraq than the more intensive patterns of land use which have followed technological improvements . . . developed by modern central government . . . (R. Fernea, 1970:37)

or, for that matter, by ancient ones.

But the die was cast. Ancient Mesopotamia moved into the dependency and exploitation of life in the city.

Chapter 12

Liberation of the Individual

The purpose of this chapter is to show that ancient Mesopotamia—where seclusion, that most individual-denying of customs, began—paradoxically had strong tendencies to try to extract the individual person out of clan and tribe.

We have already seen that progress to the urban-state level of social organization requires a weakening of the clan in order to alienate its traditional landholdings. Something else is alienated from the weakened clan: the individual. For an expansionist state, this is also very fortuitous, so fortuitous, indeed, that one cannot say which came first, a gluttony for liquidated land or a gluttony for alienated individuals. Undoubtedly, "the dissolution of the kin core of society was a key condition for the emergence of privately owned elite estates" and "the forms of labor utilized by these public institutions," namely, the temple and palace economies, "differed sharply from that employed by the kin groups. The relations of production were not those of kinship but those of subordination" (Zagarell, 1986b:416-417)*.

The individual and the values that make him tick, that turn him away from his clan and family, have not always been there, just waiting to be discovered and liberated. They must be created, created on the left side of the brain by cultures in linear desperation. This may be the most difficult of all steps I am asking the reader to take, this stepping aside to view individuation objectively. It is the very water in which we fish swim.[1]

---

*Excerpts from Zagarell (1986), "Trade, women, class and society in ancient Western Asia," *Current Anthropology* 27:5, pp. 415-429, copyright 1986 by the Wenner-Gren Foundation for Anthropological Research, all rights reserved. Published by the University of Chicago Press. Used with permission.

A History of Women's Seclusion in the Middle East
Published by the Haworth Press, Inc., 2006. All rights reserved.
doi:10.1300/5666_13

THE HUNGER FOR THE INDIVIDUAL

First we shall address the question of why it is that the burgeoning state has a cannibalistic longing for the liberated individual. Primarily, the individual, or even "the lone household torn from village and kin, has only weak defenses against the expropriation of its surplus" (Illich, 1982:168) to the purposes of the state.

Without tribal constraints, individuals can best practice their talents for the benefit of the main thrust of linear society. The very best leader of armies is not often the son of the last great general (who has grown soft living on his father's booty). A new general is more likely to be found in the garden of the palace at some lowly occupation, as was Sargon the Great of Akkad (c. 2316 BC), about whom the tale was told:

> My mother was a changeling, my father I knew not.
> The brothers of my father loved the hills . . .
> My changeling mother conceived me, in secret she bore me.
> She set me in a basket of rushes, with bitumen she sealed my lid.
> She cast me into the river which rose not over me.
> The river bore me up and carried me to Akki, the drawer of water.
> Akki, the drawer of water, took me as his son and reared me.
> Akki, the drawer of water, appointed me as his gardener.
> While I was a gardener, Ishtar granted me her love,
> And for four and . . . years[2] I exercised kingship. (Pritchard, 1969:119)

The Roman writer Claudius Ælianus (fl. 222-235 CE) tells the origins of the Babylonian hero named "Gilgamos" as he knew them. Flung from a mountaintop by his kingly grandfather, the infant was caught by an eagle and carried to safety in a garden, where the gardener raised him as his own (Pauly, 1894:XIII:1363). There's no telling how early these details entered the epic; they are not in the early cuneiform tablets that have been uncovered, but that may be the accident of discovery. Nonetheless, we have here a similar myth for a character who dates back even further than Sargon, to c. 2700 BC. That similar tales were also told of Moses, Krishna, and Christ should not surprise us (J. Campbell, 1949). In cultures struggling hard to free the individual, tales like these play an important role. They tell the young man looking forward to life that no birth, however ignoble, is an excuse for not fulfilling one's individual destiny. Work hard, excel—ignore your "changeling" mother, if need be (she is a great hurdle to be overcome in all epic poetry)—and you, too, may be a leader of men. The linear society loves such men and benefits greatly from them. Any gardener's son is a potential winning general or king. He has divinity in him that can come out if only he escapes the shackles of kin, especially female kin.

Clan elders are skilled at being ambivalent. Ambivalence allows room for all the variety of human beings their clan needs to perpetuate itself. "The hallmark of leadership," of modern urban leadership, on the other hand, is a lack of ambivalence. "A lack of ambivalence cannot tolerate complexity or compassion. . . . The State-that-is *trains* its sons [and more and more, its daughters] in this lack" (Morgan, 1989:173). It is inconceivable at this stage of the game that we can now escape the individual and his benefit/deficit bind. Our options are now too limited. The point is, the cult of the hero is maladaptive in the extreme. It condones the abandonment of children, exploitation of cultural resources, limitation of cultural options, and, hence, is bad.

In the Middle East, the veil maintains ambivalence. It is ambivalence that covers even a raised eyebrow or a rolled eye, in half the population at least, which is better than in none.

A second reason to press for unattached individuals is that such people find it easier to create and join organizations that span a larger community than the clan and therefore are more powerful. Without such organizations, trade is very difficult, if not impossible. This may, in fact, mark the difference between a village and a town: the existence of "external *relationships*." Very importantly, the relationships of clanless individuals can work more efficiently than a clan, which has broad interests and obligations to people of all types—from infants to grandmothers—and every possible variation on these types. The non-kin association can pick and choose the people it wants to have working for it, even so far as to the defining of their values, and nothing could be more efficient in allocating resources to one particular goal, to the neglect of all others, than such an association. Such associations, working under the spearhead individual at the top, are loosely called "bureaucracies."[3] The decisions the bureaucrat makes on the job and the time he devotes to it need not (in many cases, had better not) reflect the needs or sometimes even the existence of a family at home. This facilitates "multi-community organization for cooperative competition, particularly for competition in the form of war" (Harner, 1970:69). Again we find trade and war in such close proximity as to their needs and goals that we cannot help but see them as opposite sides of the same expansionist coin.

Trade and empire cannot increase without the strengthening of bureaucracy and other "voluntary" associations at the same time that kin, in Marx's term, "withers away."[4] When such erosion has taken place, or is in the process of doing so, the position of women with children, who have depended on the support of family, will be in jeopardy.

Non-kin associations are stronger, it may be argued, because of the element of choice in them: their members really want to belong and base these choices on genuine affection in their relationships. First, I must submit that most human desire and, yes, even affection, is either created or strongly mediated by culture. Cultures have made people desire just about anything under the sun, from hara-kiri to self-castration to the love of certain individuals above others, and that very strongly. Paradoxically, I believe, greater individuation (and its ultimate end, non-kin associations) actually leads to fewer and weaker relationships of the face-to-face, egalitarian variety.

"In an urban environment," we transact goods and labor "on a rational and commercial basis"—filial piety having ceased to be coin of the realm—and any consensus "is based not on implicit understanding, but on a formally specified contract." Contracts in a society such as that of the United States are given more power, and yet they can be—indeed, are made to be—broken, bought, or fast-talked out of. In the urban environment, it is rare that "actions are undertaken by one individual on behalf of those others who participate with him in the same society." The main thrust of society teaches each individual that he "exists in a state of competition with all others" and that an interest is to be taken in other members of the community, even of his own family, "only in so far as and as long as they can further his own interest." The opposite of these selfish motives existed in that blessed "natural and original form of human society and seems to lose out generally the more linear and nonkin societies become" (Layton, 1972:377).

It is difficult to understand the compulsion that could lead such non-kin arrangements to progressively extend "the scope and autonomy of their institutional spheres so that today they mould the actions and aspirations of vastly the larger proportion of mankind" (Wheatley, 1972:601). No doubt being lumped together as the lesser "them" was a small price of pride for some clans to pay when the only other option was starvation in some drought year 5,000 years ago. "Once divided into classes," it is easy to see how this could extend until the people of the earth came to experience what it means "to be differentiated according to sex, race, creed and color, and the sum of their worldly possessions" (el-Saadawi, 1980). It has a snowball effect. However, for peoples used to the "relatively egalitarian, ascriptive, kin-structured groups," the transformation "into socially stratified, politically organized . . . societies" cannot have been easy.

THE URBAN MESOPOTAMIAN CLAN

Evidence that such a weakening of kinship was indeed the case in ancient Mesopotamia comes from, first, archaeological remains, and second, kinship terminology.

One archaeologist remarks that "the well-known plastered skulls, which are found at Ramad and Beisamun as well as Jericho, suggest a preoccupation with lineage" (Oates, 1977:461) in prehistoric Palestine and the Levant that seems totally lacking in Mesopotamia. She goes on to give further evidence of just how strongly Mesopotamia contrasts with the patriarchal tribal traditions of the Old Testament. "The fact that the city 'belonged' to the god," she says

> did not mean that all land was directly owned and administered by the temple—this view has long been abandoned—but it did mean that the focus of loyalty was the city. "People were identified as citizens of this or that city, and not with a clan or some other kin-related group." (p. 474)

> As cities grew in size and complexity the strong sense of community identity tended to minimize extended family ties so that there are no vestiges of tribal organization in later Mesopotamian cities . . . [although] the older form of extended family ap-

pears to have remained characteristic of country areas throughout Babylonian history . . . (p. 478)

It is very telling that "status stratification was almost entirely economic"; Mesopotamians came very close to having a single criterion
be the means of deciding who belonged where.

Our second point comes from the language spoken between the
two rivers and their kinship terminology. Sumerian is still imperfectly
known but it seems likely (Sjöberg, 1967) that it, like Akkadian and
other languages in the area, had a kinship system of the "descriptive"
or "derivative" type, in which kinsfolk are distinguished by which
side of ego's family they come from, mother's or father's. However,
when clans are of overriding concern to the society, the different
terms tend to be elementary. They are not elementary, but derivative
in Sumerian: e.g., (Sum.) šeš-ad-da = *ahi abi* (Akk.) = father's
brother, šeš-ama = *ahi ummi* = mother's brother.[5]

On the other hand, neither Sumerian nor Akkadian had attained the
simplicity of "Eskimo" terminology. "Eskimo" is what anthropologists generally call the simplest of kinship systems, but it must not be
assumed that "primitives" such as Eskimos alone have simple families nor that complexity of kinship evolves parallel with complexity
in any other phase of culture. Modern English speakers also share this
simplest of classification systems, "devolved" within the historians'
view from the more complicated Anglo-Saxon sibs, which, for example, had a different word for father's brother *(fædera)* than for mother's
brother *(eam)*.

There seems little doubt that the "withering away" of kinship
groups as owners "of the scarcest essential means of production"
(typically, but not always, land) and the transfer of this means "to a
power elite" (Harner, 1970:82) leads to a parallel moribundity of the
terminology that had been used to regulate previous relationships. Attention is given now to such titles as "chief assistant bottle washer";
titles that have nothing to do with kin. Symptomatic of the further
progress of such moribundity in modern American society is the tendency to drop the titles "aunt" and "uncle" altogether and to refer to
such people by their first names alone. No obligations or responsibilities differentiate parents' siblings from other friends anymore; they
usually have much less influence, in fact. This will likely be the case
whenever either the physical environment is merciless on the family,
as is the case with the Eskimos, or when the cultural environment is

similarly merciless—when pressure exists toward the complex of empire at the expense of the clan.

Now, ancient Mesopotamians had not lost their variety of terms. However, they did allow bilateral inheritance, something that contradicts the use of distinctive kinship terms. Such terms usually indicate that great importance is attached to which side of the family a person is from because that indicates whether he or she will inherit or not. For all Muhammad's goodwill (and budding urbanism), many another Middle Eastern society with the same kinship distinctions manages to sidestep bilateral inheritance today. The bilateral inheritance practices of high Mesopotamian civilization and the derivative nature of its kinship terminology are an indication to me that the distinctions were of either new or wavering tenacity. It is quite conceivable that elaborate kinship terms had been done away with or never evolved in Mesopotamia, and that forces of an "anti-progress"—one might almost say, for all the modern connotations, "pro-family"—nature induced their creation or re-creation. Certainly, as long as women were "helpless" and secluded, the family must continue to play an important part in society, whatever the expansionists' desires for bureaucracy and mass organization. In the next section, we will come upon other examples of movements toward Mesopotamian lineality that are curiously and powerfully counterbalanced by factors involving the family.

HOW MESOPOTAMIAN CULTURE EFFECTED INDIVIDUAL ALIENATION

As with the alienation of land, the alienation of the individual finds a great spur in the creation of written, promulgated law that comes to take precedence over custom and tradition. In an ancient Roman parallel, it is found that the early patrilineal kinship groups "lost their legal sovereignty" with "the development of legally valid procedures and criteria for the differentiation of personal status and roles." The process is called "emancipation." I question that terminology, but not the process: The ancient Roman clans were converted

> into stratified orders whose central law regulated individual rights and preserved individual opportunities for the creation of further rights by contractual relations or other procedures of role

differentiation. . . . The initially exclusive ascriptive division of the community . . . proceeds by the gradual . . . if incomplete extension of legal and political rights and obligations to all as citizens, and by their ultimate incorporation in a common cult. (M. Smith, 1972:571-572)

It is no coincidence that a Mesopotamian, Hammurabi (c. 1792-1750 BC), usually gets billing as the first lawgiver, the ruler who first devised the tenets—like Roman law—that might be placed upon a group of individuals to supersede their ancient clannish, customary laws. Of course, it is well-known that Hammurabi had numerous precedents dating back almost as far as we have written records and no doubt promulgated by word of mouth before then, but Hammurabi will do just as well for us to hang a handle on. He indicates the very strong tendency present for this movement to law as opposed to custom in our region of interest. The briefest perusal of these laws will serve to show just how often they seek to step into the family and regulate matters there, often for the good, it seems—but so do many of our "pro-family" legislative measures seem at first blush.

THE PERSONAL GOD

At the end of this theoretical discussion of the role of law in liberating the individual, I feel the need to provide a practical example. The examples I can think of are mostly negative: Let's give that of the husband having the resources and shrewdness to hire the best lawyer while his wife, not from stupidity, but from priority of other values, remains innocent of such issues and goes like a lamb to divorce-court slaughter. It does seem to me that any attempt to improve the lot of women by legislation of relationships between individuals as equal but mere individuals cannot help but backfire. Laws actually favor male individuals, not female individuals, and especially not female "individuals" that are really "families with dependent children."

At the beginning of this chapter I made mention of the use to which myths of heroic origins can be put by a society looking for a way to avoid the cycle of kinship. Let us look at this means in more detail.

Parallel "heroic ages" have been found everywhere from ancient Homer to Serbia of the last 200 years. A telltale sign of such an age is the creation of an epic poetic tradition. According to Chadwick (1912), a further "outstanding feature" of these "heroic ages" was

> the weakening of ties of kinship and the growth of the bond of allegiance. In political organization [their] chief feature was the development of an irresponsible type . . . resting upon military prestige[6]. . . . In religion the predominant characteristic . . . was the subordination of chthonic and tribal cults to the worship of a number of universally recognised and highly anthropomorphic deities . . . (p. 442)

> The triumphs for which the heroes of heroic poetry hope and for which they are celebrated in the poems are primarily of a personal character and gained by personal prowess, even in times of national war; and all the stories alike are permeated by the spirit of personal adventure. Sometimes we find this spirit indulged with a reckless disregard of consequences. . . . Not infrequently of course the object with which such adventures are undertaken is the acquisition of wealth. But wealth itself is desired . . . so . . . that the hero may be able to outshine all his rivals in splendour. Desire of personal glory—often coupled with love of adventure for its own sake—appears to be the leading motive in all the various types of heroic poetry . . . (p. 441)

Joseph Campbell's (1949) popular declaration that the quest of the hero is at the base of religion throughout the world is only half right. Paleolithic, "true" religion as we saw in Chapter 5 was meant to draw a protective embrace around natural resources and other potentially exploitable assets against the "dissolving power" of the linear, questing, goal-oriented mind. The literature contains examples of the remnants of such mythologies, but they are infrequent and poorly studied. They are lyric poetry as opposed to the sagas and heroic epics. It's a matter of conjecture whether the seeming universality of the hero myth is due to prejudice by field-workers as to which half of a culture was worth recording, inability of those schooled in dogma-centered religions to see the myths woven by lyric poetry as opposed to the heroic, or by Campbell's concentration on "world" religions, i.e., those that have already proven themselves more imperial than the local sacred grove.

In any case, it's quite clear that hero myths, by my definition, are not actually "religions" at all.[7] They give the blessing—and the power—of religious sanction to the heroic individual who rides the dissolving logic of his mind through any number of barriers and takes the goal with a well-aimed arrow instead of in a protective embrace. The hero myth is, in fact, a justification to abuse everything from stands of ancient trees to children, and belongs to history rather than prehistory; history as we know it is in fact just one long heroic epic. Our "acutely terminal testosterone-poisoned" version of events condemns everything else to the irrelevant—precisely because it is not "heroic" enough to be worth the attention. To prove that the myth is very much at the center of the values we feed our children today, see any popular movie house in your neighborhood. To see a fine explanation of how it leads directly to terrorism, both of "legitimate" states and of the more "conventional variety," see Robin Morgan's *The Demon Lover* (1989).

The rise of the hero myth can be pinpointed, at least in its fullblown variety, to a certain stage in cultural development, a stage at the edge of history in most regions. It is incidental, although not peripheral to our argument, that, in spite of Campbell's handful of female examples, the hero myth is male territory. Females are either "the mother he rejects, the temptress he conquers, the wife he subjugates" (Campbell, 1949:77), or, if she goes along with his bolt of linear thinking, the woman must be humble and grateful; he allows her to come along with him.

The Epic of Gilgamesh can be added to the list of heroic poetry, hindering female temptress and all. This epic held such a place in ancient Mesopotamia that it rivals what Homer was to the Greeks in terms of establishing values, being recited on every street corner and to every youth as his elders tried to form his character, serving as copy material for the young scribe. We can see what sort of character the Mesopotamian powers that be were looking for, lurking there behind stylus and reckoning tablet: the ostentatious builder, quick to fight, to ignore elders, to use women and then discard them, to consider his own immortality first and ignore anybody else's claim even to life in the pursuit. *The Epic of Gilgamesh* is, like Homer, the hallmark mythology of Mesopotamian culture; it found its way throughout the ancient Near East wherever Mesopotamian culture strode.

A final way in which ancient Mesopotamia helped to motivate and individuate its youth was by the addition of "personal gods" to the pantheon. The personal god has been defined as "the personification of a man's luck and success" (Jacobsen, 1949:219). Success in Mesopotamian culture was still "interpreted as an outside power which infuses itself into a man's doings and makes them produce results. It is not a man's own ability" (as it shall become in our own day) "which brings results, for man is [still relatively] weak and has no power to influence the course of the universe to any appreciable degree" (p. 219). Nonetheless, I think the importance of this invention for the freeing of the individual can readily be seen.

Two proverbs[8] say "When thou dost plan ahead,[9] thy god is thine; when thou dost not plan ahead, thy god is not thine" and "A man must truly proclaim the greatness of his god; a young man must wholeheartedly obey the command of his god" (Jacobsen, 1949:219). When a man had success, the Mesopotamian expression was that he had "acquired a god." That the individual could become his own god is a later development, but this is all a step along the road.

Nonetheless, evidence suggests that powerful counteracting forces were at work, trying cautiously to hedge such a development. Millions of years of stable human life cycles were not about to break all at once into full lineality; a sixth sense lingered, hinting with all the force of the most primitive taboo where lineality unbound might lead. Only as much was loosed as the individual, in his blind press for resources, was forced to dare.

For example, a curious bit of Mesopotamian taboo is that a man may not have sex with the priestess of his own personal god (Kramer, 1963). Is this for incestuous reasons, or to keep him from gaining too much control over this guide in his life? A verse can be cited in which the personal god is made equal to the force of a family in bringing fortune: "To the man who has a [personal] god, to him who, in his wide extended family, has been dealt a good fortune" (Sjöberg, 1967: 203).[10]

Elsewhere, the power of the clan is extolled in the literature on its own. One curse states: "May you be one that has no father, no mother, no brother, no sister, no heir, no adoptive child, no concubine, no family" (Sjöberg, 1967: 203). A term that may be translated as "clanship" is listed along with "the kindling of fire," "the extinction of fire," and "work" as one of the divine *me* that the goddess Inanna stole from the god Enki (p. 203). It is difficult to say how close this comes to the puppet rhetoric of modern-day presidents and other political groups who say America is built on strong families when the statistics more honestly show that at least half of marriages end in divorce, and the plight of abandoned children and the elderly tells another story.

We will consider one final ancient proverb. It says "Accept your lot (and) make your mother happy! Act promptly (and) make your (personal) god happy!" (Gordon, 1959:114). The mother would rather her children, both the weak and the strong, share equally in the inheritance, or that her son lives out a long but quiet life and does not play in the dangerous games of war and politics. On the other hand, the personal god—may we demythicize it as a man's "ego"?—"helps those that help themselves." Perhaps reciters of this couplet meant to ridicule the man who was tied to his mother's "apron strings"; only intonation could tell us for certain and clay tablets don't give us that. Nevertheless, it is important that both positions were recognized with equal time at least, and that the Sumerians were aware of some power that could—and should?—be wielded against the "personal god." The Mesopotamians, it seems, were not able to develop quite the linear view of history nor its corollary of a "revolution of rising expectations" (Bray, 1977:388) to really give the final spur to an individual to leave the old ways of his family. But they tried. And seclusion pulled in the opposite direction.

Chapter 13

Cities of Power

It's hard when folks can't find the work
Way they was bred and born.
When I was young, I always thought,
Well, I'd bide wi' me turnips and corn.
But I've been forced to work in towns,
So here's me litany:
From Hull and Halifax and hell,
Good Lord, deliver me.

I've seen fog creep across Leeds Brig
As thick as Bastille soup.
And I've lived where folks was stowed away
Like rabbits in a coop.
And I've seen snow float down Bradford Beck
As black as ebony.
From Hunslet, Hull, Beck, Whipsey, Sleck,
Good Lord, deliver me.

(A folk song from England's Industrial Revolution)

The city's appearance in the archaeological record in ancient Mesopotamia is

> marked by a sudden increase in [hierarchical] power in every
> department and by a magnification of the role played by power
> itself in the affairs of men. . . . The city played a special part . . .
> in stepping up power . . . , accumulating it and storing it in sym-

A History of Women's Seclusion in the Middle East
Published by the Haworth Press, Inc., 2006. All rights reserved.
doi:10.1300/5666_14

bolic forms, and transmitting it from generation to generation. (Mumford, 1961:569)

Beyond the simple fact of having so many more people to put somewhere, anywhere, certainly one of the reasons "urbanism appeared on the scene [was] as a means of organizing and controlling the increased population" (T. Young, 1972:839). In the city, humanity invented "a new . . . container for concentrating and storing human energy" (Mumford, 1961:569)—a remarkable springboard for the power of linear thought. Picking up the image of the city as container, feminist historian Elise Boulding (1976:191) remarked that "it seems to launch men." It is mostly women it contains. "It is impossible for a man to shut up his wife when he is living under a tree or in a tent which is always open on one side. [Besides,] he requires her to work, to fetch water and firewood and to herd the goats" (Thesiger, 1959: 177). This quote, although overemphasizing the power of men in carrying out this custom, underlines what has become almost axiomatic in the study of women in the Middle East: nomads who veil are generally those with the closest contacts to the cities, and city dwellers who do not veil are those so poor that their women must perform heavy physical tasks. The life of a pastoral nomad is a harsh one, precluding the use of a veil but promoting many other unique human adaptations, so the theory goes. As we saw in Figure 2.1, with veiled, pre-Islamic nomads, and Figure 3.12, with the modern divisions of a Bedouin tent along gender lines, seclusion hasn't left the desert alone for at least 2,000 years. Exactly what the parameters are must, I think, lie in understanding that the desert does not exist without the sown in the Middle East. Nomads don't merely invade and settle; town dwellers seek escape in the desert and take their sense of purity with them.

For now, I propose that urban life, although a man-made environment, comes with its own set of harsh realities that human social creativity must rise to meet. Is it only coincidence that the city is the symbol par excellence of statecraft and civilization in the first millennia or so of historical Mesopotamia—the very time when we can first find firm traces of women's seclusion? I think not.

Many urban stresses could be investigated as possible causes of seclusion. The noise, dirt, congestion, crowds of untrustworthy strangers, and loss of privacy encountered in a city are but a few of them. Indeed, it is quite common for the last two reasons to be cited by modern Middle Eastern women, new immigrants to cities. They wear the veil in the city, but discard it on visits to their native villages where everyone is either kin or well-known to them since childhood (E. Fernea, 1976b). But there is more.

"Certainly Mesopotamian population was increasing" at the time we first see the cities,

> but within the Mesopotamian heartland, there appears to have been in-migration, not out-migration. . . . Significantly . . . during the Late Ubaid and Early/Late Uruk [c. 4000-2100] there were large-scale movements of populations (for example, movements from the Susiana plain and from Eridu to Nippur and the Uruk region). . . . These movements seem to represent massive population displacements and are certainly, to some degree, to be explained politically, that is, as movements from less successful, more unstable[1] chieftains to more successful ones. (Zagarell, 1986b:418-419)*

We have seen what forces drive the dispossessed to leave their farms and flock to the cities. They come in search of power, *their* power and *their* wealth vanished; they aren't quite sure how. However, the city certainly does seem to have something to do with it.

Power is an ambiguous term. It conjures images of swords and shields, armies and police forces. These are but the outward trappings of power: more succinctly put, it is the control of resources and their distribution. Again, let us begin with parallels from our present situation and work backward to ancient Mesopotamia from there.

The plight of many third world nations even in this time of superior transportation and technology is described thus:

> Contrary to popular notions, most transfers of food and livestock feed in world trade have been to secure the nutritional affluence in [developed nations. For example,] Japan and Europe, which together contain about one fifth as many people as China and India, import more grain. China's, India's and most African

countries' food imports are modest in relative terms, and are counterbalanced by food exports. Other developing nations, under strong economic and political pressures, export their high quality foods and thus increase internal malnutrition. Affluence and excellent transportation are creating a greater imbalance in the world's maldistributed food base than in any period of man's history. (Dando, 1980:102-103)

When I see peaches and grapes in my neighborhood store in January, I cringe. The sign says "From Chile." Wonderful for us that we can break the natural laws like this, but how many of the people who picked that fruit for our tables can share our peaches and grapes in September? What better proof could there be that trade is the result of shortages, even if only perceived shortages, in the superpowers.

I understand that even in modern Britain, people in small farming villages are least likely of all Britons to enjoy fresh vegetables on their tables. Driven by economic necessity, they specialize in one crop but then find that the major distributing forces, the food chain corporations, will not spend the time and expense to transport the very small quantities of fresh produce such a small community would require back to them. Unless they shop in the cities, or are at leisure to plant a patch for themselves, people in the country must be content with canned goods. Even in the most advanced countries, then, good, nutritious food, never mind the aesthetics of minutes-old fingerling carrots or petit pois, is a privilege of a very few.

The culprit? Our very modernized, centralized distribution system, to which everything else must bow. Ancient Mesopotamia's urban distribution flourished on the elite's ability to store the grain their trading reaped. The people of the nineteenth century discovered that the removal of the germ from flour vastly improved its keeping quality (E. David, 1977:34-35). Hence the powerful could gain control over all distribution up to the milling, whereas the Mesopotamians had to be content with grain stored in its unmilled state and armies of women at their grinding stones. The next century's addition of preservatives and refrigeration to extend shelf life has moved control into the bread itself. All the consumer needs is his or her teeth (or system-provided dentures). Isn't it interesting how the consumer "prefers exactly what the . . . industry prefers that she should prefer" (Berry, 1987: 40)—in this case, fully processed white bread.

The sense we have that famines of recent history hit the farmers, the very producers, is true: famine is usually the scourge of the farm-lands, not of the urban centers. When the powers of a city can draw on many ecosystems to sustain them, they little care if one of these happens to fail. It is to the cities that the starving come in time of famine. They are right: that is where all the food has gone, and all the fertility of their soil. Agricultural problems always take a backseat to issues such as world conquest in the eyes of multinational powers—an attitude that tends to aggravate the farmers' problems. We may want to add monocropping to the end of a scale of agricultural methods that elevates from long fallow through multicropping.[2] Monocropping, when possible with more than one crop a year, is the phase of agriculture resorted to when cities are demanding the produce. The farmer is encouraged or obliged to leave the variety of crops that kept his family alive throughout the year to specialize in some cash crop such as cotton. One cannot eat cotton. If a failure occurs in his region, he cannot buy his food from his usual sources.

Such was the cause of the Irish potato famine. For years the Irish people had been encouraged or forced by their landlords to turn their land into pastures to provide wool for England's insatiable factories. For personal consumption they turned to potatoes and little other than potatoes, and only enough to keep body and soul together. Come the blight, the shipping by the monolith's rules of all the mutton out of Dublin to England's manufacturing centers, and disaster struck.

Modern farming techniques are of doubtful efficiency. Yet unequivocally they enrich "the city by weakening and impoverishing the country" (Berry, 1987:35). They would not be allowed to survive in the world of cities if they did not.

As a girl growing up in a small village in Germany, I watched with interest one very large and very poor family. Although not agriculturalists themselves, they were able to eke out the father's meager income by frequent trips to the forests and wild places for mushrooms and other edibles. Had they lived in the city, this would have been impossible, at least on a regular basis and without paying bus fare. In England during the enclosure of the eighteenth century, we have already seen that people were forced to the factories and the cities against their wills because the communal lands where many of them had gained much of their livelihood were no longer open to them. In the United States, a friend of mine describes how the coming of many wealthy urbanites, "weekend farmers," to his rural Virginia county has put much stress on the natives. These newcomers insist that trespassing rules be enforced the way they are in the city. Many a family used to supplement their sharecroppers' diets with a "possum" or two caught on these lands. They now find their subsistence threatened.

Let us consider two points. First, that ancient Mesopotamian city-states and their transportation systems were of such a scale that if one portion of their hinterland should fail, any other place from which food—except grain—could be brought in time to be of use against famine would likewise be stricken. The divorce, then, of producers and consumers was somewhat, but not quite, what we know today. Indeed, the ancient literature includes descriptions of cities in famine. However, the redistribution system that could gather the resources to built ziggurats and massive walled cities also insisted that rulers and their armies were fed first. If they wanted to see their children fed, women would have to throw their lot with such powers even when, in the long run, such powers worked against their interest—unless they could manage claims on that power and at the same time build their own impenetrable walls against it.

We can see, then, that given the society we can re-create for early Mesopotamia—and for our present world society, too, although Westerners have hardly had a chance to see it stretched to such a degree yet—it is generally better to face a state of poverty in the country than in the city. In the country, the resources are at hand and available to all—if the powers that be have not totally siphoned off all resources, as has become possible only recently. However, if there are no resources, due to drought or locusts or some other factor, men, women, and children—rich and poor—suffer equally.

The raw materials for everything an urban population consumes must be brought in from the countryside, even if they are manufactured or receive final preparation in town. The distances involved preclude most people from going to fetch their necessities every day and, besides, it is part of the economics of a city that transportation be consolidated and made efficient with carts and mules—or trucks and trains. During England's great urbanization in 1767 (which didn't happen until 5,000 years after the Mesopotamians had been driven to it) John Mitchell wrote rather simplistically but no less emotionally, "Upon land, people can only want through negligence, but in towns they starve for want of employment, which they often cannot get" (quoted in Dando, 1980:123). Unfortunately, the man able to produce the capital and organization necessary to bring the wool into the town is also very likely to be the man in charge of hiring in the workshops. In other words, not only access to the goods, but access to the means of obtaining those goods—a wage—are completely out of the average person's control. In fact, if "the Man" uses his trucks to carry vegetables and fruit as well, a woman can find herself in a very vulnerable position indeed. A man in the same circumstances is also open to exploitation, it must be admitted, but the women may have the added disadvantage of children to care for,[3] and her labor may be considered worth only half that of a man. And a man can always up and leave.

Anna Rubbo (1975) describes the effects of concentration and capitalization on women in Colombia, driven to the cities by ever-greater consolidation on the land.

> Whereas a peasant woman could combine farming and child-rearing with a degree of emotional and economic stability for all, the poor townswoman struggles to earn a living and to raise children as she would like to, that is, as *formal* ("polite") and worthy members of society. For peasants, especially the women, householding includes domestic work, childrearing, and farming, and in a very real sense these are organically interconnected. For the townswomen, however, these basic concepts of life are structurally differentiated, and, what is more, seem incapable of synthesis. (p. 353)

"Politeness" may be translated from the Colombian here to a sense of responsibility for the rest of the clan. It is a value that an interest-based economy does not bother to fit into its system or, if it does, only at the very bottom where other considerations can quickly replace it in priority when things get rough.

As the words of the song quoted at the beginning of this chapter indicate, "the age-old attractions of the city have always been greater for the visitor who is economically independent of its machine, and who can leave it at will" (Reynolds, 1972:407). A trip into town from the rural estate (where *our* apricots are blooming nicely this year) to enjoy the famous (and terribly expensive, but who's counting?) apricot concoction of some superb pastry chef is one thing. Having to buy one's apricots (one should waste money on apricots when the children are starving!) when one has no apricot trees, and no roof to dry them on if one did have them, is quite another.

Here are some insightful comments on the subject.

> The use of flat roofs on dwellings must have been dictated by other criteria than ability to shed water efficiently. . . . Concrete evidence of flat roofs only appears in the form of pictures and models at a period when the development toward urbanization had gone a long way and one is tempted to see the flat roof as a feature dictated by urbanization itself. With increasing cost of land within the city only the wealthy could afford gardens or courtyards, yet a clean level area was vital to the economy, for only in such spaces could many domestic chores such as beating bedding or drying fruit be carried out. Indeed, in many parts of the Middle East today the flat roofs perform not only such functions as these but, because they are all at much the same level, they provide a means of moving about the town or village clean shod [or relatively secluded] which the streets do not.[4] (Hodges, 1972:526)

I think these comments are vital for an understanding not only of the Middle Eastern house but also of the nature of urbanization and what it does to women. If she cannot afford even enough space in which to set her apricots out to dry or process her wheat into couscous (never mind enough land to gather or grow her own food[5]), the woman is just that much more at the mercy of the system. She must pay the workers—and some middleman—to do that work for her now. No doubt she will be sucked into that army of workers in order to pay for what had once been any woman's birthright.

The modern American city dweller feels something similar when he or she yearns for an apartment with a balcony—or maybe just a room with a view. We have overstepped the line without seeing it. The line was blurred by the promise of technology. We all wanted washing machines and dryers for the convenience. Now they are necessities; for the babbling brook to wash in and the breezy, sunny meadow for drying are luxuries beyond almost anyone's reach. They are necessities one must leave one's children and go out to work for, for even the resources of housework have been taken out of our hands.

For her Colombians caught in the urban trap, Rubbo (1975) sees little hope of escape from the situation besides revolution. But no one who has watched the innumerable revolutions that have happened throughout the world since the spread of capitalism can really imagine that women and their children can be helped by such violent upheavals. Any man strong enough, "linear" enough, to win such a battle is bound to replace the former hierarchy with one of his own, at least as oppressive to the souls on the lower rungs of his ladder as was the former. It is the same sorts of people—women, children, the old, the handicapped—who will find themselves on the lowest rungs.

Urbanization gives lineality its greatest boost. It turns its great power to making decisions for a broad area, and they are decisions made from the view from the city wall, looking inward instead of out. More and more they refuse to take the land into consideration. They are decisions made by people who never held a hoe in their lives, who eat the fruit of the vine but cannot tell that vine from morning glory.

Perhaps the most blatant indication of this is when cities take on what has been "termed 'rectilinear' or 'geometric' planning where the advantages of efficiency accruing to the straight line are sought." This lays the streets out in the renowned "grid" pattern. Earlier settlements, even cities, "accept the site as far as possible and [proceed] along the natural levels so that communication is wandering rather than direct" (G. Wright, 1985:162). The grid pattern of urban development seems not to have been reached in Mesopotamia until the appearance of several massive settlements the Assyrians built from scratch. Certainly it seems to be symptomatic of

> totalitarian foreign rule and the disruption of native traditions. Furthermore it [eventually extends] from specialized contexts (Palaces etc.) to the everyday world. . . . It is worth noting that the two types of town plan here adumbrated, the informal contour plan and the formal geometric plan, correspond to the two worlds or world orders which appear to man—the curved and the square, the world of sense and the world of idea . . . (G. Wright, 1985:163-164)

When Assyria imposed grids on several Palestinian cities, it was able to do so because it was "a foreign-based, world power [and] absolutist, thus well able to disregard local interests and replan the city on rational lines" (G. Wright, 1985:164). It was to Assyria's advantage to do so. For example, spies can see better what's going on down a straight street; armies can move with more ease. Poor natives hiding in dark alleys have more difficulty hijacking the wealthy shipments passing by.

It is no coincidence that ancient empire builders as early as the mid-first millennium BCE put out the propaganda that they were spreading "equality" and "freedom" as they metastasized like their modern counterparts, making the world free for trade according to their rules to keep the artificially elevated standard of living at home. The Assyrians forcibly removed whole populations from lands the natives understood through tradition and used with room for renewal. The conqueror set their conquered peoples down where the empire could dictate what work was to be done when. They leveled all local cultures' ways of supporting their women and children as they brought them all equally under their exploiting monolith. "In this way, the imperial government established groups within the subject population entirely dependant on the authorities" (Thompson, 1999:183), owing nothing to "those behind them," their wives and children, the land. Also, "by convincing enemy populations that the purpose of the state was to spread civilization and a higher moral code, they substantially lowered the cost of imperial conquests" (M. Harris, 1979:110). Modern empires try the same thing today, and we seem even less able to see through the calls to "win hearts and minds."

To this day, most Middle Eastern towns preserve the jumble of "blind" alleys of their forebears (to be flattened by modern "Assyrians" imposing their "liberation" on "insurgents" otherwise protected by the twisting alleys—in Fallujah, Iraq, even as I write this). Perhaps this preservation is merely a result of the collapse of the great empires, but it may also be linked to the ideology behind women's seclusion. Perhaps the practice of seclusion helped limit total disregard for the land to this extent. Certainly this jumble form of town planning is not merely the gratis chaos made by uneducated minds (more nonlinear minds, perhaps, and in that sense more undisciplined), but plays an important part in the social organization. Such alleys are not public places but are semi-private amenities for the use of the immediate neighborhood. The emphasis is on private and not public uses, for the use of women. Public uses, such as temples, often mean merely a center for indoctrination by the masters. How women, like insurgents (better: freedom fighters, fighting against the monolith's view of "freedom") use the "chaotic" spaces in the modern Muslim city has been well documented.[6] A parallel the reader may find more understandable is found in the winding roads and cul-de-sacs of our suburbs. Our one-sided world mocks the "bedroom community" now, too, but such streets in their original conception in the 1950s at least were the province of women and children. Even then, of course, in America they were removed by a good hour's train ride from the centers of power, and isolated from them, which has in many respects led to their disparagement. To do away with the central-city jumble in the Middle East would be tantamount to doing away with women's seclusion, and women have kept enough say in these societies that this is not done—yet. But how will the conquerors rebuild Fallujah?

Other indications suggest that the rights, nay, the very basic needs, of the environment were already beginning to be threatened in earliest Mesopotamia. The new power was isolated by the artificial environment of the city from concern with fertility, reproduction, and nature that characterized the old village culture. "Without this communal identification and mothering, the young become demoralized: indeed, their very power to become fully human may vanish, along with Neolithic man's first obligation—the cherishing and nurturing of life. . . . When these primary bonds dissolve, when the intimate visible community ceases to be a watchful, deeply concerned group, then the 'We' becomes a buzzing swarm of 'I's'" (Mumford, 1961: 15). Traces of nature are found in ancient Mesopotamia's gods, but their ability to destroy a whole city at a word if it suited them expressed the new ideology of power (Mumford, 1961). The power of these new gods is not unlike that of the rulers of the time—at least, of the sort of power to which they aspired. All other wants and needs were beginning to have to give way.

An urban geographer noted that

> the contracts of the city may indeed be face-to-face, but they are nevertheless impersonal, superficial, transitory and segmental . . . . The superficiality, the anonymity, and the transitory character of urban social relations make intelligible, also, the sophistication and the rationality generally ascribed to city-dwellers. . . . The city [is] . . . a crucible for the transformation of personality, producing such characteristics as reserve, blasé attitudes, indifference, . . . competitiveness, self-aggrandizement, exploitative attitudes, frustration and irritation, nervous tension, instability,

insecurity, . . . approval of efficiency and innovation, and a high degree of personal disorganization. . . . Such qualities of social organization as the importance and interdependency of specialists rather than of individuals; impersonal, transitory, superficial, segmental, and utilitarian social contacts; deterioration in the integration of social organization . . . ; an emphasis on time; predatoriness; formal controls; anonymity; a flexible caste structure counterbalanced by an intensified and ramified differentiation by income and social status; . . . involuntary segregation of racial, linguistic, income and class groups. . . . Importance of symbols and stereotypes; standardization of products and processes, gearing of facilities and institutions to the average user; subordination of individuality; weakening of kinship bonds; decline in social significance of the family; loss of traditional bases of solidarity . . . (Wheatley, 1972:609-610)

Well, the list goes on and on.

Here is a list of the city's qualities from the tablets of ancient Mesopotamia:

> [The city] grants not long days to the braggart,
> Allows no evil word to be uttered against (the divine) judgement.
> Hypocrisy, distortion,
> Abuse, malice, unseemliness,
> Insolence, enmity, oppression,
> Envy, (brute) force, libelous speech,
> Arrogance, violation of agreement, breech of contract, abuse of (a court) verdict,
> (All these) evils the city does not tolerate . . .
> The city endowed with truth,
> Where righteousness (and) justice are perpetrated . . .
> Where the older brother honors the younger brother, acts humanely (toward him),
> Where the word of the elders is heeded, where it is repeated in fear,
> Where the son humbly fears his mother, where eldership endures . . . (Pritchard, 1969:573-574)

I can only imagine that the ancient poet "doth protest too much." Or perhaps this is an example of an ancient vacation brochure. It was written for the city of Nippur, which was something like a Mecca or a Jerusalem for all of Southern Mesopotamia. We've already noted that, as with trade, setting oneself up as a pilgrimage center is a good way to get resources from elsewhere. This has the added benefit of causing the pious to fund their own caravans and bring the goods to you instead of having to go out after them yourself. We have no record that the kings of Nippur joined with the other city-state rulers in the power struggles that disrupted the peace in these early times. So perhaps this city was, in truth, as the poem suggests, free from the usual urban ills that people even 5,000 years ago noticed and of which they could complain (Falkenstein, 1974:16)—by using the separation of religion to shove these ills to other regions.

So now we must ask the question, to whom should the woman dependent on this urban structure turn? The man at the top only understands the rule of the monolith and that rule is profit and its power. Western women today can't have their menses without deferring to the hierarchy, the good graces of Kimberly-Clark. In Colombia, Rubbo (1975) saw a desperate turning by the women to sorcery as their only means of power; Rausch (2000) found a similar phenomenon as a traditional Middle Eastern society is revised along Western lines. Unfortunately, as few of the men were believers, and the magic could make no claim on new, international Islamic belief, this conversion had little, or even a negative, effect on women's station. Still, if any hope at all exists, I think this magic gives us an inkling of what it might be.

I would suggest that if there is a second, parallel network of power opposed to the city's monolith, with rules of its own *(and with strong holds of honor upon the members of the orthodox power hierarchy)* constraints it behooves their ambition and prestige to uphold (and magic as well as other belief systems have at times fulfilled this need)—then women and their children have a chance to survive the urban center relatively unexploited. Otherwise, the end is linear and inevitable. As runs the Middle Eastern women's proverb, "To whom do I appeal when the executioner is my judge?" (Morgan, 1989:243); or as Ivan Illich (1982:36) said: "There is a Tanzania for the Nyerere, and Israel for Begin, but no Amazonia in sight. The [urban] nation-state is invariably sexist." "Institutions of religion, business, war, the

State," the city—all, as feminist Robin Morgan saw, are inextricably and inescapably "patriarchy" where

> the wife will excuse in her husband what she would not excuse in herself. And so the daughter will yearn after her exciting father, forsaking her mother's dreary life model. . . . And so the "liberated" wife will become sole breadwinner, support her husband, and call it modernity. . . . She makes his quest her quest, his system her system . . . which means, ironically, she may then survive—but as someone she will no longer recognize. (1989: 75, 79)

Chapter 14

Vernacular Gender

As she dabbles in history (or prehistory, which, as a woman, is more her provenance), the feminist becomes aware that most human societies—before our own—did make compensation to women for their bind of being born an "honest" cell. In many instances these compensations are just the "inequalities" that her feminist sisters—and perhaps she herself—have been misunderstanding and railing against for so long.

Perhaps the greatest cultural protection against female exploitation that early hominids developed was sexual division of labor. Ivan Illich calls it "vernacular gender" and gives it much broader scope than that of mere labor. What developed at this crucial time was, in Illich's words, "the eminently local and time-bound duality that sets off men and women under circumstances and conditions that prevent them from saying, doing, desiring or perceiving 'the same thing'" (1982:90). In other words, as human intelligence developed, the sexes were each given a different linear agenda to work (and play) with *in order to counteract the adverse effects of that lineality.* Most vitally, "no personal authority" of any sort was created to stand "above the two domains" (p. 90). Unlike territory, but like estrus (with which its development is tightly connected), "vernacular gender" has "no parallel in the world of primates" (p. 106). This is the human and humanizing "imperative."

Of course, such a dividing line drawn as it is first and foremost by culture must be practically invisible to the prehistorian's spade. Illich (1982) gives us these beautiful descriptions of "vernacular gender" as it is found in historical cultures:

> Each village does its own dance to the tune of its own regional music. (p. 108)

A History of Women's Seclusion in the Middle East
Published by the Haworth Press, Inc., 2006. All rights reserved.
doi:10.1300/5666_15

The contours of spaces and schedules determine who does and who uses what and when. Gender demands that the Berber woman lean on the inside of the east wall of a house while the outside of the wall is for man. . . . In one valley of the Alps, they meet on the threshing floor, he with the flail and she with the sieve. Farther down the river, this place is men's exclusive domain. As they are divided, so genders are also interwoven differently in each culture and time. They can rule separate territories and rarely intertwine, or they can be knotted like the lines in the Book of Kells. Sometimes no basket can be plaited, no fire kindled without the collaboration of two sets of hands. Each culture brings the genders together in its unique way. (pp. 105-107)

As the warp runs on and on lengthwise in the fabric, and the woof crisscrosses it at right angles to tie the threads together, so the actions that engender the home, the actions that engender life space, are necessarily different depending on whether they leave traces from men or traces from women. (p. 122)

Gender is not confined to the present. . . . To this very day in Thrace, men speak about the dead and their deeds, but only women can address them. Only the women can shriek, lamenting those who have passed away and invoking their protection. Gendered action stretches into the past, into the beyond. (p. 98)

Of course, cultural sexual dichotomy is a well-known phenomenon to anthropologists who usually, like government policymakers—heavily imbued with Western values—are quick to condemn it as a block to modernization.[1] In their fascination with the fluidity of gendered activities from culture to culture—the fact that in one place only women are potters, in another either sex may perform the task, while in the third place only men work with clay—most anthropologists have ignored the implications of the fact that some labor and worldview distinction is universal—except in our own modern culture. Bent on proving that, by primitive precedent, women can do just about *anything,* from healing to house-building, theorists fail to note that never, even in the simplest of societies, are they forced to do *everything* necessary to keep a household running. "*Balance* is the key . . . to describe the interdependence of the separate male and female domains," Illich (1982:115) says, and therefore, "traditional female-male" equanimity is "threatened [not helped] by the growing similarity of male and female roles in the home and on the job" in modern times.

Gendered labor, space, worldview, is not, in any "primitive" culture, comparable to the division of labor between, for exampe, doctor/nurse or executive/secretary in ours. By no means do I advocate the passage of laws to make these jobs gender specific when I find "vernacular gender" attractive. The "primitive" woman is never required to simply fulfill the more-valued, higher-trained, higher-paid male's orders more or less mindlessly. Nor does she mutely take dictation, bursting like revelation from the boss's lips, type it in triplicate, and carefully file (or shred) the evidence. It would also not help equalize a situation if a certain number of doctor's name tags are reserved for women, either, as long as decisions concerning funding or who may obtain what procedures are in the hands of a male-dominated legislature—or "the marketplace." Nor will it do to return to a female monopoly of the kitchen, for example, as long as the woman in the kitchen is isolated from other women in other kitchens by male-built "conveniences," or as long as other options for an honorable dinner exist for any man. As long as he can get better/cheaper/more glamorous/faster food from a male-owned and -operated establishment downtown, the man in the West is free from the restraints of vernacular gender—and the woman is the victim of the exploitation we've replaced it with.

Why one culture divides the world one way, and the next another, is a fascinating question. It is one that has been barely touched upon, and one I hope to begin to answer for the Middle East specifically. Environmental variations seem the most obvious place to start the search, and I believe this proves a fruitful source for the explanation of seclusion. At the moment, let me make the following observations concerning cultures in general. Fishing from a quiet bank in odd moments seems more compatible with the biologically determined female occupation of childbearing and nursing than large-scale fishing operations in boats on the high seas for days and nights on end, subject to the immediate demands of weather and marine migrations.[2] However, in other cases, we see it is the women who traditionally take long trading journeys with both infant and wares strapped to their bodies, or engage in other difficult, even dangerous tasks. In these cases we must suspect that the environment is dangerously close to overpopulation and that either removal of the women from their marital beds or exposure of child, mother, or both to hazards is one means the society has at its disposal to enforce birth control.

Whatever the precise nature of the arrangement, whatever other purposes it serves, there is one major function of this key aspect of human culture, this complimentarity which "is unique about *Homo sapiens* . . . , the constant *incarnation* of the symbolic duality of gender" (Illich, 1982:76). It is to render a man without a woman (either his sister, wife, daughter, or mother—by no means do I want to imply that sexual, romantic relations are the all-important ones) an anomaly, warp without woof, unraveled cloth, a lifeless pile of threads. This man was still in existence in the early eighteenth century when

> you could recognize the bachelor from afar by his stench and gloomy looks. From notaries' records, we know that solitary men left no shirts or sheets when they died. . . . A man without a woman . . . could barely survive. . . . He had no way to make, wash and mend his clothes; it was impossible for him to keep chickens or to milk a goat; . . . he could not eat butter, milk or eggs. He could not cook certain foods even if he had the ingredients. (Illich, 1982:67)

In short, culture must make the plight of the womanless man not simply a case that the nearest brothel can cure, but something approaching what the abandoned honest-cell-with-highly-dependent-human-child becomes because of her biology. In any society (until ours), any person alone was considered an object of pity, deserving of special help and consideration (as long, of course, as he upheld the rest of culture's values). The widow, for example, could get her tools sharpened by the blacksmith without charge.

Some would suggest that my vision requires every woman to be a mother. Not so. Not only does vernacular gender make the physical survival of the next generation possible, it also, more vitally, protects cultural options for that generation.

> When, from infancy, men and women grasp the world from complimentary sides, they develop two distinct models with which they conceptualize the universe. . . . Not only do they see

the same things from different perspectives and in different hues, but early on they learn that there is always another side to a thing. (Illich, 1982:128)

As long as tradition protects both sides, options exist for the individual outlook as well as for the community as a whole.

Cultural inducements to family responsibility, vernacular gender in particular, were such an important development that we may be sure only the most dire of circumstances could let this responsibility for the future be set aside for the necessity of the moment during our early prehistory. Certainly women's contributions to the common food store rarely flagged—71 percent of the calories consumed by the !Kung are the product of women's gathering activities.[3] Their first priority was always to the future of the species they toted everywhere (estimates are in the thousands of miles per child in the first three years of life), strapped to their backs.

Look at the expansion of possibilities a division of labor opened up to early women and men: every member of the community need not "learn" (or have present in their instinctual repertoire if we are at the preculture stage) every skill, but could devote time and energy to the specific skills of his or her own particular labor. Although it is popular among feminist prehistorians to see our ancestresses carrying spears and bringing down the big game, this need not be a necessary part of our self-esteem. Let the words be reiterated that

> too much attention has been given to the skills required for hunting and too little to the skills required for gathering and the raising of dependent young. The techniques required for efficient gathering include location and identification of plant varieties, seasonal and geographical knowledge, containers for carrying the food and tools for its preparation. Among modern hunting-gathering groups this knowledge is an extremely complex, well-developed and important part of their cultural equipment. Caring for a curious, energetic, but still dependent human infant is difficult and demanding. Not only must the infant be watched, it must be taught the customs, dangers, and knowledge of its group. For the early hominids, as their cultural equipment and symbolic communication increased, the job of training the

young would demand more skill. Selection pressure for better brains came from many directions. (Slocum, 1975:46-47)

A sense that "merely" grubbing around for nuts and berries is not worthy of "superwomen" is probably a product of recent unification of the sexes, grown maladaptive, and of appraisal of everything in terms of the dominating, individuating value system, now being allowed a free hand at exploitation. Certainly, "the chances of productive failure, everything else being equal, are halved by a mixed hunting-gathering economy. A group can fall back on the alternative technique when necessary" (Woolfson, 1982:30).

To underscore the importance of the cultural as opposed to the individual evolution, the !Kung and many other simple modern societies have mechanisms to see to it that no individual's superiority becomes his alone, that he shares it among his social group. These include laws as to the sharing of all resources and, among the !Kung, this example bears repeating:

> Say that a man has been hunting. He must not come home and announce like a braggart, "I have killed a big one in the bush." He must first sit down in silence until I or someone else comes up to his fire and asks, "What did you see today?" He replies quietly, "Ah, I'm no good for hunting. I saw nothing at all— maybe just a tiny one." Then I smile to myself because I now know he has killed something big. (Lee, 1979:244)

"If a hunter has had a particularly good series of kills," we are further told, "he may even voluntarily cease hunting for a matter of weeks so as not to outshine too far his fellow-hunters" (Woolfson, 1982:27). Perhaps, also, not to overhunt an area.

These acculturated values are of particular importance between the sexes. The !Kung do not make the mistake of Westerners in devaluing the work of women. The men freely admit that without the contributed vegetable resources of the women, they wouldn't have the strength to carry out the hunt. Although they do not hunt, the women's "knowledge of the environment gained on gathering trips is valued by the men" (Wolfson, 1982:28) and drawn on when discussions concerning the next hunt are held. Most importantly, heavy socialization seems to work against compartmentalization (over linearization) of "one's motives, feeling states, and (most of all) actions" (Draper, 1975:104). The society demands that all its members "remain in continuous communication" (p. 104) and avoid all "kinds of ostentation" (p. 107). Finally, "there is an extremely low cultural tolerance for aggressive behavior by anyone, male or female. In [other] societies where aggressiveness and dominance are valued,[4] these behaviors accrue disproportionately to males, and the females are common targets" (p. 91).

Patricia Draper does much to show how, with the coming of settled life to these people, these gentle values and the status of women quickly deteriorate. Altruistic teaching in this case can do little to alleviate the realities the !Kung now face in a world of Western creation.

Whenever we—men or women—leave our homes to work, we can hardly help becoming either the exploited or the exploiter; the latter is sought after because it is physically less objectionable but it cannot be any less objectionable morally. It is by not undertaking actions within the system that we can keep our homes from becoming mere residences. "Residence," says Wendell Berry (1987), is

> from the Latin *residere,* "to sit back" or "remain sitting". . .[a place] in which the residers do not work. The house is built, equipped, decorated, and provisioned by other people, by strangers. In it, the married [couple's] . . . domestic labor consists principally of buying things, putting things away, and throwing things away . . . In such a "home," a married couple are mates, sexually, legally and socially, but they are not helpmates; they do nothing useful together or for each other. When such spouses say to each other, "I will love you forever," the meaning of their words is seriously impaired by their circumstances. They are speaking in the presence of so little that they have done and made. . . . (pp. 119-120)

Essayist Berry describes a sunflower a friend had grown all alone, apart from others. "There is a plant that has 'realized its full potential as an individual,'" the friend said. "And clearly it had," Berry continues.

> It had grown very tall; it had put out many long branches heavily laden with blossoms—and the branches had broken off, for they had grown too long and too heavy. The plant had indeed realized

its full potential as an individual, but it had failed as a Maximilian sunflower. (p. 115)

People likewise reach their full potential as human beings not alone, but in relationship with other human beings. "More and more," Mary Catherine Bateson (1984) wrote, "it has seemed to me that the idea of an individual, the idea that there is someone to be known, separate from the relationships, is simply an error" (cited in Berry, 1987:115).

The Middle Eastern system of women's seclusion forces relationships between men and women upon a society that would fain do without them. It demands that men and women, at least, are not allowed to be interchangeable and replaceable, insists that men and women "find their common ground and be somewhat harmoniously rejoined, not by some resolution of conflict and power, but by proving indispensable to one another, as in fact they are" (Berry, 1987:122).

Chapter 15

Slavery

Aggression against one's neighbors follows an interesting evolution. Self-sufficient hunting-and-gathering tribes tend to have systems of mutual raiding or highly ritualized warfare, which are part of their traditional mechanisms for population maintenance. Although people at this level of social complexity

> identify with the territory in which they were born, they don't have to defend that territory in order to earn their living. Hence acquisition of additional territory through the rout or annihilation of enemy forces is seldom a conscious motive for joining battle. (M. Harris, 1977:149)

Under such circumstances, captives, among other booty, serve as tokens of the raiders' prowess but are of little economic value except in the symbolic marketplace of scalps and battle scars. As a matter of fact, "taking prisoners and making slaves of them is impractical for a society that cannot intensify its system of production without depleting its resource base and that lacks organizational capacity to exploit a hostile, underfed labor force" (p. 55).

There are cases among the Plains Indians, for example, when "slaves" were taken, but this word is the word of the white men recording the action. Such captives were usually children, taken and adopted "into families who had lost their children either by war or sickness" (R. Flannery, 1953:98). By no means could these people have engaged in true exploitative slavery, for "Their entire mode of existence is dominated by the need not to expand in order to preserve the favorable ratio of people to resources" (M. Harris, 1977:55).

Subsistence farmers—most are, as I have shown, ultimately not self-sufficient—may also move aggressively against their neighbors

A History of Women's Seclusion in the Middle East
Published by the Haworth Press, Inc., 2006. All rights reserved.
doi:10.1300/5666_16

when they feel the pinch of resources. New Guinea provides a fine example of how ritual warfare continues to play a part in population maintenance. However, at this stage warfare probably does "become more frequent and more deadly. Certainly the scale of combat [increases]. Permanent houses, food-processing equipment, crops growing in the fields [sharpen] the sense of territorial identity" (M. Harris, 1977:50). If they are strong enough, the farmers will wipe out their enemies and appropriate sometimes their women but mostly their land. Usually there are mouths enough to feed already. Therefore, agricultural villages, too, lack the slavery dimension of aggression.

With the coming of the state, matters take on a very different face. Aggression at this level clearly involves

> the attempt on the part of one state to raise its standard of living at the expense of others (although the underlying economic interests may be covered up by religious or political themes). The form of political organization which we call the state came into existence precisely because it was able to . . . conquer territories [and] subjugate . . . enemies. (Harris, 1977:54-55)

It takes great faith in and even greater dependence on systems of capitalistic trade to covet not only one's neighbor's land but one's neighbor himself as a means of production. Inviting (even when the invitation is chains—or illegally across a dangerous border) total strangers to share one's board seems a contradiction if resources are scarce. Therefore, when slaves are a part—often the major part—of the interest in aggression, not only must milking the local resources take most or all of the average person's day, but the capitalists' brilliant discovery must already have been made: that the exploitable and inflatable quantity of a commodity, à la Marx, is the labor power involved. It seems reasonable that a good prod in this direction can be given when land is alienable and it has been alienated from one's neighbors—i.e., they come begging or are sold for food or for work, and one learns (it is not obvious at first) that by juggling the arrangements of this relationship—giving the worker not what his labor is worth but only what he needs to keep on working—one can really help oneself.

All slaves are not created equal, however:

> To force a detachment of captive slaves—i.e., former free warriors—to work in the field with copper hoes would demand about double the number of armed soldiers to watch them, because in an armed conflict a copper hoe was not so very different from a copper hatchet, which was the usual warriors' arms of that age. . . . Therefore all male prisoners of war were usually brained on the spot, and only female slaves were used in any number in the state economies. (Diakonoff, 1972:45)

Gerda Lerner's (1986) study of the history of "The Woman Slave" in *The Creation of Patriarchy* is very good reading. She points out that since part of being made a female slave was being raped, not only were women less physically inclined to rebel, but it soon became in the best interest of their children to be subservient.

Many scholars with no interest in women's history at all have illustrated the difference between men's and women's slavery in very early ancient Mesopotamia. For instance, already in the earliest Protoliterate tablets we have a word for female slave—a drawing of a vulva with three mountains, to indicate her foreign origin. (About half of the women in one study of ration lists had non-Sumerian names [Maekawa, 1980:90].) The word for male slave does not occur until later.

We are given these telling facts: "In the Bau [temple] community . . . there were from 250 to 300 slaves, of whom the overwhelming proportion were women. One tablet alone lists 205 slave girls and their children" (Adams, 1965:96). The Sumerian texts often call these women *lukur,* a term which sometimes appears in a combined form meaning "concubine of the king" (A. Oppenheim, 1948:78), but which in later epochs becomes interchangeable with the Akkadian *nadîtu,* woman "dedicated to a god" (Uchitel, 1984b:271).

One may debate, I suppose, as to whether the fate of these women's husbands and brothers (probably death[1] or blindness for those few kept alive if the Sumerian name given to them, *igi-nu-du,* "the blind ones," is to be taken literally) was better than the women's ongoing exploitation. Perhaps males were taken to serve by pulling shipping up the river or in heavy industrial workshops in the suburbs, in which case their ration records may be rare because they are situated away from the city centers archaeologists prefer to excavate (and away from the conquerors' women).

Another very good possibility is suggested by the fact that women on the ration lists are much more frequently listed with female children than with male, and that sometimes when a male child is listed one year, he vanishes the next. This leads to the suggestion that to "deactivate" the sons of slave women, so to speak, they "were separated from their mothers and were castrated just before they attained puberty when they were given 15 *sila* of barley" (Maekawa, 1980: 112). Their names appear as haulers of ships from Lagash to Nippur (upstream); also, the names of many overseers in the temple workshops are those of eunuchs.

Let us take a look at a building excavated at Eshunna/Tell Asmar in the Diyala region of Mesopotamia. Its main-level floor plan is reproduced in Figure 15.1. The excavator dubbed it the Northern Palace (there was already a larger, more elaborate palace discovered at the site), and he was at pains to describe its division into public rooms and an inner "harem." This "harem" description first attracted my attention to the edifice, but aspects of that identification did not sit well with me. To name but the most glaring, room 19 with its bench or sleeping platform in the northeast corner was called the lord's bedchamber. The southeast corner, just inside the door, has tiles and a drain where, it was suggested, all visitors to the chamber, being profane, would have to undergo a purification before entering. This really would have thrown a wrench into the works, for it stands my understanding of the harem on its head. But consider the path the woman chosen for the lord's nightly pleasure would have to take from the harem, identified as centering around the large room 6! She would have to go through room 17, which marks the only link between the "harem" and the public space. Then she must parade through corridor 8, lined all on one side with what were thought to be lavatories of a rather communal sort, into room 10—a very public space, all but in the main court—through rooms 9, 2, 16, and finally to 19. I should think she would need purification after that jaunt into public spaces!

I was gratified to find my suspicions confirmed by the better interpretation of Delougaz (1967). The first issue that bothered Delougaz was the "unimpressiveness of the entrance." Tucked away off street 9 and coming into the hallway in square E:14 numbered 1, it seems almost the entrance to a harem and not the monumental entrance one would expect from a palace. Oh, for some writing in this Protoliterate period!

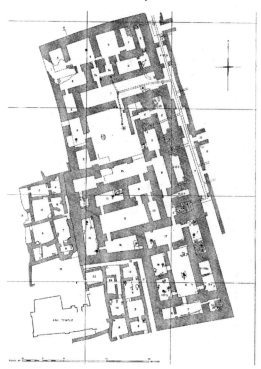

FIGURE 15.1. Textile factory in the Tell Asmar temple complex. *Source:* Delougaz, Hill, and Lloyd (1967). *Private Houses and Graves in the Diyala Region.* Chicago: The University of Chicago Press. Copyright 1967 by the University of Chicago. All rights reserved. Used with permission.

Fortunately, there is a clue from above. Built directly above this building is something Akkadian tablets found there have identified as a "'women's house' in which presumably several hundred women lived and worked" (Delougaz, 1967:197). It was a "manufacturing establishment," Delougaz concludes, "where various artisans practiced their crafts in close proximity to one another, perhaps for a common patron, either temple or ruler" (p. 198). None of the finds indicates weaving or sewing, but the great number of tile floors and the intricate plumbing system make Delougaz think of leather tanning. Dyeing might also be possible. These two occupations are often associated with men, but there can be little doubt as to the femininity of several of the finds, discovered particularly in the rooms first called the "harem." A number of carnelian beads were lost in the cracks of the tiles here and "a copper toilet set consisting of a ring from which are suspended a pair of tweezers, a piercing instrument, and a tiny spoon for cosmetics" (Hill, 1967:192),* an ivory comb and other such objects were found in room 9. It is not at all impossible, therefore, that women could have been the major workers at this factory; perhaps the heaviest tasks were carried out by men kept at a safe distance from the women in the northernmost cluster of rooms. One or (at most) two guards placed at the doorway could easily keep the process inside running smoothly.

Much that we have gleaned from later texts would confirm this identification and it suggests a very important aspect that must be added to the formula of female enslavement as envisioned for Mesopotamia. This is the fact that the major destination for these captive women was not the fields or irrigation works where men with their copper hoes would have been expected to do better; there retired the victorious foot soldier with his family as a reward for a job well done. Nor were they destined to be nannies and ladies' maids to the idle wives of the victorious generals, although certainly some (the fairest, to double as concubines?) found their way there. The majority of these women with their babes in arms and toddlers clinging to their skirts went to toil in the ancient versions of sweatshops, making the luxury textiles that were the very lifeline of Mesopotamia's merchants.[2] The markets these merchants were trying to break into, remember, were basically self-sufficient. They had all the grain, wood, stone, metal—all the products of "male" labor—they could use with their simple needs. What they didn't have were luxurious wants—and these the merchants hastened first to create and then to provide at the all-important surplus value. Of course, were the neighbors already urban and "sophisticated," they hardly needed inducement to crave such items, or anything else as long as it was "new," rare, and expensive. This observation is very telling: "there was a strategic concentration of [female] slaves in precisely those institutions which characterized Mesopotamian urban society as distinguished from preurban society" (Adams, 1965:103).

Not all scholars are agreed that the women whose names appear on the Mesopotamian sweatshop ration lists are to be seen as slaves. When we have monthly records from the same shop for a year or more, certain names are permanent while other names appear for a few months, to be replaced by a new group of women the next few months (Uchitel, 1984a). The conclusion is that such women were part of a corvée workforce, free women, but perhaps the flotsam and jetsam of the splintered clan system: widows, orphans, and divorcées. Then again, they may still have had the support of their clan, but it is a family debt or tax they have come to work off. In any case, they come with their children who are too young to be left at home. The case of one woman, Šaša, may represent an early day care provider (unless she was left with the orphaned children of a sister or two or a co-wife, perhaps). Šaša is listed with a large number of children, and the number fluctuates (Maekawa, 1980).

Whether they were the destitute or women helping ends meet for their clan, if they were indeed free women, we must confess that ancient Mesopotamian lords were able to rid themselves of some of the onerous responsibilities of slave ownership, just as modern bosses have done. The ration lists become the temple corporation payroll, and it is a subsistence, minimum wage most of these women receive. After their excess labor had been extracted in this part-time job (or if they were too old or sick to work), the women were returned to their families; the lords felt no compunction to support those who could not work.

The clan, on the other hand, is not so ready to welcome the returning laborer. She'd been working for other men and had nothing to show for it (her wage having vanished to keep her and her children alive). Suppose she has caught a glimpse of luxury and is not content with things as they are in the round of clannish life. Or suppose—and this is more likely—that without her menfolk to protect her, the young woman had been compromised by her bosses. As far as reproductive rights go, in the capitalist state, women are in a double bind. Hunter-gatherer societies support women's desires not to be burdened by more small children than they and the environment can handle. In clannish agricultural societies many children are desired, and the clan is willing to help the mother out with them. The urban capitalist state wants many children to feed its expansionist and labor hunger. It is, however, reluctant to support them until they are of an age to join the army or the workforce. "That's the family's responsibility," it says. Well, the family is not so sure. Its women and their labor have been out of its control for a while. Even if the woman has not been physically raped, even if the menfolk she returns to believe her when she tells them so, her labor has been forced; there's been a wedge driven between the old sacred bonds of vernacular gender. In a perverse, even terrifying way, the state and its bosses like it that way. It is these groups of workers,

> predominantly nonlocal and to a large extent female, that represent the earliest stage in the emergence of [capitalist[3]] production, the production mode that formed the backbone of the emerging public power. . . . The greater the use of encumbered . . . (often female) productive labor, the greater the central organized power [the bosses] over the kin base. (Zagarell, 1986b: 420)*

because they now have access to the labor of the kinwomen without the responsibilities of kinsmen. The bosses are the sneakiest of sneaky cells, and the women they employ have no traditional kin as a defense against this exploitation.

As female work thus became subsumed under the monolithic heading, we must imagine that early Sumerian women chafed as it is recorded women did in an industrializing town in Germany in the first half of the nineteenth century. Suddenly, men "ordered them around at work, a totally new experience for them" (Illich, 1982:174). But in neither the German economic structure nor its social structure could these recently exploited women find a way to thwart their fate, unlike early Mesopotamian women who had a firmer base to stand on. And so, to their daughters, this German male dominance was accepted as traditional and "the way it is." Historians, Illich writes, "have woven a tapestry to make us feel comfortable in our sexist environment, but the fabric has been manufactured out of industrial fibers" (p. 177). Ancient Mesopotamian women clung to enough strong fibers of their own to construct a defense, but they knew well enough that what they

---

were about to construct would have to be a strong defense, woven more tightly than any other male/female barrier in history.

It seems to me no coincidence that the fortunes of similar empires were also built on the labor of sweatshop girls. Tablets in Linear B from Bronze Age Greece give lists of slave women and their children from many different places of the eastern Aegean, including what might be interpreted as Troy. They are recorded as doing menial tasks, particularly preparing flax, a backbreaking chore, and spinning. "The predatory nature of Mycenaean expansion in the eastern Aegean" (Wood, 1985:159), Homer's refrain that the goal of the Greek heroes was "the city and its women" and that Odysseus's booty is elaborated as no more than "treasure and women," the fact that the pivot of the Trojan War is possession of a woman, all captive women personified in one Helen, now gains vividness and steps down from the realm of myth to economic reality.

> The presence . . . of slaves[4] from Lemnos, Chios, "Asia," Miletus, Halicarnassos and Cnidus, working in highly organized "state industries," shows us that the world of Agamemnon was one which constantly needed to seize slaves in war, or buy them from its slave ports. It was a society where surplus expenditure at the top—treasure, royal cult, royal graves, war gear—was so enormous that a great pyramid of labour was needed to sustain it, labour which had to be constantly replenished—even though the women slaves bred children—for the life expectancy of such people must have been very low. (Wood, 1985:248)

Certainly the pyramid of labor found in the factory towns of Northern England in the nineteenth century, East Side New York in the early part of this century, and God-knows-what dens of Hong Kong, Seoul, and the Mexican border where all those little teddy bears in tutus come from today present parallels in more aspects than one.

Once the tricks of female enslavement (wage slavery or otherwise) had been learned in ancient Mesopotamia, males could be brought into the force, as certainly they were at least by classical times. Still, even then we hear of their greatest numbers on galley ships and in the mines where they could still serve the purposes of the entrepreneur but where they could nonetheless be fiercely guarded—and incidentally would pose no threat to the conqueror's women.[5]

The antebellum American South is an example supporting the notion that men can only effectively be enslaved in the most barrack-like of conditions or by technological superiority, i.e., when their copper hoes are no match for the overseer's rifle. The capitalist must therefore take another step if he is to reach the full flower of that idiom, and this step seems to have more success when one begins to try it out on the men rather than the women. Because they cannot be raped and made to care for their future under the whip by the stirrings of new life under their ribs as women can, men must be the subjects of an ideological enslavement instead, an ideology that can break the back of clannish balance. The capitalist must create a linear future for his labor to aspire toward instead. This may take the form of a freedom to be bought or earned as occurred in ancient Rome or medieval Islam, or the ideology must become so powerful and so full of promise as to sidestep the stage of "slavery" altogether.

We have seen what this meant in ancient Mesopotamia as new ideologies were sought to replace the clan system. In the West, religion has become the tool of the left side of the brain; nothing is truly right-sided and (by my definition) sacred anymore. Christianity and its individual salvation were a beginning, and each reformation since has added more and more divine sanction. As Gilbert states in his study of *Religion and Society in Industrial England* (1976), evangelical nonconformity, Methodist, Baptist, and other denominations which developed at the same time as Western industrialism are part of the ideology resource-starving superpowers must put in place to survive on their terms.

> In a society just emerging from a situation where the maintenance of a standard of living not far above the subsistence level had been a realistic economic goal, men . . . had to embrace new values. They had to learn to value the profit motive as opposed to the motive of subsistence. They had to be acquisitive. They had to accept the novel concept of work not as a necessity for survival, but as an avenue to socio-economic advancement. If from the perspective of a modern industrial society these values seem self-evident, then it is salutary to remember the problems that early industrial manufacturers experienced in inculcating a capitalistic work discipline into the new industrial work force, problems with parallels wherever industrialization and modern-

ization have taken place in economically undeveloped societies. (Gilbert, 1976:85-86)

In ancient Sumer and throughout the Middle East until the twentieth century, women stuck to their guns and their harems, insisted that men keep their side of the bargain, and refused to justify slavery with this ideology.

Chapter 16

Honor

In the balance of genders maintained in the Middle East even in the face of forces pressing for androgynous slavery, women seclude themselves. Men are expected to reciprocate by protecting their honor.

Honor. What is it? We think we know what it means. Yet we are tempted to go to the dictionary to confirm our rather vague feeling. Anthropologist Julian Pitt-Rivers, one of the authorities on the subject, notes that Northern Europeans are "bashful" in discussions of honor. He suggests that we must find it uncomfortably "archaic." When the hero of the late-night movies in which honor plays a supporting role in lace-trimmed gauntlets and pearl-handled pistols manages to find the mandatory alternative, something more "rational," more sensibly calculating of the bottom line than sunrises in the mist of the Tuileries, and the soundtrack blares in triumph at the civilized denouement. In linear society, the press aids us in the comfortable conclusion that honor is passé, nay, positively barbaric, when every tidbit it feeds us is some version of the headline "Irate Father Slaughters Own Daughter to Salve Honor." When the presence of honor (not its absence) does play a part in crimes in the United States, we are much too civilized to notice.

Our discomfort with honor nears Marc Antony's irony: "So are they all, all honorable men." We are uncomfortable, perhaps, because we don't know what it means and feel we ought. Or perhaps it is because when men call on honor to justify themselves here in the West, we are uncomfortable with what this emotion has made them do. One great capitalist of the nineteenth century, Jim Fiske, who made a fortune on the miseries of the Civil War was able to congratulate himself that in his scam he lost nothing but his honor and hence was still a part of the American dream (Bledstein, 1976:51).

A History of Women's Seclusion in the Middle East
Published by the Haworth Press, Inc., 2006. All rights reserved.
doi:10.1300/5666_17

The first thing that must be recognized is that when we in the West say "honor," we mean someting different from what people in the East mean. English-speaking anthropologists who study the Middle East and surrounding regions appropriated the term for a bundle of emotions that seemed very similar—it is usually modified as "Mediterranean honor"—but close inspection has demonstrated important differences.

"The Anglo-Saxon term *ar* and the old Nordic *eir* [both meaning "honor"] don't speak of veneration and worship. . . . They speak of granting peace instead, and of protection and luck. They embody the beneficent will of superiors towards their dependents, who, by providing peace for others, gained honor for themselves" (Strecker, 1996). Gone is the worship, gone the place for women in the honor of American culture's direct ancestors. The Puritan religious reformation solidified these differences between north and south, and, in the process, paved the way for modern full-blown capitalism to develop as it had not been able to under the constraints of Mediterranean honor.

> The Puritan's rejection of the flamboyant conception of honour which still reigns in southern Europe and centres upon patronage and women was bound up with their particular notion of egalitarianism, their condemnation of sensuality and their thrift. Within such a complex of values, possession, stripped of its significance as a means to enhance their honour by establishing domination over others, became an end in itself as a sign of Grace and aimed thenceforth at accumulation rather than conversion into prestige through redistribution. The conflict between honour = precedence and honour = virtue was resolved [for the Puritans] in favour of the latter and honour was felt as religious conscience and manifest in financial solvency; earned no longer, so to speak, with lance in hand but with cheque book in pocket. All their attitudes: to display, to women, to lying, to literacy, even to Time, are to be explained simply as (Pitt-Rivers, 1977:36)

a response to this sense of honor. No wonder we are a little uncomfortable with this sort of honor!

Mediterranean honor, on the other hand, "derives from the domination of persons, rather than things" (Pitt-Rivers, 1977:36). "Domination" is perhaps not the best word to use here. Perhaps "support" is better, when seclusion is in place to maintain the supported woman's right to at least some of her own decisions. A "Mediterranean" man works hard so that he can gain dependents, either wives and children or clients. He works, as did the chiefs of the northwest native tribes, in order to redistribute the wealth in a sort of potlatch. Without other people to lavish his wealth on, it is meaningless. This is, "needless to say, a goal which is inimical to capitalist accumulation" (Pitt-Rivers, 1977:36). It is the maintenance of this view of honor that kept the wolves of Middle Eastern capitalism at bay for so many thousands of years.

Mediterranean and Puritan honor

> differ as to whether men should or should not compete for the favors of women over whom they have no rights. The Puritans believed that women should be distributed equally in accordance with the Christian ideal of monogamy, and so does the Catholic Church, but in the Catholic countries of the Mediterranean, as we know from the remarkable proliferation of dramatic works on the theme of Don Juan [as well as in polygynous Islam] this ideal has not gone unchallenged at the profane level. The kind of honour attaching to personal preeminence and the possession of women runs counter to the Christian ideal. Yet be it noted that both codes accept the same initial premise: that, whether honorably or not, men *do* compete for the favors of women. (Pitt-Rivers, 1977:75)

Following Puritan egalitarianism to its ultimate conclusion (which has taken several hundred years) we now have the situation where, whether honorably or not, women also must compete for men, either for their favors, or, as is more common (we have not nor, I believe, can we most of us be liberated from this need) "for their protection" (Pitt-Rivers, 1977:75). Mediterranean honor is not unisex. Women are off the hook in this, as in the competition for most other forms of male honor.

A man in the regions where Mediterranean honor holds sway "may think it perfectly right to seduce someone else's wife or daughter, yet think it very immoral if someone else seduces his," an immoral act of such magnitude that it warrants the death penalty, if not for the adulterer then at least for his wife. "Such a man is applying a double standard," we say, one for himself and one for others. Pitt-Rivers has difficulty with the term *double standard.* It suggests, he says, "that those cultures that contain 'double standards' are somehow not morally respectable; decent English-speaking people, it is implied, have single standards" (Pitt-Rivers, 1977:75).

This is, of course, patently not true. Some Marines who will fight to the death to keep small, dark foreign men from invading the land where their wives and mothers are think nothing of doing unspeakable things to the small, dark foreigners' women. When an eighteen-year-old on welfare and crack with four children finds herself pregnant again by her abusive boyfriend and gets an abortion, her actions are called murder by the "moral majority." However, when she's put eight or nine months or eight or nine years into that child and he dies "of causes incident to poverty"—perhaps even if she neglected him while she went to seek a miserable job—it is called "market economics." No charge of murder is even considered against the man who might have hired her through a lower personnel officer, who has amassed a fortune according to the rules of the "market economy" and consistently thrown his vote against higher taxes and social programs. Finally, and most critically, there is a double standard even more vital to Puritan honor: it is a point of honor that a man buy at a lower price than he is able to sell. "If double economic standards were disallowed," writes Pitt-Rivers (1977:74),

> it would be the end of commerce just as the phrase, applied to sexual morality, condemns promiscuity altogether. I would not wish to be thought to be opposed to marital fidelity nor to prenuptial virginity, nor to sexual freedom for both sexes either, nor blind to the arcadian charms of the subsistence economy, my objection is only against the use of this phrase ["double standard"], for it expresses no more than the attitude of the speaker toward the values of an alien culture.

By assuring that a large percentage of women are selling, not buying, Mediterranean women can set the prices in their favor, making the cost of being a sucessful sneaky cell prohibitive to all but the honorable.

Whenever resources are scarce, reality gets fiercely polarized, and the goods and bads become more starkly black and white. This is a major premise of our thesis. Because in reality there are very few black-and-white situations, double standards must grow as competition and rivalry grow. In the Mediterranean case,

> there is competition for the favors of women because they are a source of prestige as well as of personal satisfaction and the competition is only keener [because] the rarity of these favors is ensured by the value attached to female purity. (The special glamour accorded by seventeenth century gallants to the seduction of nuns surely derives from this scarcity-value among other things). (Pitt-Rivers, 1977:74)

Morality is the most difficult of topics to maintain objectivity on. We all know in our bones "what is right" and even when we can see ourselves clear to opposing economic colonization, we often still wave the banner of moral colonization. Let us recall again what we have defined as good and bad in this study: If it protects flexibility and both sides of a set of polarized values, it is good. If it tends to shove all humanity onto one pole or the other, it is bad.

Now look at Mediterranean honor again. Pitt-Rivers calls it the "*moral* division of labour." Honor in the Mediterranean regions "is not a single value but a complex of values united at the level of social relations rather than at the conceptual level of ethics." Male honor and female honor are disparate, but they are "complementary as the active and passive manifestations of the same principle. . . . In each marriage . . . , two different strands of honour come together in order to provide the honour of the nuclear family thus formed" (Pitt-Rivers, 1977:74). As the external and internal facets of the same honor, male honor and female honor "imply each other in the sense that female undefended can be taken not to exist while in its absence male honour cannot be transmitted" to the next generation. Without his women, no Mediterranean man has honor. He is as pathetic a case as was the seventeenth-century French bachelor we met earlier. Mediterranean

> men think themselves responsible for the behaviour of their women because this is where the essence of *their* moral honour resides. . . . This is clearly visible in a fact which would otherwise appear anomalous: that the greatest insults that can be addressed to a man refer not to himself at all but to his female kin, especially his mother, also his sister. (Pitt-Rivers, 1977:74)

An even fiercer verbal attack can be made by one man upon another's honor. Pitt-Rivers tells of this attack in the altercation between a Spanish carpenter and another man of the village. This was not the suggestion that the second man tried to cheat him, or that his mother wore army shoes, or even that his wife was carrying on behind his back. No, these statements that we first think of in questions of honor paled before the attack on a man's reputation made by the suggestion "that he was cruel to his daughter, his only child, and that he intended to abandon his wife and go off with another woman, not that *his wife* had unfaithful intentions" (Pitt-Rivers, 1977:26). Male honor is most closely associated "with the family and the qualities necessary to defend [and maintain] it rather than with the morality . . . of sexual conduct" (p. 28). Men require of their wives, daughters, and sisters

> moral qualities which they do not expect of themselves [because] after all, a man cannot afford to have too fine a moral conscience or he would not be able to meet his obligations to his family in the struggle for existence, but a woman having no such responsibilities can be the epitome of moral worth. (p. 79)

In the West where the struggle to maintain our standard of living has forced every hand into that struggle, [passive] honor—honor that is morality derived, as it is among women in the Mediterranean sphere, "from the world within, that is to say, from within the house or even within their bodies" (Pitt-Rivers, 1977:79)—is indeed passé.

Because of the Mediterranean division of moral labor, "men, though they are the focus of authority within the family, are forced to give way to their women in certain situations," particularly in situations when the women feel "from within" that something is wrong (Pitt-Rivers, 1977:80). Feminine power in this world

> is not overt, but, due to their participation in the familial honor (as the repositories of its moral and sacred aspects) women hold in their hands the power not merely to put pressure on their menfolk but actually to "ruin" them. (p. 80)

Some feminists complain that all their lives little girls were told to be "good" while the little boys were allowed to do as they pleased. Such feminists rebel. They demand everything boys have, including their form of honor. If women are not allowed to join their brothers in the pursuit of the perfect orgasm then life is not worth living.

Female honor having been done away with, men are under no obligation to maintain that part of their honor. It is a debased form of honor we are left standing with, the honor of thieves and war in which all is fair in the pursuit of glory. To be female under such circumstances is to begin in dishonor in exploitation.

The case, I think, is made, as to which culture maintains the more adaptive system.

Modern Western discomfort with honor exists, some observers might say, because we have outgrown it, grown too logical to be duped by such "superstition." Are we not rather embarrassed at the mention of honor as we are in the face of all true religion, as we are at the mention of a parent we've consigned to a nursing home and haven't had time to visit for a year or two? "Alzheimer's," we justify ourselves. "She wouldn't recognize us anyway." Mystical visions and honor are forces beyond our ken, beyond scientific control. We say, therefore, that they do not exist. Yet things are still out of control. We never consider that it is perhaps in the acceptance of the irrational that control comes.

Honor deserves accreditation as religion if we have no word for something deeper and more powerful, yet more irrational than modern religion. Islam, much to its credit, has done the least to eradicate the underlying base of honor, the most to incorporate and disseminate it. Of course, honor finds itself at home among most of the heirs of the Hellenistic/Persian world, including their descendants from as far afield as Latin America and Indonesia. Everywhere it stands opposed to all attempts by linear religion and written law to eradicate it. Honor, Pitt-Rivers says, is part of a triad of sex-religion-honor, where it is very difficult to tell where notions about one idea begin and the other leave off. Honor is almost synonymous, in cultures in which it is practiced, with virtue, with righteousness; the dishonored man, the cuckold, shares many symbols with that primary symbol of evil, the devil.

In Spain one sees a great division. On the one hand are the middle and upper classes, whose interests are with the wider industrial economy or with a more universalizing, linear Catholic Church; they are as much swayed by honor as your average North American—hardly at all. On the other hand are the lower classes in Spain who are notoriously "anti-clerical and . . . irreligious" (Pitt-Rivers, 1977:28)—but who cannot take a breath without honor. Clearly, one form of religion cancels out, stands for, replaces the other in Christian lands, which have been much more effective (probably because they are much farther from the original core of seclusion) in linearizing than Islam.

Honor views "the adulterer and the cuckold not in terms of right and wrong, but in terms of sanctity or defilement" (Pitt-Rivers, 1977: 24). The assumption is that if a man does everything in his power to faithfully provide his womenfolk with all they need, both emotionally and materially, willing to share his good fortune with them as well as the bad, they will have no desire either to take a lover or earn their keep in a brothel. A necessary part of each sex's method of saving face is invested inextractably, inexchangeably, in the other.

The home where women are (and there cannot be a home without them) is a sanctuary, granting to the man under threat of assassination a haven much as did the horns of the altars in temples in biblical cities of refuge. When we read of the Moroccans' association of women with magic and the supernatural to such an extent that men stand in fear of them,[1] this, too, is emblematic of the religious nature of seclusion and its form of "virtue," honor. Fear and veneration are expressed by men toward women as supernatural figures in the Middle East. Veils as devices to "increase the sense of mystery and remoteness of the wearer" (Murphy, 1970:304) have been seen among the men of the Tuareg, and "this remoteness serves to increase the status and power of" the individual. Some researchers do not believe that what is true of Tuareg men can possibly be true for women in purdah, but I think they are trapped by Western values and do not consider alternative power (such as religion that prohibits the wanton deforestation of forest lands) as true power. Also coming under the influence of Western values are Eastern men who lose this sense of veneration toward their secluded women. Having found their honor in balancing power with the West, they can no longer invest it in their women. They insist that their women be mute supports to their larger struggle. I can only hope that the centuries of strength these women have enjoyed makes them equal to this new balancing act.

Whether as sorceresses, magicians, healers, or just plain women, women in the traditional Middle East do not play by the rules of the male world. It may not be scientific to spend time considering the alternative power, but I think it must be anthropological. Part of our misunderstanding of veiling and seclusion comes because of this:

> The paucity of ethnographic descriptions surrounding the relationship of women to the religious system in general, and the supernatural in particular, suggests more a lack of interest on the part of ethnographers than it does a lack of concern on the part of the actors in Middle Eastern Islamic societies. . . . There is a firm belief [for example] that God's anger befalls the whole community as a result of any sexual misconduct on the part of women. (Nelson, 1974:557)

This is an awe-full power indeed and one, if it is not to be considered Islamic because it is too "superstitious," should nonetheless be considered religious. Understanding the religious origins of the Middle Eastern position of women in the goddess temples puts this into perspective.

Religion is not to be limited to a rote creed of "I believes" given in high abstraction. Indeed, much that is condemned as "magic" and "folk superstition" is indeed religion when religion is defined not as "that which is highest in man"—jargon that naturally begs for a male-dominated hierarchy—but as that which protects humanity from the dissolving power of its own mind.

Women under honor are accorded holiness, a holiness such as was once accorded to the Mother Goddess. She, too, did not play by the rules of men. Indeed, in this light, it is easy to see how honor could be the very religious impulse that first gave us the edge over other apes in far-off times. Just such a culturally learned emotion would be necessary if early women were to be freed from the necessity their apish cousins face, that of foraging on their own with an infant in tow, foraging as an individual among other equally independent individuals. Honor obliges the addition of the male to the nuclear family unit, thereby giving the woman (and the man) the extra time they need to devote to a highly teachable, highly vulnerable next generation.

Obviously, this scenario cannot be wholly true. The cultural distribution of the peculiar phenomenon anthropologists call Mediterranean honor, although broad, is yet not broad enough or ancient enough to be basic to humankind. Other types of cultural inducement of a similar yet much weaker vein suffice when culture is simpler; it did suffice for the tens of thousands of years we were human, yet not urban. It is with the intensification of culture after the Ice Age, particularly with its culmination in urbanism and empire, that the strength of honor became necessary in order to preserve a prehistoric independence and interdependence of the sexes at the same time. Therefore, not only may we see honor as a religious impulse, but as religion of a very basic type, a holdover from a time "when God was a woman" (Stone, 1976), preserved like canned soup in a highly condensed, compact form, easy to transport, easy and quick to use, perfectly sustaining when you don't have direct access to field peas yourself.

Honor represents the mystical hold women in seclusion have upon men. Their seclusion demands it of them. Honor is the credo that makes seclusion possible, hence the women's eagerness to inculcate it in their sons. Yes, honor is irrational, emotional. But any other device conceived of by courts and hammered out in the black and red of account books could not fulfill its same purpose. When energy is being devoted to the next generation, either in the form, most obviously, of children, or more subtly in the preservation of values that stand in opposition to the present monolith, such devotion naturally appears in the debt column of today's one-dimensional ledger. Honor is the credit a man receives to counteract his desire to eradicate that debt, as other taboos have served to protect his forests or hunting grounds (while there were still forests and hunting grounds left to preserve), also with the next generation in mind. Or, to look at the metaphor in the looking glass, honor may be the brake to running up massive national debt for future generations to pay. The more the interests of that next generation are allowed to fade from view, from consideration among the figures on the computer screen, the more archaic honor will seem.

Honor is a powerful force to preserve vernacular gender under powerful pressure to dispense with it. "Under the reign of [honor], men and women collectively depend on each other; their mutual dependence sets limits to struggle, exploitation, defeat. . . . Where men mutilate women's bodies, the gynaeceum . . . knows excruciating ways to get back at men's feelings" (Illich, 1982:178), ways we in the West, without honor, have forgotten.

I mourn the death of my sisters in crimes of honor from regions of the Mediterranean. I mourn them as I do the death of the unborn child of a woman who must seek an abortion today, of those children unaborted who die of poverty or, from long ago, of those infants who were offered up to Moloch, those virgins sacrificed on the altar. However, I know that morality cannot be forced. Many people—and they include any number of feminists—insist that all we need is "kinder, gentler" hearts and this will lead, as the arrowhead leads the shaft, to a kinder and gentler world—and we reserve the right to force such hearts on others while at the same time we rob them of their livelihood. No, rather than change of heart, we must understand that

> Reproductive pressure, intensification, and environmental depletion . . . [are] the key for understanding the evolution of family organization, property relations, political economy, and religious beliefs. . . . Sexism will cease to be practiced when [its] productive, reproductive, and ecological functions are fulfilled by less costly alternatives. (M. Harris, 1977:xii, 97)

The simple expedient of having fewer children per woman, supporting the childless couple and career woman does nothing, however, to protect other values for cultural flexibility into the future.

I tend to believe that traditional, preurban birth control methods were more successful than they are given credit for. As the state grew more powerful, it tended to take matters out of the control of women, too. The new immigrant to the city has lost her connection to her grandmother's wisdom and stands of wild carrot. The state, wanting cannon fodder, likes to keep it that way.

One estimate, however, suggests that under normal circumstances without modern birth control methods in settled agricultural or urban environments, "almost 50 percent of the females born must be prevented from reaching reproductive age if a population initially in reasonably good health is not to suffer severe cutbacks in the quality of life in a very short time" (M. Harris, 1977:68).

Palestinian men in Gaza and the West Bank father the highest birthrate in the world[2] while at the same time murdering an average of one teenaged daughter a week in matters of honor.[3] I find it hard to condemn the feelings of honor responsible for both unfortunate circumstances without admitting some responsibility for being part of the (Western) world community that put these men in their present situation. Theirs is a situation in which male honor has none of the traditional outlets, no access to jobs, land, or any of the other outlets honor would constrain these men to share with their families. All that is left them, really, is the passive honor of women.

Before condemning this as merely a problem of the East, I must weigh it, too, against the crisis of boys in the United States, a society that has removed the means of production from their hands for more generations than it has done the Palestinian men. Money is touted as being the only true success. The young American boy sees that those who make the most money resort to steroid use, insider trading, or dissolution of their workers' pension funds. His choices are to take this path of advancement in new and creative ways. Or he may choose a life small but honorable which he is constantly urged to leave by advertisers.

In closing out this section on the religion of honor, I would like to make the observation that religions remove to the hereafter what they can no longer promise their followers in the present. Christianity promises food, warmth, and peace to come because it cannot promise flesh sacrifices that gave earlier believers meat, on holy days at least. Religions that have developed in the industrial revolution often promise their faithful that they will have their families with them in heaven because they demand that they neglect them while they run hither and yon fulfilling the demands of an urban industrial lifestyle. If this is a constant truism, isn't it curious that Muslim men are promised the services of a garden of doe-eyed houris as their reward? Having no personal experience of a secluded sex life, I cannot say for certain; but surely this does indicate that, contrary to Western mythology of the dark Eastern lecher, the Muslim honor must be given compensation for putting something else—such as the welfare of his family before prurient satisfaction—first.

Chapter 17

Masscult

The expansion of exchange networks, coercively when necessary, increased the relative power of the new production mode
vis-à-vis other modes both quantitatively and [what is important
for this chapter] symbolically. It legitimated, indeed, demanded,
the expansion of the bureaucracy and control over resources . . .
including the use of writing, numerical controls, inventory, access controls (seals), scribes and administrators. By competing
with the kin base, this new production mode created instability
where there was order and then recreated order in the form of
administrative integration. (Zagarell, 1986b:420)*

In other words, it was to the burgeoning capitalist's advantage to
destabilize anything that wasn't in his image. We have been working
mainly in terms of life's "necessities," but this term "necessity" has a
capitalist cast to it. In order to maintain clannish social systems, elaborate symbolic systems in art and ritual are necessary; hence they become "unnecessary" to the marketplace.

However, in a feminist history, what holds true for resources of
food and clothing is likewise true, although perhaps not quite as devastating to human life, for the resources of the soul-renewing force of
nature (a vacation to the Adirondack Mountains, for example), the
arts and aesthetic enjoyment, intellectual achievement, and, most vitally, the propaganda such control can wield over the very minds and
souls of the powerless. It is a rare modern (or Sumerian) urbanite who

---

*Excerpts from Zagarell (1986), "Trade, women, class and society in ancient West-
ern Asia," *Current Anthropology* 27:5, pp. 415-429, copyright 1986 by the Wenner-
Gren Foundation for Anthropological Research, all rights reserved. Published by the
University of Chicago Press. Used with permission.

can indulge in the days on end of singing and dancing that any Kalahari Bushman is allowed. Any European peasant woman of a century ago with half an inkling could express herself through weaving, embroidery, or stenciling. Her husband enjoyed wood or leather work. Not so the urbanite. If she is fortunate, she may buy such items to grace her home or her person. She surely has little time herself to indulge, and all but the wealthy must be content with the purchase of mass-produced items lacking all personal or artistic merit. The walls are painted landlord green, and clothes must be for success. In most cases, the Powers have removed the arts from the individual home altogether, relegated them to the temples and palaces in ancient Mesopotamia, to the art museums in our society. The average citizen gains admittance to these shrines only very rarely, and then only at the behest of a powerful foundation. The colorful sarong of native dress now graces the coffee table in some businessman's guest room (dusted once a week by the foreign-born maid), while the woman who wove it cannot afford the work of her own hands. She must be satisfied with a used Mickey Mouse T-shirt.

The once-hallowed grounds of religion that protected the rights of Nature and the weaker members of society have in the urban state been invaded so they will preach the exploitative agenda of the powerful. So has the world of art, which once went hand in hand with that first protective device. In ancient Mesopotamia, the archaeological record shows how more and more of the art had to go to supporting the urban superstructure. It had to glorify the individual king. It had to make his palace impressive with all the tricks in the dramatists', architects', sculptors', and painters' bags. Similarly, the Roman towns in Britain "were provided with civic centres and market places, baths, temples . . . and some place of amusement" (Trigger, 1972:589) at no little expense and quite in excess of what the local population had required before the Roman conquest. We have Tacitus's statement of the purpose for all of this: it was not Roman beneficence, ancient foreign aid, as it were (most modern foreign aid, I suspect, plays the same role). Rather, "it was to 'persuade a people previously scattered, uncivilized and, therefore, prone to fight, to grow used to peace'" (quoted by Hassall, 1972:858). In other words, Rome and other empires before her provided civic centers as ancient propaganda.

Those who protest that the Sumerians were the first to lay pen to paper (rather, reed to tablet) and that this must have been a boon to the writer (before there was writing, how could there be writers?) should know that of the volume of tablets found, only a fraction of a percentage are what we might generously call "art." Then as now the great majority of characters went down to the evermore precise controlling of resources by those in power. "The tablet says you owe; you are ignorant and cannot read; the mind can easily forget, clay cannot; you owe." Adams put it well: "innovations like writing . . . facilitate administration and assure the pre-eminence of a few of the many strands of unrecorded tradition" (1972:735). So does Diamond (1974):

> Writing provides the ruling classes with an ideological instrument of incalculable power. . . . An official, fixed and permanent version of events can be made. . . . Those people who *could* write, the scribes and priests, . . . were rarely disposed to record the attitudes of those they taxed, subordinated and mystified. (p. 4)

Education for the expertise the literate empire needs allows certain kinds of thinking to flourish and others it forces to wither and die. You may be sure that the strands that win out are those most likely to support the ideology of the system in power, run by the most power-hungry of the pseudo-individuals.

> The main work of any administration is to obtain and collate the information which is the key to decision-making at state-level— and this process was kept firmly in the hands of government officials who were drawn from the noble classes. (Bray, 1977: 386)

Modern computer technology is but the latest extent to which the powerful will go to keep their billions of little flashes of information under control. It is the most recent step in reducing every human relationship to one of credits and debits.[1]

It is instructive to our particular problem to note that during the first few hundred years of records, women do quite often appear as scribes. As history "progresses," however, they write less and less with their own hands and finally become only the subjects of this powerful manipulative tool.

Some room was left for individual artistic expression in ancient Mesopotamia, including folk arts and crafts. Surely there were avenues of artistic exploitation as yet untried until our day. But certainly, in the higher circles at least, a theory of art was struggling to evolve that wanted this power kept in the hands of a few.

> We've come to believe that if an image or subject is humble, humorous or simple, it must be superficial; if it's stately, tragic or perverse, it must be profound. . . . Women's art for millennia has been considered "craft" (because the quilt, the pottery bowl, the basket also have a daily *function,* to warm, to feed, to carry). . . . "Fine art" is defined as something magnificently unuseful, thereby "pure." (Morgan, 1989:111)

The traditional ways of making bedcovers and clay pots took longer, but they obliged even common folk to take the life-renewing force of art into their lives. Once it was possible to visit rural American towns and be served in tiny cafés food with personality by strongly individualistic women. Now the waitresses are all trying to be the latest starlet on TV and, if they do not know in their hearts, they show in their very carriage that not only has the fertility of their soil and wealth of their material life been leached into big cities, but so has their artistic and spiritual life as well.

Art can be murdered in many ways. Of course we think first of the life of the artist in communist countries. Milan Kundera (1984), for example, deplored the "kitsch" in art under the communist rule in his native Czechoslovakia. But the West has more than its share of "kitsch," too. Direct censorship is but the most clumsy way to kill art, like killing your prey with a bow and arrow when you have stealth bombers at your disposal. More modern methods include

> isolation of the artist into irrelevance, trivialization, proscription of subject matter, commercialization, and—one of the most effective means—manipulation of art into a mode of propaganda. When this is done swiftly and blatantly, it's absurd enough to be recognizable. (Morgan, 1989:110)

I remember hearing an interview with a Soviet-bloc poet whose work hadn't been allowed to see the light of day for years. Surprisingly, he wasn't bitter, and the interviewee asked him why. "Simple," he said. "Everyone here knows it's a lie, it's all a lie, so I am never seen as a failure." Propaganda culminates not behind the former Iron Curtain but here in the West where the powers have learned to make the lie invisible, and the artist perishes in her lonely bitterness. The West has accomplished this slowly but "steadily for aeons" until propaganda has become "virtually inseparable from . . . art, and is not so easily identifiable" (Morgan, 1989:110). Corporations, having taken the best artists for their own marketing departments, leaving no one able to afford the luxury herself, have "infiltrated the core activities and institutions of childhood" (Schor, 2004:12-13). Born to do little else other than buy, our self-confidence whittles to nothing unless we have the latest—until we turn on the television again, primed to bolster our souls with the next mass movement.

Does the collapse of the Soviet bloc change the point I'm making here? On the contrary, it only makes it more terrifyingly monolithic. Time was when a Soviet artist could express his individuality by whispering democracy. He could fill his closet with works unacceptable to the government, and invite a few trusted friends over for wine and show them. Praise given in such a gathering had the validity of a million-dollar check in the United States. Now artists in the former Soviet Union find themselves in the same bind as we here have known for years, where to validate the government and the values of the masscult is to win financial security, to counter them a sure sentence of obscurity—"It will never sell!" Recently I heard a Soviet artist complain: "Now when I invite my friends over for drinks, all they ask about my work is how much I made in New York or Paris."

Granted, not every personality craves the tension of art in a primitive sense, but such individuals, I protest, have this craving in their genes. Art is part of the original survival mechanism of our species. When such "artistic" individuals are forced either to do the proverbial starving, take (prescribed or otherwise) drugs to numb their sensitivities, or join their art to the universal praise of the good and better (surely no toilet tissue was ever touted as the "so-so") then that culture is jeopardizing one or more possibilities of human existence for the sake of "totalitarian kitsch."

It was the eighteenth century in the West that saw the final breakdown of the barriers between high culture and folk culture, barriers that had meant for all of previous history a defense against a single point of view taking over all power of symbol making. "Masscult" has come to replace these parallel traditions. And "while folk art is created by the people when there is community, masscult comes from above *to* the people when there is a mass-atomized man. . . . This is the difference between participants and consumers" (Rapoport, 1969: 127). Masscult has the terrible power to break down folk arts and their symbolic systems so that they can no longer communicate. Seen in this light, "the lack of 'taste' shown by new products and buildings" is more horrible than mere eyesore. It reflects confusion of symbols at the grassroots level, "an inability to choose outside the framework of traditional forms" (p. 128), an erosion of confidence in old participant values and hence a terrifying susceptibility to molding from above.

We live in systems that are becoming more centralized, laments feminist Robin Morgan (1989). Here diversity and individuality are replaced by the "sameness" reinforced by global media and corporations whose advertisements seek to create one homogeneous consumer market. The privileged of each society use the same, abstract terminology ("poverty" and "homelessness") to "disguise who the poor and homeless are," the same political tricks to keep such systems in place, and the same technology to enforce them. This, therefore, "is the bureaucratic machine 'which excludes all judgment and all genius' in its drive to localize all powers in itself" (R. Morgan, 1989:45).

It is one of the artist's main functions to hold up a mirror to society. "But," laments Morgan, "the Demon Lover's soulless reflection by now is invisibly omnipresent" (p. 110) when she tries to do so. A major part of women's vulnerability in the face of the Western social system is their inability to create powerful systems of symbols in which to communicate. Other oppressed peoples at other times, such as

> slaves living in an environment controlled by their masters and physically subject to the masters' control, could maintain their humanity and at times set limits to the masters' power by holding on to their own "culture." Such a culture consisted of collective memories, carefully kept alive, of a prior state of freedom and of alternatives to the masters' ritual, symbols and beliefs. (Lerner, 1986:222)

Certainly it is a dreadful aspect of masscult that it is heavily male and that its powerful men take

> the half for the whole [whereby] they have not only missed the essence of whatever they are describing, but they have distorted it in such a fashion that they cannot see it correctly. . . . As long as men believe their experiences, their viewpoint, and their ideas represent all of human experience and all of human thought, they are not only unable to define correctly in the abstract, but they are unable to describe reality accurately. (p. 220)

In Marxist mode,

> class struggle can be described as a struggle for the control of the symbol systems of a given society. The oppressed group, while it shares in and partakes of the leading symbols controlled by the dominant, also develops its own symbols. These become in time of revolutionary change,[2] important forces in the creation of alternatives. Another way of saying this is that revolutionary ideas can be generated only when the oppressed have an alternative to the symbols and meaning system of those who dominate them. (p. 222)

For feminist historian Gerda Lerner, this alternative, alas, has not been open to women since Genesis.

For a number of women, increasing at first very slowly but, in the past 200 years growing much more rapidly (paralleling the rise of "masscult") I agree that this is so. However, I have arguments with Lerner's feminism.[3] "What wisdom can there be in menses?" she asks rhetorically (p. 224). "What source of knowledge in the milk-filled breast? Can one generalize while the particular tugs at one's sleeve?" Infinite generations of our ancestresses found it possible—witness the plaster reliefs of breasts encasing vultures' skulls at Çatal Hüyük or the strange primordial versions of "Little Red Riding Hood" where the young girl learns to hold her own against the seductions of wolves. But Lerner's call that we demand time for ourselves to create these images, that we all shuttle children off to day care and take private offices on quiet university campuses, is as impractical as it is male, and as male as was the seventeenth-century bourgeois Frenchman Perrault's addition of a woodcutter to help Little Red Riding Hood and her granny out (Zipes, 1983).[4]

My arguments with Lerner's view are perhaps most clearly exemplified by her call that women take on male hubris—"that of intellectual arrogance, the supreme hubris which asserts to itself the right to reorder the world" (p. 228). This, to me, is a call to give up the most powerful of feminine symbols, the symbol of giving life not by reordering the world to but by giving in to labor pains. Lerner's path is to bow to men's images with nose to the ground. I'll agree it's a great temptation to be arrogant when all the goods in the world are going to the arrogant. However, it is, in the end, the paradox of a most terrible humility. Lerner says that in patriarchy "men hold all the important institutions of society and that women are deprived of access to such power" (p. 239), but her definition of "powerful" seems woefully male. To her, segregation "always has subordination as its purpose" (p. 242), and it is here that I wish most strongly to disagree.

Cultures undertake every minute of every day to define, in effect to shut down, possibilities of being for their speakers. Classification of ideas, items, and people in the world helps the people of societies make decisions, as in the example Needham (1979:17) gives of the classification between edible mushrooms and poisonous mushrooms. The proverbial twenty-one Eskimo names for snow or the hundreds of Arabic words for our single classification "camel" seem clear adaptations of these cultures to their particular environments. I'm sure it is very important to an Eskimo when he looks out of the igloo to be able to classify what he sees down to minutia and with one word conjure up past personal and group experience to tell him what his chances of finding game that day will be, what equipment he should take for such conditions, and so on.

Under conditions of stress, classification tends to ever-sharper dichotomy and occurs with ever-sharper limitation of the options between poles. The leisure for areas of gray does not exist. The ancient Israelites chose the tyranny of a king, even when they were warned that taxes and other evils would follow, because they were threatened on all sides by other peoples whose energies and resources were already concentrated in a single pair of spearheading hands. Germans in the twentieth century felt that, in the face of fearsome inflation and the merciless bleeding of their resources, the clear vision of a Hitler was needed.

It has been suggested (Needham, 1973:111) that the more "lineal"—that is, hierarchical—the social system, the firmer the symbolic classifications may be and the tighter the hold of the one upon the other.[5] As a society hardens the line between the relevant and the irrelevant in speech, it reinforces by parallel divisions in the structures of social groups and organizations. It is the evolution of lineal thinking to such a pass that makes feminists such as Robin Morgan (1989:51) exclaim that "if I had to name one quality as the genius of patriarchy, it would be the capacity for institutionalizing disconnection."

Our conclusion is therefore that under stress, ecological stress, societies (and individuals in those societies) tend to line up their poles of (in particular) dichotomic classification more and more rigidly in their thought and social systems in self-defense. In addition, they tend to tolerate less and less deviance from these systems. Furthermore, under stress, categories tend to become mutually exclusive and, at the same time, become more expected to cover every possibility. The extent of sexual physical dimorphism is shown to be "related to the extent of danger in the environment" (Boulding, 1976:39) among apes. We may expand the rule to humans and to socially approved sexual dimorphism. When this rule fails to be maintained, the culture will not be flexible in the onslaught of those dangers.

The Middle Eastern seclusion of women is classification gone wild—or rather intensely domesticated. It is a heady distinction not between clannish moieties, but between the most basic and inescapable duality of all—that between the sexes. It is the most dimorphic, the most "advanced" and "scientific" system around, the quantum mechanics of gender politics. It is a system which does allow the observation and preservation of both "wave" and "particle" aspects of human nature at one and the same time.

In ancient Mesopotamia, as big men lavished more and more art upon their own glorification and used it to further their own aggrandizement, women knew they must do something drastic to retain some control over the self-expression even the humblest had in her art or craft. Mernissi (1994) remembers fondly, from her native Morocco, the individual taste traditional women brought to the clothes they made or dictated to their dressmakers instead of the other way around. Women even resort to spirit possession to justify clothing preferences (Rausch, 2000) for what lies under the uniform chador. These women decided that when the looking glass was held up to them, they should be invisible, yet omnipresent, and, with this magic trick, safe from further exploitation.

Chapter 18

Women's Tongue

Concerning women's potentials for independent expression, we will now consider seclusion's effect on a language spoken in conjunction with the practice. Arabic is fairly straightforward and points to a high degree of sexual consciousness even from its origins. It is perhaps the most "gender-loaded" language in the world (Beit-Hallahmi et al., 1974; Bodine, 1975) on a scale where English, which has received such impassioned criticism from feminist speakers of the language, ranks only "very low." Arabic's gender-based conjugations and adjectival agreements make romance languages, with which readers may be familiar, seem positively egalitarian. In Hebrew (closely related to Arabic), one cannot say the first-person pronoun without declaring one's sex.

So far as we can tell, however, Arabic and Hebrew were not the languages spoken by the first women to close their grilles against exploitation. More complicated, but closer to the point and perhaps more interesting in this light, is a brief study of the world's first written language, ancient Sumerian. In Sumerian, gender is not distinguished. What linguists term a "gender" does exist, but it is rather poor terminology forced on our study by Indo-European languages: grammatical paradigms are made with a difference marked between beings with souls, i.e., gods, demigods, and humans, and those without, i.e., animals and everything else. It is as if English had a single word for "he/she" and then an "it" of such powerful consequences that it demanded a different conjugation for all verbs.

This lack of Sumerian gender has bothered some (Falkenstein, 1974:68), particularly for a culture in which "the difference between the sexes" appears to have been so important.[1] Even when "the distinction is vital, the masculine and feminine are distinguished by different words (e.g., *lugal* 'king', *gašan* 'queen')" not, as is often the

A History of Women's Seclusion in the Middle East
Published by the Haworth Press, Inc., 2006. All rights reserved.
doi:10.1300/5666_19

case in English, by feminine suffixes that make "princess" only another (and somewhat lesser) sort of "prince." This should be noted
especially in light of the Sumerian way of seeing kingship and
queenship as essentially different powers, different *me,* or gifts of the
gods, as Sumerian mythology puts it.

"Even in some instances where the distinction is *necessary* none is
made, and the noun is of no gender (e.g., *dam* meaning both 'husband' and 'wife')" (Falkenstein, 1974:68). I italicized "necessary"
because obviously the difference was not "necessary" to the Sumerians or they would have done something about it. Marking the difference between a husband and a wife linguistically is certainly not necessary for the life and survival of a race in the way that, say, a source
of potable water is. Indeed, modern American application forms
seem to be managing very well with the single word "spouse." As a
matter of fact, Sumerians did sometimes find the distinction necessary. In such cases a word of unequivocal sex may be added, as in
dingir = "god" and "goddess"; *dingir-ama* = "god-mother" = "goddess" (p. 68).

Do I mean by this discussion to hold ancient Sumer up to the modern equal-opportunity activist as a guiding light of what unsexing language can do for a society? Not at all; at least, not in the way the activist may hope. For it must be noted that Sumerian, while being
remarkably unconscious of gender in its grammar, cannot be discussed without considering the fact that it, in reality, consisted of at
least two dialects. A number of other dialects have been proposed and
investigated—a sailors' dialect, a shepherds' dialect—which we may
call jargons, such as those spoken today by doctors or computer programmers. However, it is the two major dialects that will concern us
here, "one of the most controversial topics within Sumerology"
(Whittaker, 2002:633): eme.ku or Emegir, the "main dialect"[2] in
which most inscriptions are written; and eme.sal,[3] or Emesal.

Emesal was a form of the "main," or rather, male dialect, spoken
peculiarly by women: goddesses, and priestesses and their atten-
dants, including eunuchs. Indeed, Assyriologists are often helped by
this fact in deciphering their tablets. If the name of the speaker in a divine exchange between Inanna and her consort Dumuzi has been broken off a clay tablet, but part of the speech remains and it is in Emesal,
it may certainly be ascribed to the goddess. Certain lamentation litur-
gies are always written in Emesal, "even though recited by male

priests (although the latter may well have been eunuchs)" (Hayes, 2000:7), and on occasion a cow (Schretter 1990:170), a fly (Mark Cohen, 1981:88-89), a demon (pp. 76, 81), and even a temple (she says, "Oh, my hierodule," pp. 70-71) are humanized, we may say *feminized,* with Emesal speech.

The two complementary languages that were spoken in Mesopotamia 5,000 years ago were actually quite close, with "scarcely any grammatical differences" (Diakonoff, 1975:114). The main differences were phonetic: every time the male dialect would use the sound *n-* at the beginning of a word, Emesal would use *š-*. In main dialect *-ḡ-, d-, g-, -g* became *-m-, z-, d-,* and *-b* respectively. Also, a limited number of nouns were completely different from the names for the same objects in the main dialect (cf. Emesal *gašan* for Emeku *nin,* "lady" or "queen").

Here I will examine one specific difference between the Sumerian dialects that will help us begin to clarify the purpose this linguistic "boondoggle" served. The ceremony or gift by which a betrothal was sealed was called *nì-mí-ús-sa* by men. Women called it *èm-mu-lu-ús-sa.* This difference has been declared to be "inexplicable" (Falkenstein, 1958), for by no known rules of transposition does Emegir *mí* go to Emesal *mu-lu.*

However, let us look at the word more closely. It is a compound word.[4] In the men's dialect, *mí-ús-sa,* the usual word for brother-in-law (from the wife's family's point of view) means literally "he who follows or accompanies the woman." *nì* or *níg* is the common Sumerian prefix used to make abstract nouns, so we might say that brideprice is the state which allows a man to accompany a woman—in the language of men.

mí is the common word for woman, the determinative preceding names of women. In its original form the symbol for this word was a drawing of a vulva—*sal,* mentioned previously. Let us look at what Emesal replaces this with. *ém* is the well-known Emesal version of the *nì* or *níg* particle, so all we have really replaced is *mu-lu* for the word for woman. Even with no knowledge of Sumerian, it does not take much inspiration to realize that the bride-price does not allow a woman to accompany a *woman.* For women to use this terminology is to be party to making oneself an object. It would be as sexist as is— well, the English term "bride-price." So what is *mu-lu?* Emesal *-mu,* according to the phonological rules just stated, should be Emegir

-$\bar{g}u$, but it is also a common Emesal reading of *giš*. Commonly, *giš* means wood or tree and is the determinative used before the names of trees or objects made of wood. However, it is also a euphemism for the male organ, as in *giš-zu* = "to know the penis" = "to be wed" or *giš-nu-zu* = "unwed,"[5] said of young girls. This suggestion is given further support by the next element, the very common word for man. The use of *giš*, while being quite graphic and certainly focusing attention to what must be the central aspect of marriage for Middle Eastern women, might have had the further benefit of being misunderstood by children considered by their culture too young to hear talk of sexual matters.

This translation adds important information to our understanding of how early Mesopotamian women's society worked. The betrothal ceremony or gift was seen by a Sumerian woman quite logically as that which permitted her to accompany a man sexually. Female use of the male term would border on the ridiculous, and would certainly be nothing short of a full-scale acceptance of the men's view of the world. Whatever else it did, it is my contention that Emesal served very effectively to allow women more control over the creation of the symbols with which they described their world. After all, where do our symbols first take root but in language?

Sexual dialects such as the Emesal/Emegir dichotomy that existed in ancient Sumerian may seem very bizarre but in fact they are not unheard of among the world's languages.[6] Let us look at the data from other world languages that use sexual dialects.

Japanese is very important because it exists in written documents covering a thousand-year period; we can watch the development of sexual differences:

> in general the sexual identity of the characters . . . in *The Tale of Genji* (written [by a woman] somewhere between [AD] 1001 and 1010) cannot be made on the basis of their speech style. . . . The distinction in the writing style can be traced back earlier . . . but it seems to be [generally] agreed that the distinction between male and female speech style began to be widespread after the fourteenth century, and became rather firmly established with the emergence of the Tokugawa shogunate at the beginning of the seventeenth century. (Kitagawa, 1977:296)

The rise of sexually distinctive speech therefore coincides with the time when class distinction began to be the basis of social order in Japan. Class and sex distinctions did not appear at once, but the former fed the latter in a slow, yet dependent progress. The sexual distinction in speech style in Japan is more of an urban phenomenon than a rural one. In farming communities, women constitute an important part of the labor force, and are not as dependent on men as their sisters in cities.

The dialect's inception, as far as we can glean it from the old sources, was during the Heian period (middle of the first millennium AD). This first flourishing of literature in Japan was spurred by a great influx of learning and scribal art from China. Official documents, histories, and religious tracts were heavily dependent on Chinese orthography and the attendant lexicon. Women never wrote such things; they were totally barred from these genres.

Men, on the other hand, "considered writing in Japanese to be beneath them and devoted themselves to the composition of poetry and prose in Chinese" (Shibamoto, 1985:162). This left the native language unoccupied, as it were. This the women appropriated to themselves and used it to write masterpieces the entire culture acknowledged.

If women did not have access to "male" genres,

> it is equally true . . . that men did not have access to the genres used in diaries and novels. In fact, men who wished to write, for example, diaries, did so, but most often in those cases they wrote as women. *Tosa Nikki* (The Tose Diary) written by courtier-scholar Ki no Tsurayuki (868 CE) is perhaps the most famous example. (Shibamoto, 1985:162)

In this diary, Tsurayuki takes on a feminine persona that enables him to give expression to a fear of pirates and to "excessive"[7] grief over the death of a child. These would otherwise be unseemly in the person of a very powerful and "macho" precursor of the samurai. He brushes the whole thing off by closing his work with the comment, "Well, well—this must be torn up at once" (Ki, 1981:133)—but he didn't tear it up.

This dichotomy of the genres continues to some extent today. As recently as the 1970s it was deemed unseemly for Japanese women to be caught reading newspapers (which use male dialect) in public places such as trains or subways. They were encouraged to confine themselves to reading paperback novels or magazines (usually written by men, but in supposedly female dialect). Political speeches are characterized, among other things, by the use of language forms women are constrained from speaking. Surely this limits a woman's effectiveness in this sphere. In addition, if a female newscaster read the news "one inevitably became doubtful about whether she was telling the truth. . . . They read [therefore], not the news of violent current events, but items in the cultural line or small topics" (Shibamoto, 1985:163).

The main problem here as I see it is not that women are barred from these genres, but that these genres have become the only sources of power in a monolithic society and that, in this monolith, men have taken for themselves the powerful genres once limited to women alone *by their use of dialect*. The fact that Tsurayuki did not tear up his diary and the fact that he wrote it at all let us know that the feelings he expressed in it were very real and important. In the polarization of the sexes at the time, he could only give vent to them by resorting to a women's genre. But note: Novels and diaries in Japan at this time were unique women's genres. They were not then incorporated as the lowest rungs of a male genre power hierarchy as are modern paperback novels and women's magazines.

In light of this, let us consider this general statement by Ivan Illich (1982:139):

> Feminine and masculine features of language are its most tender and vulnerable aspects, even while the language is still very much alive. . . . These features seem particularly to have been abandoned when a language became the instrument of empire, when it became a trade language, a language of administration that had to fit areas with very different gender divides. The feminine and masculine traits are the first to be threatened when language is standardized, and what tends to remain is mere grammatical gender, out of touch with old dualities and now mainly used for discriminatory speech.

Our third example of a language with sexual dialects is Ottoman Turkish, although this is not generally recognized as being so. It was, of course, the men's speech, the language of dragoman and vizier, that attracted the attention of European merchant and diplomat in early centuries. The world that the women's language described and moved was so totally separate and secluded as to have left almost no mark on the other, public world which, in the end, won out.

A bias against scouting out even what vestiges of the harem's dialect may linger today is fostered by the government that has actively sought to repress all but the "true" Turkish tongue Atatürk imagined. *A Frequency Count of Turkish Words* (Pierce, 1964a) for example, relies heavily on military manuals and responses to a questionnaire given to illiterate soldiers in the Turkish army. Even when some respect for dialectology is expressed, conflicting reports exist. This same Pierce (1964b:75) who admits to being a great believer in "language as a reflection of culture" could not understand why in the small Anatolian town of his study where the spheres of men and women are so separate, "there is almost no sex . . . differentiation in the language." Perhaps because he is a man, he was accorded less access to women's lives and their natural speech. A woman of my acquaintance (Wasilewska, 1987) declared that, indeed, no difference exists between men's and women's speech in the large Westernized towns[8] where the spheres are more closely aligned. Alhough she had no trouble understanding the men during her stay in rural Anatolia, the women were almost incomprehensible. Their vocabulary differed drastically from the men's and from what textbook study had taught her. Their speech was also very high pitched and rapid.

Foster's observation of palatal umlaut in the modern dialect of Istanbul, which is "perhaps somewhat more operable in women's than men's speech"(1969:216) would, if pursued, probably display the class-consciousness, not sex-consciousness, of the women in Labov's New York (1966) and Trudgill's Norwich (1972). Yet there remain two references to prove my point.

The first is that given by nineteenth-century traveler Lucy Garnett who tantalized us: "The speech of the serailis [women in the harem] is a sort of dialect differing from that of the outer world, and their extraction can always be at once detected by this peculiarity" (1891: II:385). More clues than that she doesn't give.

The second is more recent research done on the archives of the imperial seraglio. "All the girls in the palaces," we are told,

> knew how to read and write. . . . However, we should admit that these ladies did not have a good education. Their letters are full of spelling, grammar and construction mistakes, . . . That their

> pronunciation was bad and irregular is clearly seen from the
> written words in their letters. Apparently they wrote the words
> as they spoke them. (Uluçay, 1959:398)

Apparently. However, that this appearance should lead us to the conclusion that their education and pronunciation was "bad" is to view
the evidence from a modern, male-valued perspective. The first step
in correcting this perspective is to consider that the "girls" did write
what they spoke, that this was quite different from the way men (and
the women when they were being official) wrote and spoke, but that it
was the *right* way to speak—for a harem woman. Studies on the earliest folios of Shakespeare's plays indicated that he wrote words the
way he spoke them and that he maintained the dialect of his native
Stratford-upon-Avon to his dying day. For all the bad press trend-
setters in London might give to "lesser" dialects, in this case certainly
they cannot be said to have hampered the genius of the man. The
same holds for the attitudes of speakers and writers in the modern,
"main" dialect of Turkish. In fact, in both the case of Shakespeare and
of the women of the harem, a different perspective on life from the
given masscult can only have helped.

The second step Uluçay or another Turkish researcher might undertake to help us understand Ottoman Turkish women's speech is to
go over the archives again and try to determine just what these "irreg-
ularities" were, if some sort of consistency can be determined. At the
present state of our knowledge, I may suggest that, given the foreign
origin of most of the women in the imperial harem, perhaps certain elements of foreign accents were accorded high status. Women from
the Caucasus were thought to be the most beautiful. "Farms" actually
existed in Caucasia where promising girls were trained and groomed
for the imperial harem. Such women were most likely to win the favor
of the sultan and therefore were most likely to end up as Queen
Mother and in other positions of great power. Is it too much to suggest
that part of the serailis' "dialect" may have included aspiration of ini-
tial consonants or the glottalization of all consonants, which is typical
of Turkic languages exposed to influence from Caucasian peoples
(Menges, 1968:176)?

Although at this point we cannot follow the course of the Ottoman
Turkish women's language development, it is clear that the power
they wielded inside the sultan's realm and beyond by virtue of their
being women was nothing to sneer at. "But," the Westerner may say,

"they were secluded, and the fact that we have little written in their dialect screams out their powerlessness." The Turks understand their own culture better: they call a period of close to 200 years of their history "The Reign of the Favored Women."[9] As for the demise of this dialect, surely it can be dated to the time of Atatürk when women of the serai were paraded out of their luxurious and comfortable seclusion and sent back to live with the families they hardly knew (and, it is noted in some cases, they could no longer understand) in impoverished villages. Women walking through the streets in the veils that protected their separate way of life had those veils torn from them. Overnight, through Atatürk's craving for a "pure" Turkish language, the male intelligentsia (because their Turkish was heavily arabicized) became illiterate, if not altogether speechless. Even today this revolution cramps those seeking to study Turkish dialects. If it silenced the men of letters, how much more so their female counterparts!

Modern American and British women who try to fit their language into the monolith they feel encroaching upon them enjoy no such separateness of expression or power. This is made clear by many attempts to discover an *obscenic* voice not only by radical feminist writers but by third world writers who feel a similar crunch. The word *obscenic* was coined from "*ob* (in a relation of friction with) + *scena* (the space of ritual and communal enactment)" (Dunton-Downer, 1989:8). The dominant "scene" will find what is written in *obscenics* uncomfortable and obscene, but the speakers and writers who make these attempts to find an alternative tongue know only too well that "the scene is unable to contain [them] or provide a home for" their expressions; they will never honestly "recognize themselves in the scene and its language" (Dunton-Downer, 1989:8).

It is my conclusion that Sumerian Emesal represents an expression of female solidarity that cuts across a growing male monolith of power. In my model for the historical beginnings of women's seclusion in Sumer, I see women changing their speech as a reaction to the development of urbanism and class hierarchy that threatened their ability to create their own images and value system.[10] As a demonstration of this (or rather, counterexample) I would like to take a large corpus of writings in Emesal, namely the cultic poems of Enheduanna, the daughter of Sargon the Great of Akkad (whose dates are ca. 2371-2316 BCE).

Enheduanna is a great favorite with feminist historians because she is among the first women in the world to get her name in print, to figure as an individual in the parade of mostly male ambition. As he brought more and more of Mesopotamia under his rule, Enheduanna's father placed friends and family in influential positions wherever he went. Enheduanna herself was made High Priestess (propaganda agent?[11]), first of the moon-god Sin's temple in Ur (in the *gipar*) and then of the temple to An in Uruk. With Sargon's influence, the Akkadian language was spreading and sounding the death knoll for Sumerian—except within the protection of the temple. Enheduanna worked part of this protection by composing quite a large corpus of hymns and poems in the sacred language, women's Emesal. Unfortunately, I agree with others who percieve her work as mainly propaganda in favor of her father, his conquests, and the rigors of male empire. I will argue, however, that it is precisely these attributes that caused her works to receive the attention they did in later, even more imperialistic years and, indeed, to have them preserved to this day. They became schoolboys' copy texts, copied over and over because of the "patriotic" sentiments they express as much for the obscure examples of a dead sacred language—and its women's dialect, no less—that they contain. I cannot help but think that poetesses were grinding out Emesal hymns in Mesopotamia's temples for centuries, but those poems with a tone less favorable to male power were certainly never copied as often, even if they did reach the mostly male medium of the clay tablet. Examples of "true" Emesal have not survived because it did not suit the curriculum of male-dominated scribal schools.

Enheduanna's betrayal of her sex, her manipulation of female genres and symbols for male ends, is merely a sideline of the great secret, verbal tradition in Emesal that women in seclusion were fostering. This is not to gloat, but to sympathize: we have still the laments Enheduanna wrote when a man other than her father came into power and she tasted the bitter fruits of her support of linear power.

Of more promise is the career of Forūgh Farrokhzād, arguably the most important poet working in the Persian language in the past fifty years. She was branded a heretic—and worse—by her critics of the male establishment. Her images certainly are disturbing to anyone raised in a world of The Truth, whether Zoroastrian, Islamic, or

Judeo-Christian, a world exorcised of feminine and divine nature.
The following are excerpts from some of her poems.

my body's an altar
ready for the rites of love[12]

*   *   *

Ah, do you see
how my skin is bursting
how the milk is congealing in the blue veins of my cold breasts
how the blood
is beginning it's cartilaginous growth
in my patient womb?

I am you, you
and the one who loves
and the one who finds, suddenly
a mute alliance within herself
with thousands of unknown, estranging things
Once more I am the ardent passion of the earth
that draws all the waters to itself
to make all valleys fertile, rich and geen[13]

*   *   *

Give me sanctuary, O you simple whole women[14]

*   *   *

swallows will lay their eggs
in the nest of my inkstained fingers[15]

*   *   *

The flowers' bleeding ancestry is what's committed me to life
The flowers' bleeding ancestry—have I made it clear to you?[16]

No one can deny the power of these images, their vibrant harkings
back to a time and religion of strong femininity we thought we had
lost; nor, ultimately, their reality.

I do consider it something of a blasphemy to try to pin down and eviscerate the sources of artistic inspiration: a very linear occupation. It is quite conceivable that a poet of the caliber of Farrokhzād came to her work by instinct, discovering with a sixth sense where the rigid categories of her society could be pricked. On the other hand, I cannot resist the temptation to suggest that she may have been trustee of symbols and images that her mothers may have kept inviolate behind veils and harem walls since the ancient Persian goddess Anahita herself went underground, images that hark back to the wellspring of Emesal and beyond. Farrokhzād represented the first generation—perhaps the last?—of Persian women to be raised outside, under a monolithic system. As such, it was her calling to bring these images to the light of male-dominated printing presses and literary journals. Naturally her reception was hostile. It may ultimately prove fatal to those precious values to demand that they compete for the bottom line with more comfortable doctrine.

In conclusion, we may say that seclusion, becoming more severe as masscult pervaded, was not masscult's tool but its counterforce, protecting this most important access of women to symbols, often revolutionary, of their own. They could not succumb to the blandishments of masscult. They must, and behind harem walls are allowed to, have their own music, dance, stories, expression. I believe that, where women's symbols are secure, so are those of any minority.

Chapter 19

For Men Only

The harem needs scribes, storytellers, merchants, healers, readers, and interpreters of the Qur'an. They are not educated in formal, male-sanctioned schooling, but by other women, with a female slant to the knowledge. The ambitious mother puts her energies to finding good matches for her children, dropping their names to the wives of men who can further her sons' careers. If any woman has the gumption, skill, and energy, I am convinced no harem wall is going to stop her. I would like to cite one example that the pilgrim Hurgronje (1931) gives from his stay in Mecca in the nineteenth century. Here a woman, married to a starry-eyed, absentminded scholar, ran the house, the servants, and most of the neighborhood as well as one of the most thriving businesses in the city while her husband shut himself up with his books. Come to think of it, this was similar to the case of the Prophet Muhammad and his first wife Khadijah. Even in the Middle East, then, in the holy city of Mecca and under the roof of a holy man, the division of the sexes is not ultimate. The harem presents many directions for the ambitious woman. They are not the same directions as the men are sent in, perhaps, but they are directions that can earn the aggressive soul her sense of self-worth and accomplishment. The only thing that may not happen is that her skills and energy be syphoned off to otherwise "male" ends. There are men for that.

The flexibility of ambitious women to take on various tasks in the strict dichotomy of seclusion has been provided for; the "woman's woman" is so by definition. Let's turn now to the men. Patriarchy, up to and including female infanticide, is a function of populations pressing the limits of their resources (M. Harris, 1974, 1977, 1979): One man can keep a dozen women procreating, so devaluing women and their fertility, emphasizing the importance of the male, and sending his aggression out to get more resources for the clan is a good pol-

A History of Women's Seclusion in the Middle East
Published by the Haworth Press, Inc., 2006. All rights reserved.
doi:10.1300/5666_20

icy. When a woman's reproductive tasks are so devalued that she must turn her efforts to the male, merely productive side of the monolith, there is no reason her talents cannot flex to encompass that as well, stretched as she may be. She does what she must.

It may come as a surprise when we look in the mirror and see that a unisex, technologically enhanced world, contrary to what we may have expected, may come close to making obsolete the very males who set the pace in the first place. If a woman can, in fact is encouraged to, push the button on a smart bomb as well as the next guy, and she can stir her own gametes in a test tube to take care of the reproductive part, the male is indeed in danger of becoming redundant. The only task that cannot go to either sex for the most basic continuation of the species is the honest-cell nurturing.

Populations as close to being asexual as we on the American continent have made our culture "expand more quickly than sexual ones" (Cherfas and Gribbin, 1984:4), rather like the aphid having suddenly discovered an uncolonized[1] rosebush who happily clones her female self all summer long. Indeed, although I have no statistics to back it up, I get the feeling that this sense of redundancy is rampant among American males. I see a huge proportion of husbands among my ambitious, well-educated girlfriends who, confronted by women who landed and kept better jobs than they did, have basically checked out of the rat race. The wives now support them as well as the kids—unless they go to the trouble of getting a lawyer to dump the dead weight. Other women have found no male with the necessary "commitment" and so have resorted to sperm banks. The woman basically replicates herself—a unisex, or multisexed organism, if you will, one of whose appendages is an atrophied male appendage who's simply provided his sperm to the concern—just like the aphid. Among their sons, the phenomenon finds a new generation in a surprising number of teenage boys who cannot make themselves get out of bed in the morning.

Feeling the hot breath of redundancy on his neck, the male with a fierce patriarchal streak instinctively tries to keep women out of competing in his sphere. "Stay in the bedroom and kitchen," he may order, whether fundamentalist Christianity or Islam has won his favor. However, it is no use insisting on that half of the equation if he doesn't pick up the honor side of the parallel. He may not leave behind him a welfare mom or two with no support (even if they aren't his own castoffs, except he gave them not a second glance while they waitressed in that fancy restuarant last night) while he sneaky-cells on to his next trophy wife.

The aphid's instincts tell her the roses do not bloom forever. Come winter and the withering of her resources, "in the long run . . . asexual populations are doomed by their inflexibility" (Cherfas and Gribbin, 1984:4). The aphid will finally lay eggs, to get her genes through the dearth in offspring balanced and flexibly male and female again.

Bad as a unisex monolith is, in the long run, even for those who shortsightedly set the rules in the first place, I will not spend any more time on the "man's man." Ambition and energy, I assume, need no protection; they will take care of themselves. A worse problem seems to be what to do with the, say, one-quarter of the male population who might find the emphasis on ambition a difficult fit? Dreaminess and softheartedness really are out of place in the male world, and it would be a cruel society indeed that did not offer an out for the gentler soul. Ancient Mesopotamia was not such a desperately cruel land.

As a matter of fact, as we have hinted, not all speakers of the "women's dialect" of ancient Sumerian were women. Emesal was spoken by three classes of people: (1) goddesses and other women of mythical proportions, including priestesses who often acted in the role of the goddess; (2) "messengers and servants of the goddesses," (when Sumerian was a living language, this included all women); and (3) a class of male incantation singers called *gala* (in Akkadian *kalû*) (Diakonoff, 1975).[2]

The easiest path to understanding this latter class of men seems to be to work backward from classical times when the Latin *gallos* or *gallus* became the general word for "eunuch" throughout the Roman Empire. Lucian's description of the galli in the cult of the Syrian goddess in Heiropolis in his day (second century AD) is the most famous description from Hellenistic times. It is certainly the most graphic:

> Of all the festivals I know about . . . the greatest is the one they hold at the beginning of spring. . . . On appointed days, the crowd assembles at the sanctuary while many Galli and . . . holy men . . . perform the rites. They cut their arms and beat one another on the back. Many stand about them playing flutes, while others beat drums. Still others sing inspired and sacred songs. This ceremony takes place outside the temple and none of those who performs it enters the temple.

On these days, too, men become Galli. For while the rest are playing flutes and performing the rites, frenzy comes upon many and many who have come simply to watch subsequently perform this act. I will describe what they do. The youth for whom these things lie in store throws off his clothes, rushes to the center with a great shout and takes up a sword which, I believe, has stood there for this purpose for many years. He grabs it and immediately castrates himself. Then he rushes through the city holding in his hands the parts he has cut off. He takes female clothing and women's adornment from whatever house he throws these parts into. This is what they do at the Castration. (Lucian, verses 49-52; translated by Attridge and Oden, 1976: 53-55)

This practice "is without doubt very ancient in the religion of Asia Minor."[3] It may even find descendants in the modern-day mourning for Hussein and Hasan, as practiced with self-flagellation among Shiite Muslims during the month of Muharram—without the castration, of course. Doubtless, it is precisely the rites of the Syrian goddess that the biblical writer reacted to with such horror in Leviticus 22:24-25: "Ye shall not offer unto the Lord that which is bruised or crushed or broken or cut . . . because their corruption is in them, and blemishes be in them: they shall not be accepted for you." It is impossible not to see the etymological grandparent of the term *gallos* in the Sumerian *gala,* the Akkaddian *kalû.*

The human beings in this class may have originated as the sons of the slave or (probably not) corvée women who went to work in the temple and palace workshops (Maekawa, 1980). Castrated male slaves would pose no threat to the captor's women. If this is the case, we can imagine that these men were pivotal in facilitating the concentration of honor on their kinswomen and helped them to maintain their integrity and to give it mystical power in the face of exploitation. We can begin to understand how the first men of this class became violently energetic in the defense of their mothers and sisters—and, also, of the traditions (perhaps matrilineal) that they brought with them from the far land. This is a tradition that held after the ties of kin had gone, even down to the nineteenth century.

The Akkadian *galas* were dirge singers. Castration would do much—in a very awe-inspiring way—to attach a *gala* to the sense of loss he was supposed to portray for worshippers through his laments!

At the same time, this was supreme "union with the divine" (Gruppe, 1906:1542). The god was a woman, yet "all people are women before the god." Both views are and were possible in the kaleidoscopic images of religion, but castration is not absolutely necessary to attain the high-pitched voice postulated for these priests (Silvestri, 1976).

Support is added to the castration theory by pointing out that certain Sumerian proverbs depend for their irony on the "powerlessness" of the character of the *gala* (Diakonoff, 1975). "Should a *gala* [beget a] son, (he would say): 'He will surely build cities like me, he will surely make the land live, like me!'" is one such proverb in which there is a "perverse use of men's and women's dialect" which defies translation (Gordon, 1959:247). This "truly royal speech of the *gala* is in men's Sumerian" (p. 247), a language he would not use! It is no wonder that the Akkadian translation of this proverb on the same tablet replaces the Sumerian *gala* by a she-mule, which cannot, of course, have any progeny at all.

Irreverence such as this proverb shows toward a member of the clergy, even of the pettiest grade, is difficult for us to understand; proverb lists were used as copy texts for students in the elementary levels of a scribal education. One might hope for more edification from the school system!

It seems to me that the ancient author of this proverb meant not just any *gala* but an *ambitious* one to be the butt of the joke and of high-minded scorn. Expansion of one's dominion either through numerous offspring or the fruit of a well-tilled field were not the values a *gala* was supposed to hold up to the youth of Sumerian society. His prerogative was different, something more akin to a perpetual "Inshallah!," the Arabic "as God wills."

I do not mean to suggest that the Sumerians were somber puritans—far from it. However, from these examples we can see that their humor meant to underscore the fact that a man who chose (or was chosen) to become a *gala*-priest was not to be like other men. His association was with the women whose speech and dress (as far as possible) he was meant to imitate, and ambition was supposed to be foreign to him—yet he was still a man to command respect.

On the other hand, some scholars do not hear the sarcasm in the proverb at all (Jacobsen, 1959), and others point out that the children of *galas* are documented elsewhere, sons even following in their father's profession (Renger, 1969:192-193). Records show that some *gala*-priests had wives. "Evidence of a female *gala* in Archaic Old Babylonian times" (Whittaker, 2002:635; see also Black, 1991:26-27) also exists. Are the children conceived before induction into the priesthood? Are they perhaps adopted children? Are we wrong about the castration altogether? Clearly, we do not know everything about this priesthood position.

For that matter, we have records of married Ottoman eunuchs and descriptions of how they and their wives were able to enjoy sex sometimes with more success than women enjoyed with whole men (Croutier, 1989:135). Although sexual enjoyment in such a marriage is not something the ancients thought worthy of recording, there exists a record of one ancient marriage that I particularly like. It is found on a series of tablets from Sippar where the wife[4] of a *kalamahu* (chief dirge singer or *gala*) repeatedly borrows barley and silver from the same *naditu* woman (R. Harris, 1975). This reminds me of some of the contemporary couples I mentioned previously, where the husband—usually an artist, a musician, a photographer, a writer—is basically incapable of supporting himself, let alone a family. Music (or art or writing) is such a consuming passion for him that he can think of nothing else, and in these couples it is the wife who must deal with life in our society for him. This is how I imagine the ancient dirge singers, although also from Sippar are records of *kalamahus* as creditors, so this was not a universal trait. Perhaps castration was not a necessary prerequisite for entry into this priesthood. I do feel, however, that it was necessary for the applicant to espouse this set of values that stood in opposition to the newly discovered power of the Mesopotamian city and to help maintain the system of checks and balances. That women's religions had to borrow powerful reinforcements from the other half of the scale only goes to show how much in favor of linear forces the balance had tipped.

To eke our notion of the *gala,* let us add images from closer to our own time. Our word *eunuch* comes from the Greek *eunoukhos,* originally nothing more exotic than a "bedchamber attendant." By the courts of Byzantium, eunuchs—in the later, castrated sense of the word—had become ubiquitous and powerful figures indeed. Because of the seclusion women enjoyed, only eunuchs could have direct access both day and night

> to the person of the ruler or the master of the house, . . . even during the master's private hours. Even the sons [and presumably

heirs] of the master, who so frequently had different mothers [and rarely the same woman as she who currently shared the master's bed], could not, from a certain age onwards, enjoy that privilege. (Ayalon, 1979:68)

In the Byzantine court, eunuchs played a pivotal role:

Eight honorary titles . . . are reserved for the eunuchs, and the patrician eunuchs in fact occupied a position superior to that of the other patricians. . . . No office, however high in Church and State (with the single exception of the imperial dignity itself) was withheld from the eunuchs on principle, and many of the patriarchs,[5] statesmen and generals who distinguished themselves in Byzantine history were eunuchs. There were, however, a number of court offices which were normally, though not without exception, held by eunuchs. The most important of these were the office of the *parcoemomenus* who slept near the imperial bed-chamber and who was usually one of the Emperor's most trusted confidants . . . and the office of the *protovestarius,* the head of the imperial wardrobe. (Ostrogorsky, 1957:221)

We recall that Byzantine Christian parents, even those in line to the throne, often had their sons castrated as infants in order to qualify them for powerful government posts. A neat piece of irony is found here: that ambition would drive people to create beings who were trusted in positions of power because they had no dynastic ambitions themselves (Bridge, 1978)—an irony very characteristic of how a system of severe sexual dichotomy works to balance itself.

During medieval Islam, the "institution developed special characteristics, which made it—in spite of the obvious existence of a wide common denominator and numerous other similarities—quite distinct from its parallels in other civilizations" (Ayalon, 1979:68).

Eunuchs were often addressed as *ustadh* ("master" in Arabic) and their post was not without honor, indeed power, from Muslim Spain to Mamluk Egypt to Mogul India. However, the original function of eunuchs did receive serious compromise when it was decided that no Muslim should be castrated and slavery from beyond the realms of Islam became the main source of these principle guards of the harem.

Eunuchs in other civilizations had not been necessarily slaves. Side by side with foreigners a very substantial part of the eunuchs in those other civilizations belonged to the local population, and had very strong local roots. Their isolation from that population, and sometimes even from their own family and relatives, must have been much smaller than that of the eunuchs in Islam. Furthermore, in Byzantium, for example, eunuchs could be found in various strata of the society, including the Royal family. Nepotistic attitudes of eunuchs toward their relatives were quite common in Byzantium and China.

In Islam, because of the eunuchs' foreign origin, it occurred very rarely that a eunuch would have a relative at all . . . , this made all of them extremely dependent on their patrons, as well as grateful and loyal to them for, under the circumstances in which they lived, they owed them practically everything. (Ayalon, 1979:69-70; see also Ayalon, 1988)

The practice of total castration as was highly favored, practiced on black men by the thousands, and from which as few as a quarter survived, is indeed a blight on the name of humanity. Still we must recall, too, that such men were given perhaps the highest honor in all of Islam: that of guarding the Kaaba in Mecca as they guarded any other holy harem, and that of guarding all of the pious foundations and donations to the holy cities by the Ottoman sultans. In this way these Muslim holy places were the descendants of the Sumerian temple (Marmon, 1995).

The male *xanith*[6] of modern Oman, described in 1977 by Wikan, might be following an age-old custom—descendant of the *galu,* Islamicized, removed from his temple, arabicized. Wikan (1978) suspects (and the evidence from Mombasa at least says she may be right) that the custom finds parallels throughout the Muslim world, and that little has been said on the subject up to now because most ethnographers have been men. Denied access to the world of women, such researchers failed to notice the pastel-clad men with shoulder-length hair flitting their way through the back streets and conversing freely with the usually black-masked and female denizens of these places. The age-old custom of the *xanith* indicates that even with the influx of slave eunuchs, providing a "mediating sex" to members of a society with high sex segregation is so important that it could not be totally entrusted to slave labor.

The *xanith*'s motive in entering this station is likely to be "a desire to escape from the exacting demands of the Omani male role" (Wikan, 1977:309). Arab machismo and its demands of honor certainly have its terrors. Wikan chooses to focus maleness, as it seems the Omanis do, on the ability to perform (usually unrehearsed) on the wedding night.[7] I also think economics is part of the male Omani's terrors. Trying to succeed as a *man* in the age-old bazaars of Sohar[8] when one hasn't the funds to start a little shop of one's own or to get enough training to avoid being cheated if one did, might well be daunting and make the *xaniths'* occupation of household servant, allowed to remain like a child in the harems, attractive. Of course, we must believe that some men would rather not perform on the wedding night or any other—with a woman.

Many of the youths of Lucian's account went to the Syrian goddess's festival with no thought of self-castration. Perhaps in the Hellenistic world where other, more cosmopolitan values pervaded, they even went to the temple to fulfill idle curiosity (or to scoff) and suddenly found their lives totally reversed—if they didn't die in the process. The indication here and from the study of *xaniths* is that these societies crave that the post be filled as much or more than the men themselves desired an out. How ironic, when the societies themselves are so fierce at building the boundaries between men and women in the first place! Why should this be so?

Western values of the aggressive marketplace exist in Oman on the male side of a pair of separate but equal diametric hierarchies which the *xaniths* are pivotal in maintaining. The Omani women often value the *xanith*'s abilities in "cooking, home decoration and neatness" as superior to their own (Wikan, 1977:309). The reader who scorns or pities such valuations should examine her system of values to see how one-dimensional it must be. How lacking in a mirror image is our society! *Xanith* translates as "soft." Life in the harem is a million different adjectives: soft is not one of the first that comes to mind, except, perhaps, to the male mind. Be that as it may, why should being "soft" be a demeaning thing? Will we only allow "soft" to be a virtue of our toilet tissue? Certainly, then, ours is a society where the "hardest" must win and the soft, unprotected, are condemned to be flushed away.

In mundane terms, we learn that the demand for male help inside the harem (i.e., help that can come and go among females as only the *xanith* can) far exceeds the supply, even when out of about 3,000 adult Sohari men as many as "sixty transsexuals . . . are found" (Wiken, 1977:305).

Xaniths, like the ancient *gala,*[9] are admired for the high-pitched singing voices they cultivate. My contention that arts and religion serve to protect the cyclical from linear society latches on to this singing and indicates one major purpose transsexuals serve in a severely segregated society, a purpose that warrants their sacred status in the ancient Near East.[10] In spite of the fact that her transsexuals have lost their holy status, it is Wikan (1977) who gives the best description of their power in this regard:

> In Oman . . . all forms of sexual aberration and deviance are sinful according to religion. Young boys who show homosexual tendencies in their early teens are severely punished by anguished parents, and threatened with eviction from the home. So far, reactions in Oman are as one might expect in our society. But the further course of development is so distinctly Omani that any feeling of similarity disappears. If the deviant will not conform in our society, we tend to respond with moral indignation, but no organizational adjustments. He is disgusting and despicable, a violation of our sense of modesty and a threat to public morality. Strong sanctions force him to disguise his deviance and practice it covertly. But because we do not wish to face up to him, we also fail to take cognisance of his distinctive character. As a result, we construct a social order where men and women who are sexually attracted by their *own* sex, none the less are enjoined to mix freely with them in situations where *we* observe rules of sexual modesty, such as public baths and toilets.
>
> Omanis on the other hand draw the consequences of the fact that the sexual deviant cannot be suppressed. He is acknowledged and reclassified . . . and left in peace to practice his deviance. (p. 311)

We have utopian visions of the perfect TV personality, to which everyone must strive. Omanis, on the other hand, know that

> the world is imperfect; people are created with dissimilar natures, and are likewise imperfect. . . . The world contains moth-

ers who do not love their children, children who do not honor their parents, wives who deceive their husbands, men who act sexually like women . . . and it is not for me to judge or sanction them. . . . On the contrary, we are under an obligation always to be tactful and hospitable to people.

In other words, we are dealing with a society where the conceptualization of the person is subtle and differentiated. One act or activity is only *one* aspect of the person, and only one facet of a complex personality. No person is branded by any single act committed, and mistakes in the past can be corrected and ignored. It is bad taste to harp on them. (p. 311)

This holds not only for transsexual men, but for women. One woman in Wikan's close circle of neighborhood friends had such behavior that even Wikan's Scandinavian scruples were scandalized. Yet none of the other women sanctioned her at all. Instead, they found Wikan's increasingly obvious distaste more worthy of censure. "What wrong has she done you?" they asked. "[Is] she not always hospitable, friendly, and helpful?" (p. 312)

Modern Western society is so concerned with having the best, the most efficiently useful members of its funneled society, that individualities are called "aberrations" and chiseled away whenever possible. We are evolving, we are told, getting better, and such and such a trait is to be overcome for the sake of progress. Like our garbage, we wrap it up in plastic, and have it carted off to places far from our nice homes where, we like to think, we will never have to deal with it again. Of course, landfills will raise their ugly, toxic heads on the horizon. And so do these "aberrations" of personality. I maintain that variation in the population exists, not to be overcome, but to offer the possibilities of change and flexibility to new generations; just as, in a society that has a healthy relationship with its environment, waste exists not to be thrown out but to be recycled.

Agencies, specialists, couselors, antidepression seminars, schools of psychology, genetic engineering, and a pharmacopoeia of cheering stimulants are marshaled to the task of making useful citizens out of "misfits." It should come as no surprise that the large bull's-eye they target is comprised of mothers of young children, the class least able to juggle the razor-sharp values they are tossed, like the rest of our nimble society. Mothers must walk slowly for their toddlers to keep up, and the toddler finds the smallest stick or leaf of interest. Infants must be hugged and sung to; they cannot eat without being burped afterward. Simply put, efficiency is anathema to motherhood; hence, in our society that demands ever-greater efficiency, motherhood is a heresy.

It is no wonder that with this core wounded and rotting the rings of maladjustment ripple out ad infinitum to the rest of society. This confusion of metaphors is only a fraction as confusing as actually having to live in such a system as ours with one highly individual inborn system of drives to try and fit against but a single template of possibility. This leads if not to debilitating confusion (which is what the system would like), then to a clinging attachment to the tail of whatever blindly speeding comet of thoughtless movement is closest to hand.

The sine qua non of the Ottoman eunuch was a fearsome blade worn between the folds of his sash, in obvious plain sight, and which everyone knew he would not hesitate to use if the honor and integrity of his harem—be it some great pasha's household or the holy of holies in Mecca—were threatened. This is not an emasculated task for cowards and mama's boys. Transsexuals mediate. They speak in a language men understand of the rights of women, just as the rights of women, protected, protect the right of any man (or woman) to be different in case society, against its better rational judgement, should someday need his (or her) particular talents.

Let us close by returning to women, because that is our major interest here. "There can hardly be any other contemporary society," Wikan (1977) states,

> where law and customary rules combine to define so powerless a position for women as in Oman. They have no say in the choice of spouse, cannot leave their house without the husband's permission, are debarred from going to the market to make a single purchase, may often not choose their own clothes, must wear masks before all males who are not first-order relatives, etc. (p. 317)

Yet, she confesses with astonishment, because of seclusion and the strict vernacular gender that it and *xanith* men help to maintain:

> I have never met women who to the same degree seem in control of themselves and their situation. Omani women impress with

their self-assurance and poise. They comport themselves with beauty and dignity, as if confident of themselves and their position. This is no doubt partly because their tasks and responsibilities are clearly defined and they command the resources to perform them with honour and grace. But above all, it is so because of the fundamental respect which men accord them . . . and the preconditions that are thereby created for conceptualizing and realizing a valued identity. (p. 317)

For this valued female identity the mediation of transsexual males is in part responsible.

Chapter 20

The Fate of Seclusion in the West

By way of conclusion to this history, I want to give a different history—that of seclusion in the West. I need to answer the question of why it doesn't exist here and what this means for Western women today—indeed, for all women as our culture spreads like a plague. I can point to three main reasons why seclusion in any form failed to get a foothold in Northern Europe and therefore in North America. These are, in chronological order (the order in which we will consider them): (1) the development of Christian monasticism, in which men claimed the benefits of seclusion for themselves; (2) the development of the cult of romance; and (3) the witch hunts of the early modern period. It is by these means that linear religion made an end run around the defense seclusion had set up and finally became able to set up the unrestrained tyranny we suffer under today.

Now, Ivan Illich, a former priest, liked to see the advent of priest-supervised confession for all Christians as the pivotal event in the destruction of vernacular gender in the West. "Up until this time," he wrote (1982:152-154) "members of vernacular-gendered households had come to the Church; now the Church moved in the opposite direction, overstepping the house's threshold." It made equal transgressions of the same moral laws by both men and women and thereby did away with the sexual division of moral labor as we have seen exists still in Mediterranean honor (Chapter 16) and "laid the foundation for sexist codes. . . . It compelled each 'soul' to create this new space within itself, and to create it according to architectural rules laid down in Church law."

By no means do I intend to distract from the importance of this "prototype of the helping professional" (p. 153) with all its monolithic bureaucracy when I choose rather to focus my attention on the Christian institution of monasticism as an eroder of the benefits of

A History of Women's Seclusion in the Middle East
Published by the Haworth Press, Inc., 2006. All rights reserved.
doi:10.1300/5666_21

vernacular gender, particularly those afforded by seclusion. It seems no coincidence that the monastic movement in Christianity had its beginnings in Egypt. The collapse of the Roman Empire has properly been seen as ecological in basis and proportion (Boak, 1955; Jones, 1964; MacMullen, 1976; Tainter, 1988): the distance the Roman army could march in its search for new, desperately needed resources without rebellion was reached and surpassed, bringing predictable ruin in its wake. Egypt is where the bread half of the bread and circuses came from to forestall the political results of this collapse, to keep them away from the capital, at least. In order to keep the wheat shipments coming, Egypt's cyclical richness had to be terribly exploited. Of all Roman lands on the Mediterranean, it alone was never granted provincial status. One can grant citizenship to any number of landless unemployed, but not to the peasantry who grow one's food. Naturally, Egyptians had a great desire to flee such servitude, particularly with the lures of Alexandria and Rome in view. The punishments for land abandonment were fierce—but they were not infrequently ignored (A. Johnson, 1951; Lindsay, 1963; Lewis, 1968).

It is no surprise that Christianity, holding out the promise of a better life to come, should have gained so many early converts along the banks of the Nile, nor that the brand of Christianity that was favored was of the Gnostic, a particularly antiauthoritarian variety (see Pagels, 1979). Having seen so clearly the limits of a linear, expansionist, imperialist philosophy, the attractions of the cyclical, world-denying pole of values for the Egyptians should be clear. Because they knew little—except from the Hellenized towns, which were only for citizens—of the association of the feminine exclusively with these values in wider Hellenistic culture, Egyptian peasant men flocked to these values in droves. If these values sent them to the desert and away from serfdom on the fields, so much the better.

We see many indications that at this time and in this region, there occurred a great shuffle of old goddess values and images into Christianity: an androgyne Christ, a mother goddess named Mari, self-castration among the devout (Origen being the prime example). This shuffle ended, simply put, in men claiming a part of seclusion's power for themselves. At the collapse of the Roman Empire, this was an obvious desire, and there seemed no harm in it. In fact, its ill effects would not be seen for nearly a thousand years. In the meantime, the respite of the Middle Ages occurred.

The Middle Ages were dismissed in half an hour in a world history class I had in high school: "Nothing worth studying here." This is clear proof that it was a bad time for linear forces, a heyday for the cyclical. Female monastics enjoyed perhaps the greatest independence and economic power their sex has ever known, certainly in Western history (Harrison, 1998; P. Johnson, 1991; Venarde, 1996). Their secular sisters were not far behind, as a basically clan-centered, localized economy held sway. Land- and right-defending customs evolved and were rigorously employed. Women could not help but come to the fore when a creed of "the meek shall inherit" was in force and literally believed. Your average medieval soul was not fooled by pomp and circumstance. Mayr-Harting's article "Functions of a Twelfth-Century Recluse" (1975) shows us who had the most authority among the people where it counted—an ambitious prelate, or a woman who forswore the world and walled herself up in a tiny ancrehouse, the medieval European version of the harem. The most aggressive of popes (and we must admit that the papal see usually, although by no means always, went to the grabbiest) had to confess that he was beaten by a supplicant coming not with superior arms, but on his knees, penitent, for three days and nights in an Alpine snowstorm.[1]

The Middle Ages developed the so-called three-field agricultural system. By rotating fields on a crop-crop-fallow basis, farmers were able to maintain the fertility of the fields yet at the same time greatly increase productivity over the simple crop-fallow two-field rotation of the classical period. (Northern European soil has this advantage.) By breaking the two-gender system of Hellenistic seclusion into three "genders"—those who farm, those who fight, those who pray[2]—medieval people might have made similar improvements in efficiency on a social scale, still leaving protected a flexibility of options. However, it seems you must assign your personnel to their "gender" according to some indelible, unassumable mark, by some undeniable, incorruptible, uncontrollable lottery. I know of no such trilateral dichotomy. Otherwise, whichever "gender" appears to offer the most immediate benefits will be bought, bribed, pushed, murdered into by those with either the brains, the means, or the brawn, and a monolithic hierarchy must quickly result. We see that this is what happened to the medieval trilateral social division. As a matter of fact, the three-field system showed itself susceptible to the same sorts of forces. It was extended first to a five-, then a seven-field system in England as enclosure progressed, and now we see the average farmer willing to addict his land's fertility to the same nonagricultural economic system that grants (or denies) food to the farmer's table. A disaster of equal proportion was set in motion when men retired from public life and claimed a portion of seclusion for themselves. This was a part of Christianity that already embraced the dangerous creeds of forestallment of the good life until after death and a drastic good-versus-evil view of the cosmos.

The Middle Ages do present an idyllic culture in which men who chose to could retire from public life while gregarious women could find fulfillment as abbesses or alewives, where women were canonized as readily as men, and where the hermit was a sought-after creature. Of course such an idyll could not last forever, one of the main reasons being that, in spite of the Black Death, during the Middle Ages the population of Europe increased thirtyfold. The means to alleviate this problem were typically linear and hierarchical. When plan A—the Crusades—did not work as well as hoped, all was not lost, for the Europeans came in contact with people who'd been dealing with such problems for millennia. They offered other solutions by example: trade, an addiction to luxuries, urbanization . . .

Every indication shows that as part and parcel of the modernization program, the Orient offered European women seclusion and honor. Saladin certainly made a great impression by refusing to bombard the tower of the crusaders' Krak des Chevaliers where a wedding was being celebrated, out of deference to *al-harim* (the women).

Still, as the main site of contact was the battlefield or the bazaar, and most crusaders left their women home, there was little chance for Eastern and Western women to meet as equals as they had done with more frequency when the Greeks were colonizing and adopting seclusion. The best location for such a meeting was probably Spain, and it is from Spain that we get the first troubadour lays. The romances of the troubadours became immensely popular. They delivered a Western version of the harem tale and came close to disseminating the values necessary for seclusion to flourish. But it turned to romance instead, and romance backfired. Instead of becoming women's best defense against the linear monolith, she became objectified into its major prize (Bloch, 1991).

At first only a means of upper-class dalliance, it took until the late sixteenth century, Shakespeare in his *Romeo and Juliet,* before anyone dared to suggest that love, this blind, irrational passion that nobody pretends to control, was a reasonable excuse for leaving family and clan, much less that it offered any sort of stability on which to raise a family. Of course, since this time, all hell has broken loose and we now assume no other possible foundation to home life than this quicksand exists. Instead of an obligation to honor and protect, the cult of romance makes a sexy woman the carrot dangled before young men to encourage hard work and an adherence to the program. They make the perfect item for the treadmill, too, in that there is always a new crop of younger, prettier, slimmer girls coming up. You see them every day draping themselves over other inducements to success: sports cars, gold watches, soft drinks, paling these items in allure, for why else does one buy the expensive car or the right soft drink but with the hope that the girl comes with it? A man shakes off first parents and then older woman after older woman.

Teenaged girls, who have the country's greatest spending power, are the targets of even more advertising than the ambitious male. From the time they are hardly more than infants, they are the pursued on the treadmill rather than the pursuers. They are pursued by a horrible knowledge: If they are to have a good life for their children, they must attract and hold their father. To attract the best in this hierarchy, one must be the best, the thinnest, the blondest, the best dressed. Intelligence or skill counts for nothing, for it is the thirty-second advertising spot one is competing with. One surely must be good enough to do better than one's own dumpy, henpecked father; there are so many glamorous guys on TV.

The powers that be, of course, encourage our cult of the female as carrot. They are the greatest pimps of the cult of romance. Besides the fact that three single-person households can be sold three times as many refrigerators as three people living together, there is all that insecure, individuated helplessness to prey on. Indeed, who can say which painful ache is true love and which is the desperate fear of being so awfully alone?

"Surely one should be allowed to choose the person one is to spend the rest of one's life with," the die-hard romantic will protest my callousness.

Very well; some choice I allow.

"There is no choice of husband for the girl in an arranged Middle Eastern marriage."

No choice of husband, no. However, under seclusion, it is not the husband a woman spends most of her time with anyway. It is the mother-in-law. Not coincidentally, it is the mothers who are most instrumental in arranging their sons' marriages.[3] After all, a young man is in no position to know what is available in local harems. No more is his father. A man probably doesn't even know that his best friend has a daughter, for his honor prevents him from speaking of her and, if asked how many children he has, he may well only count his sons. The prospective groom and his father certainly have no idea how old a friend's daughter might be or if she is eligible.

Prospective mothers-in-law, on the other hand, do know. They scout the houses of their friends and relations (it would be nice to let the girl already be integrated in the neighborhood or family network), the baths on women's day. They are not looking for the thirty-second flash of makeup and glitter. They're not going to bed the girl, after all. They want to know if she's clever, witty, intelligent, kind, polite. Will she be a help around the house? A good mother for the grandkids? A considerate nurse when one is old and infirm? One will, after all, have to work side by side with her and probably leave one's prized coffee service, the pots and pans, to her when one is gone.

Under such scrutiny, a girl is encouraged to become a little more than a fashion plate. Certainly, no women love fancy clothes more than those in the Middle East. But they dress for one another in clothes they generally make themselves (at least until recently). It is a way of showing themselves adept with a needle—and part of a hierarchy independent of that of men, not slaves of men's eyes and of the male-dominated fashion industry.

Most North Yemeni girls interviewed (Dorsky, 1986) said they would rather live in a multigenerational household—that is, with their mothers-in-law—than start out alone with their husbands. The comfort of having a knowledgeable woman around with a burned dinner, a family illness, a first baby, can be appreciated: it shows a disregard for the male hierarchical "professionals" young wives in the West usually turn to. Besides, "It would be too lonely," the girls declared; male company doesn't count.

Because matches are a communal business, no individual guilt devolves if a marriage fails.[4] Indeed, in North Yemen (Dorsky, 1986) the assumption is that the first or even the first *few* attempts to match young people will fail.[5] They are, after all, young. Traditional systems are in effect so that no child is abandoned in the shuffle, no one remains divorced for long. The more times a man or a woman has been married, the more likely it is that his or her opinion in the matter will be considered.

One last event in Western history proved the final death knoll to the search for female autonomy, which was already sorely crippled by rising urbanism, male usurpation of religious retreat, and the cult of romance. This is the infamous witch burnings: between the fourteenth and eighteenth centuries, at least a million people,[6] mostly women, were put to death on the pyres and gibbets of Europe and her colonies.

It is common to dismiss this "gendercide" as medieval and Catholic. As modern Western culture is neither, we have, we congratulate ourselves, cured the disease. Actually, the witch mania was neither medieval nor particularly Catholic. In AD 1000, a papal bull declared that anyone who said that anyone else rode around on a broomstick was obviously deluded and should not be believed. As for the medieval dates, "the witch mania reached its peak in the aftermath of the Reformation—both Luther and Calvin were ardent believers in the dangers of witchcraft" (M. Harris, 1974:202). We have at least one trial account[7] on record in which the magistrate unashamedly admits that he was in the business for the monetary gain of himself and his colleagues: the goods and lands of the condemned went not to their heirs but to the court (Starhawk, 1979).

There is more early modern motive to the witch craze, however, than a scheme to finance budding capitalist ventures. The specie added to the magistrate's coffer was of immediate but only short-term effect. Another aspect of the witch craze exposes its ominous power residing with us today and coloring our every thought toward our fellow human beings.

> The witch hunt system was too well designed, too enduring, too grim and stubborn. It could only have been sustained by interests that were equally enduring, grim and stubborn. The witchcraft system and the witch craze had practical and mundane uses apart from the stated goals of the witch hunters. (M. Harris, 1974:204)

"A few people here and there hallucinating about intercourse with the Devil or casting spells on some neighbor's cow" (p. 202) would not have created the mass hysteria of torture, accusation and counter-accusation we see in the period. Rather, it seems clear

> that the witch hunters went out of their way to increase the sup-
> ply of witches and to spread the belief that witches were real,
> omnipresent, and dangerous. . . . The situation demands that we
> ask not why the inquisitors were obsessed with destroying
> witchcraft, but rather why they were so obsessed with creating
> it. Regardless of what they or their victims may have intended,
> the inevitable effect of the inquisitorial system was to make
> witchcraft more believable, and hence to increase the number of
> witchcraft accusations. (Harris, 1974:202)

"The passing of feudalism and the emergence of strong national monarchies was a period of great stress" for the common folk of Europe. "Witchcraft was related to the problems of a growing population pressing on already enclosed land" (p. 202). In the sixteenth-century Essex witch-hunt centers Macfarlane studied, tiny villages were experiencing a surplus of births over deaths as high as fifteen per year (Macfarlane, 1970:147), which meant that in less than forty years the population, which had already eaten up the "circuit-breaking" common lands, would have doubled again. New attempts were made to alleviate the population pressure. The attempts have a familiar ring to them: "The development of trade, markets, and banking [forcing] the owners of land and capital into enterprises aimed at maximizing profits. This could be done only by breaking up the small scale paternalistic relationships characteristic of the feudal manorial estates" (Macfarlane, 1970:147).

These steps were taken on a practical level, not just by the setting up of shops, but, more importantly, with a change to "a less collectivist religion, a market economy, greater social mobility and a growing separation of people through the formation of institutional rather than personal ties" (p. 202).

Macfarlane (1970:197) has brilliantly shown that witchcraft in Tudor and Stuart England was a result of tensions between the old "'neighbourly', highly integrated and mutually interdependent village society, to a more individualistic one." Witches were generally people, usually older women, who under the old system had had claim to unstinting charity. The duty to support them was imbued with something akin to holiness, inspiring the fear of God, and the women themselves could enforce this by cursing when charity was denied. Cursing was a traditional power they could use to protect themselves from their neighbor's greed, intelligence to counteract the dissolving power of intelligence. In the sixteenth and seventeenth centuries, people still believed in this power, but they had tremendous social pressures on them to make "improvements which would keep them abreast of their yeoman neighbours, . . . [to] invest their capital" (Macfarlane, 1970:205) elsewhere than in the local community, not to "waste" it on poor old women. As a specific example, we can imagine that a blacksmith might refuse the traditional free sharpening of tools to a widow in favor of paying customers. It was nothing more malicious than that. Such people found that the easiest way out of the bind of guilt was to brand the traditional power evil and to burn (or hang) it.

> By suggesting that the widow was a witch the power of the old sanctions to neighbourly behaviour . . . was broken . . . An accusation of witchcraft was a clever way of reversing the guilt, of transferring it from the person who had failed in his social obligation under the old standard to the person who made him fail. (p. 196)

One of the witches in *Macbeth* gives an example of the old woman shunned and what Shakespeare's audiences still expected might happen to them for such shunning. "A sailor's wife had chestnuts in her lap," sings the crone,

> And munch'd, and munch'd, and munch'd. "Give me,"
>   quoth I.
> "Aroint thee, witch!" the rump-fed ronyon
>   cries.
> Her husband's to Aleppo gone, master o' the Tiger;
> But in a sieve I'll thither sail,
> And, like a rat without a tail,
> I'll do, I'll do, and I'll do . . .
> I will drain him dry as hay;
> Sleep shall neither night nor day
> Hang upon his pent-house lid.
> He shall live a man forbid;
> Weary se'nnights nine times nine

> Shall he dwindle, peak, and pine.
> Though his bark cannot be lost,
> Yet it shall be tempest-tost

(Act I:iii)

What more effective way to distance neighbor from neighbor than by fanning witchcraft mania? This

> dispersed and fragmented all the latent energies of protest. It demobilized the poor and the dispossessed, increased their social distance, filled them with mutual suspicions, pitted neighbor against neighbor, isolated everyone, made everyone fearful, heightened everyone's insecurity, made everyone feel helpless and dependent on the governing classes, gave everyone's anger and frustration a purely local focus. (M. Harris, 1974:239)

By so doing, "not only were the Church and state exonerated" for responsibility for the suffering people felt, "they were made indispensable" (p. 205) in the combating of it.

The "old women and . . . midwives" who "were usually the first to be accused in any local network" were not merely "defenseless" and of the lowest class (M. Harris, 1974:206). Such were the figures around which any effective female counterbalance to the accumulation of linear power would have to cluster. I suspect that such "old women and . . . midwives" posed a greater threat to the privileged and the powerful even than the popular messianic movements of the period. These movements were generally militaristic and masculine in character, attributes the privileged understood and could cope with on their own terms: "May the best man win." That the coming of Protestantism did little to change the burgeoning power structure in Europe and nothing at all to ease the witch craze shows us how ineffectual combating the powerful with terms of linear power really is. Against the greater threat of women failing to take their proper places on the single ladder to power that was in the process of being erected, however, only sheer psychological terror would do, and on a scale unequaled perhaps even by Hitler's Germany. Simply put, the European "witch constitutes a gender-specific reaction against the loss of locally embedded subsistence," subsistence which is lost due to "repression . . . by the rising nation-state" (Illich, 1982:166).

So not only did the witch mania make us afraid to trust one another, to turn to our traditional feminine fonts of wisdom lest there come the cry of "Witch!" and the smell of burning flesh; it also deprived us of our "bravest and best," perhaps one million[8] of them. When Jacoba Felicie was tried in Paris in 1322, it was because she cured men whom numerous male doctors had failed to help (Hughes, 1943:89-92). Naturally, one is a witch if she so shows up the standards the male hierarchy sets.

Friendship, female friendship in particular, continues to be corrupted in ways that are irreparable. "Friendship," Schor (2004) tells us, used to be

> important precisely because it [was] insulated from commercial pressures. It [was] considered one of the last bastions of non-instrumentality, a bulwark against market values and self-interested behavior that permeate our culture. It's part of what we cherish most about friendships and that's precisely why the marketers are so keenly interested in them. (pp. 77-78)

Marketers teach us to view our "friends as a lucrative resource [we] can exploit to gain products or money. They even counsel [us] to be 'slick' with [our] friends" (p. 77). When a gathering of women is more likely than not to be a chance to have friendship used as leverage to purchase plastic containers, makeup, or sex toys, we see the depth of what we've lost.

That witch holocaust, that million, was a loss from which we have yet to recover. We no longer have the courage to imagine advancement through education that isn't masculine, models that aren't male, symbols that aren't phallic, progression that isn't linear. We have yet to overcome our fear of being seen to congregate, a group of women behind closed doors. We are afraid, in short, of seclusion.

Chapter 21

Conclusion

Nature, the physicists have found, "seems to keep all its options, all its probabilities, open for as long as possible. . . . It is the act of observing a system," labeling and classifying it, "that forces it to select one of its options, which then becomes real" (Gribbin, 1984:172). Why this should be so is not known. Indeed, it is all we can ask of the science of physics to tell us how it is so. Let me suggest in non-physicist terms, that it may be numbers of options that keeps the universe flexible, able to maintain and to continue to evolve. It is limitation of options, whether by the human mind, the pressures of environment, or whatever device, that leads to collapse of energy and to extinction.

"Progress," systems theorist von Bertalanffy (1968) says,

> means at the same time impoverishment, loss of performances still possible in the undetermined state. The more parts are specialized in a certain way, the more they are irreplaceable, and loss of parts may lead to the breakdown of the total system. (p. 70)

The biology of Darwin "thought of variation as a transient phenomenon" (Ayala, 1978:56), that evolution happened because of rare and fluke mutations. In recent years, however, biologists have recognized that natural populations "harbor large reservoirs of hidden [genetic] variation" and that it is this, not an occasional bolt from the blue, which enables

> them to adapt to changing environments. The greater the variation stored in a population is, the more readily it is able to adopt to a new environment. . . . How much variation exists in natural populations . . . determines to a large extent the evolutionary

A History of Women's Seclusion in the Middle East
Published by the Haworth Press, Inc., 2006. All rights reserved.
doi:10.1300/5666_22

> plasticity of a species. . . . A population that has considerable
> amounts of genetic variation may be hedged against future
> changes in the environment. . . . Laboratory experiments have
> demonstrated that the greater the amount of genetic variation in
> a population, the faster its rate of evolution . . . (Ayala, 1978:56,
> 60-61)

The human potential for rapidly changing, highly flexible, and diver-
sified culture is the basis of our remarkable adaptability to environments from ice floe to jungle. If, however, once our abstracting skills
have subdivided the whole, one or the other of the poles is allowed to
be stifled in the press, our ability to change to meet the changing exi-
gencies of the environment will likewise be stifled. The very flexibility of our capacity for culture will have been the cause of its own inflexibility.

Recently I moved into a new house. For the first few months I was
astonished by how the vegetables in my garden faced no competition.
I'd go out to weed—and there weren't any weeds. I commented on
this to the previous owner. "Oh, yes," she smiled proudly. "I always
was very careful about keeping all weeds out." She had wrapped them
carefully in plastic and sent them off with the milk cartons and meat
trays. But soon the deleterious effects of this practice became clear to
me. Although unopposed, my spinach grew weakly and had pale yel-
low leaves. It became apparent that the soil was practically sterile.

Traditional German farmers place their manure piles in the very
center of their farmyards. It is more pivotal to life than the kitchen table. Every member of the household contributes, from old Oma with
her potato peels to little Hänsel with his training pot. Instead of labeling the waste "useless" and moving it across town, the farmers put it
where it will be the first sight to greet the visitor. They vie with one
another as to the size of their piles, for a large pile means healthy, numerous cows (the most productive source of the compost), the largest
piles, the most fertile fields. One aspect of prosperity is sterile without the other.

A highly linear society would throw away everything that does not
meet its immediate efficiency, including human variation if we could.
Variation in the population exists, not to be overcome, but to offer the
possibilities of change and flexibility to new generations; just as, in a
society with a healthy relationship to its environment, waste exists
not to be thrown out but to be recycled.

The coincidence in the rise of the feminist and ecological movements in the 1960s is not so coincidental. "Enlightenment science designates nature as a woman to be unveiled, unclothed and penetrated by the light of reason" (Illich, 1982:125). Those in power have become so efficiently, abusively exploitative in recent years that those with less power—women and the environment, for example— have found their situation intolerable at the same time. Unfortunately, most attempts to rectify the situation remain ineffective partly for the reasons deep ecologists (Devall and Sessions, 1985:4) express in these terms: A movement (feminist or ecological) that would take a stand opposed to such a society must choose its means carefully, for it runs the risk of becoming "institutionalized into a mere appendage of the very system whose structure and methods it professes to oppose" (Devall and Sessions, 1985:4). We see how many of the values and individuals of the rebellion begun in the 1960s are now used to help the powers that sell records and clothes; a "lover of nature" sells more and more of a megacorporation's cereal product in an environment probably unspoiled until the cameraman dropped his beer can and his film case there; one cannot be a truly liberated woman unless one smokes a brand of cigarettes that has taken one "a long way, baby."

In modern America, agoraphobia is predominantly a "disease" that "afflicts" women. The agoraphobe is not some remote, talentless creature. She is "independent, self-sufficient and capable" before the onset, "intelligent, often highly educated and perhaps professional" (Seidenberg and DeCrow, 1983:8). In spite of their self-imposed seclusion, the names of some agoraphobes the world cannot ignore: healer Mary Baker Eddy, Jane Addams, the poet Sara Teasdale, Margaret Sanger, Carolyn Wyeth (whom some consider to be the best of all her artist family), Emily Dickinson, and Queen Victoria head the list. This last woman took to her bed with a certifiable fever when, after two years of independent rule, she was about to marry Albert. This same Albert she used as an excuse to stay in mournful seclusion for years after his death, effectively keeping meddlesome male cousins and uncles at bay so she could run the empire "the way Albert wanted it." But Albert, a German, had taken no active interest in governing Britain and her far-flung battlefields when alive. The way the deceased Albert wanted it was the way Victoria wanted it. "She became almost as unknown to her subjects as some potentate of the East," complained a subject (Seidenberg and DeCrow, 1983:81) (not quite as unknown, we may parenthesize, as that potentate's wife). We may also add that a woman who wants to run politics in a modern democracy would be unsuccessful if she refused to go out, smile at TV cameras, shake hands, and kiss babies.

Who can forget Emily Dickinson's classic description of her agoraphobia? She put on her bonnet one evening when she was twenty-one, "opened the gate very desperately, and for a little while the suspense was terrible—I think I was held in check by some invisible agent, for I returned to the house without having done any harm!" (Seidenberg and DeCrow, 1983:81).

Like Emily, many agoraphobes report that they feel too big for the world, too big for the traditional scraps men leave them. Our feminist writers are correct in suggesting that "if Emily Dickinson had not been a recluse, she probably would have married . . . and she would not have written a line of poetry" (Seidenberg and DeCrow, 1983:81). However, they are wrong to imagine that unlimited access to equal employment would have solved the problem. They criticize the primitive "feminism of the time," which urged many women "into all sorts of unnatural situations, inventing for them new forms of suffering and breakdown while it imposed upon them the norms of an inferior intellectual culture" (p. 81). This same criticism may be leveled against modern feminism, perhaps to an even greater degree. Suppose Emily had been "liberated" and taken on a high-power job instead. Such jobs leave about as much clear-minded time as wifehood. Ask any working "spinster" today. When motherhood and the job are juggled, as is the usual result of the feminists' cry, you can forget a lucid thought of your own for the rest of your life. What sort of job should Emily have taken? Should she have tried to make a living off her poetry? She would have had to compromise it terribly, for, as it was, in its radical free form and with its unpopular subjects, it was unpublishable in New England in the nineteenth century; she was told so in plain terms often enough. Rather than rail against it, then, the "restrictive" Victorian New England dictum that fathers should support their daughters and brothers their spinster sisters (Hawthorne's mother was a recluse, too) deserves a lot of credit for the Dickinson corpus. Emily, genius that she was, just added to it her own little fillip. Victorian New England treated her more kindly than she would be treated today. The publishing industry today, even more than in her day, runs on a very heavily monolithic set of values, even when the editors are women. Victorian Emily received kinder treatment than a feminist utopia would have given.

Dickinson viewed her seclusion not as a dungeon but as a liberation. Her niece Martha relates that she visited her aunt once "in her corner bedroom on the second floor." Emily pretended to lock the door behind them and then said, "Matty: here's freedom" (Rich, 1979:158). Freedom to putter around the house and in the garden, and freedom to write enough poetry to fill several trunks, only six poems of which were obliged to take on an audience until after "death kindly stopped for me."

It is a terror of shopping centers and malls that most often brings the agoraphobic case to the specialist's attention. I've known a full-tuition scholarship to a prestigious school to be turned down because it would entail moving out of the parental home, but in general "a woman who is unable to leave the house to attend a NOW meeting, to return to graduate school, or visit an art exhibit is not considered similarly ill" (Seidenberg and DeCrow, 1983:27). It is this refusal of the modern agoraphobe to take up her proper place as a consumer that makes everyone uncomfortable.

"The market may have hidden significance for a woman in a phylogenetic Jungian sense," we are told (p. 27). "Historically, and as still practiced openly in some parts of the world, women themselves have been on the block, bought, sold, traded and bartered as commodities." Men have been sold, too. It seems to me that rather than this ghostly history closing in on her, it is the present use of women's bodies in advertising (to a greater degree than men's), the virtual attack to "buy or die," targeted to the lowest of drives and intelligence that debilitates. Every trip to the store is a groveling, a shuffling into a single scheme of value with a little green piece of paper with a man's face on it balanced on the top.

When this is the state of the outside world, is it any wonder that a woman with any sort of intelligence or the inner strength to hold any sort of heretical values should seriously wonder whether the place for her, upon giving birth, should not be the maternity ward but the insane asylum? Dissidents in the former Soviet Union were locked away and given shock treatment. I suspect they are here and now, too, only the government doesn't even do you the favor of paying "mental health" coverage for you. Nothing sounds more insidious than the discussion of doctors about their drugs that will help the psychiatric patient function as she "ought to." "Chemical imbalances" they blame, with no thought as to what might cause such an imbalance or what purpose it may serve in giving our species flexibility in generations to come. If we do not glibly accept "this best of all possible worlds," then certainly let us be drugged until we can. To be drugged until you can be just what society wants you to be, or to have your fear trivialized, is the worst sort of chauvinism in the world.

"Agoraphobics may well be the most completely uncompromising feminists of our times," write Seidenberg and DeCrow (1983). "They will not be placated or bribed by small favors or grants of limited success." Much the same may be said of the "uncompromising feminism" of Middle Eastern women, but because they, so to speak, all decided to be agoraphobic at once, their husbands[1] and children couldn't threaten them with divorce or scorn. They had to succumb to women's joint and just demands.

One-woman, one-vote participation is not the answer, since increasing public wealth increases democracy, which only throws gasoline (which God carelessly hid under someone else's desert) on the one-value-system market and imperialism (Samons, 2004). Once upon a time, for a few months after the collapse of the Soviet Union, I thought the all-mighty dollar might be integrated with the unattached ruble. One currency could be used only for "male" goods, the other for "female" or more socially conscious goods—and in order to get a nurse in your old age, you would have had to put some energy into social services during your life. Ralph Nader once proposed a similar dichotomy of goods and services. It didn't happen, naturally. The man who has spent his life destroying the air to make his fortune still wants a good nurse—and can afford it, unlike others who breathe his air—when his lungs give out.

In our society, when the nation as a whole is divided into two parties to give the illusion of freedom of choice, what happens, since both basically jump to the same monetary tune, is that both become more and more centrist with less and less support for the edges. Since the illusion of two quickly reforms into one monolith after any feeding frenzy of an election, the winners—by no matter how narrow a margin—feel mandated to say, "We've won; now you must join us" rather than responding as a tradition-based Middle Eastern man might when he sees that God has made him male: "I am the boss here—and that means I must take your female needs and values into consideration because I see that indeed those behind me hold up half the sky, not to mention my honor." Wisdom exists even in a place I thought most unlikely—the Christianity of Paul, who, according to one reading (Crossan and Reed, 2004) stood against the Roman monolith of power in his day. Rather than proclaiming, as the legions did, "Let us attain victory first, then Pax Romana," Paul said, "No, justice first, then the Kingdom of God." Justice blind—or veiled. Paul did ask his women to cover their heads and keep quiet in church, didn't he?

Let modern seekers of victory in distant places who call themselves Christian take note—and let modern Western women, too. The modern Western woman sees herself exploited in the mall, obliged to pay corporate prices for fashion trends set by someone else to keep up her position on the monolithic ladder. Then she looks at the label on those garments and thinks of her sisters in textile factories in ancient Mesopotamia, in Macao and China today. The counterbalance of garment workers' unions have been sidestepped by corporate outsourcing. But how can a budding labor organization in India compete with the bosses as a union of the twentieth century did when the bosses will simply move to the next third world country? When the bosses own all the tools of rapid transport and communication? A dichotomy of powers is impossible as long as one party owns all of these tools and the other does not. A woman of conscience in the United States wonders if she has the means to work for her distant sisters. Would she stand in solidarity with women she has never met? Would she put on a veil if it would put the brakes on the exploitation of her sisters, of the environment, if it would help stop an unjust invasion? In a heartbeat—if it would work.

On the scale of values I propose, women who barge their way into America's highest boardrooms are among the most "conservative," supportive of patriarchy's values. "Equal rights in a man's world" will never offer the succor of "a totally different reality, a different language, a different attitude toward power and authority" (Adler, 1986:343) that manifests itself by women separating "themselves from society and the world of men to lead isolated lives with other women" (p. 186). Nothing could be closer in effect and, I maintain, purpose, to that of Middle Eastern seclusion. The struggle of these modern American women with the patriarchy of the English language makes them refuse, for example, to spell "woman" in any way that connects it with the other half of the species, i.e., womon, womyn. This finds startlingly close parallels with my discussion of the women's dialect of ancient Sumerian.

The parallels proliferate. In the wilds of Oregon these modern Amazons set up "moon huts" where they retire during their menses not because they are "unclean" in any pejorative sense but because they are consciously trying to be women unashamedly and not some sort of clumsy, not-quite-right men.

So far, these separatist women confess, their attempts are but weak and they call "upon women who choose to remain in the mainstream of society, or women who have no choice, to protect the separatist women until they can gain the strength to create a new women's culture" (Adler, 1986:186). Frankly, I doubt that we have the strength to do such a thing. I fear that remaining in the mainstream is not a matter of choice in 99 percent of the cases. If we haven't the strength to extract ourselves, how can we possibly be expected to buffer? How much success can even these radically separatist women have in thwarting the male tax collector of the male-dominated legislature of the male-dominated capitalist social structure?

More practical to my mind was the strategy of feminist witch Z Budapest, who "enlisted . . . a group of men, many of them gay, to protect the perimeter" (Adler, 1986:346) of an area in which she proposed to lead a large group of women in a special feminine ritual. This the men effectively did, excluding even the father and husband of two of the participants. The man, although a witch himself, did not approve of particularly feminine rituals and wanted to break in there to get his wife and daughter out. This event comes very close to duplicating the vital purpose served by eunuchs or transvestite men in traditional Middle Eastern society.

An acquaintance of mine who went to Egypt to "help free" Egyptian women left within the month, throwing up her hands and declaring their case hopeless; they'd been too repressed for too long. I maintain she wasn't too radical. She wasn't radical enough. If we stand on tiptoe and reach way, way up from the ruins our most radical thought can make of the patriarchy in which we live, our fingers may bridge the arc and just barely brush the fingers of our sisters and mothers in the Middle East.

In ancient Babylon, a man who overspent his resources would face the immediate effect of having his children sold into slavery. Perhaps it was easier for him to see through this threat to their posterity than it is for us to see the disastrous effects for the future of our nearsightedness. *X* million tons of toxic waste created per year or an astronomical national deficit are to the natural and economic resources of our children what the abstraction and exploitation of the individual—women in particular—are to their emotional resources. When faced with exploitation similar to what American women—and, more gravely, their children—stand on the brink of today, women in the Middle East millenia ago threw the veil over their faces, put up the wall of mystified honor, and said, "So far may you exploit, *but, by God, no further!*"

Notes

Introduction

1. Even so important and generally sympathetic a collection as Beck and Keddie's *Women in the Muslim World* (1978) has lapses in this direction in some of its articles. As the quote from them indicates, however, these editors themselves do not seem guilty of this point of view.

Chapter 1

1. I would like to make mention of one other example from the literature of how a different, totally unrelated society maintains its cyclical values without veiling and secluding half of its population. The natives of Western Timor are said by Claudine Friedberg (1977) to have two chiefs—a "masculine" and a "feminine" one. Although both males, "the feminine chief was the living symbol of the established order which he guaranteed. He could neither move nor act" but enforced certain ecologically sound principles such as leaving fallow land every year on which certain nitrogen-fixing weeds were allowed to grow, and caring for the seed during an enforced "cooling-off" period. It was "the mobile and active 'masculine' chief," on the other hand, who "was responsible for" policing this order, by force if necessary. One wonders how long this system can last with the Timors ceasing to be agricultural people, taking to cities in great numbers and suffering the recent and ongoing militarization of expanding empire.

2. Fernea's 1976 film and her book *A Street in Marrakesh*.

3. American blues, also the genre of an "underclass," but not so well protected and eventually usurped for the overclass's profit.

4. In 1984 (Morgan p. 525) under the repression of Zia al-Haq, there was a campaign under way in Pakistan "to decrease or deny female admission to medical school" altogether.

5. Unocal, after years of convoluted litigation, recently settled out of court with Burmese natives who accused them of using slave labor, murder, rape, and forced relocation as the corporation built its pipeline through their jungle. See Democracy Now, 2004. Can we expect any better from this corporation in bed with the Taliban than they demonstrated in bed with the totalitarian Burmese?

Chapter 2

1. The uncovered remains reveal a "life more holistic than today," with ritual and domestic functions unseparated. To ask the remains "Is this space is a shrine?" is

A History of Women's Seclusion in the Middle East
Published by the Haworth Press, Inc., 2006. All rights reserved.
doi:10.1300/5666_23

probably the wrong question, as Hodder (1998) suggests. Yet, relegated here to a note, I will include musings of mine concerning the "shrines" of Çatal Hüyük.

The temptation cannot be resisted to see in these ruins what the first movements toward urban life did with the sharp Paleolithic division of the sexes that abounded along with the Mousterian dual assemblage of tools (see Chapter 3). Following this line of thinking, Çatal Hüyük society "centered around the woman, was matrilocal and probably matrilineal" (Barstow, 1978:14-15). Perhaps evidence of men's activities are to be discovered away from hearth and home and so haven't appeared to the spade yet, but Barstow goes on:

> Every house without exception had a large sleeping platform, always along the east wall, accentuated by large wooden posts painted red; the skeletons of women and of some of the children were buried under this platform. Smaller platforms were scattered about the room in varying positions, children buried under some, men under others; but never children and men together. (p. 11)

Many reconstructions have called the men buried within a house "husbands" and "fathers" of the "wives" and "children" in the same house, but certainly there is no reason that they could not be, in true matrilineal style, brothers and uncles. I might even offer the suggestion that the shrines served as the meeting place for a woman and her husband, who most of the time lived with his sisters and their children. Of course, there is absolutely no way to prove this—and never in this preliterate period will we find any labels over the dead to let us know "daughter of," "husband of" relationships—but as I make the importance of the shrines clear this should be seen as certainly not an impossibility.

It is the shrines that have attracted the most attention to this excavation. The people of this Neolithic town appear to have been very religious, although, to put a quantitative value on such things and say they were *more* religious than their contemporaries is to argue from physical remains alone a subject that most often eludes the physical. In any case, as many as half (and nearly exactly half—this is important) of the rooms in each level were set apart by Mellaart (1967) as "shrines." What earns them this designation is the wonderful decoration that was discovered in them: wall-paintings, reliefs, giant bull horns and boar teeth embedded in the plaster.

It is possible to interpret the ruins in such a way that each single-room house had a shrine associated with it: each house consisted of a public, everyday room and a sacred room. Moving one's worship to a public site is one sure way to give up control over this important power and hand it on an offering tray to centralized authority. The ancient people of Çatal Hüyük weren't willing to make such a sacrifice yet. The family, or some of its members, retired to the sacred room on certain occasions. Perhaps marriages were celebrated here; perhaps, as I have suggested, all sexual encounters took place here. Çatal Hüyük does reveal "one of the earliest representations of the *hieros gamos,* the 'sacred marriage' . . . [showing] the union of the couple on the left and the intended result [mother with child] on the right" (Mellaart, 1967:148). Perhaps women retired there when labor came upon them, when it came time to bring a new member of the clan into the world. Female skeletons in the shrines were often sprinkled with ocher (male skeletons more rarely). One such burial is in fact "a prematurely born infant . . . , another a mother buried with a child on top of her" (p. 207). One brick discovered in a shrine fell apart in the excavator's hands and revealed the bones of a newborn infant encased inside. How many more are there that did not fall apart? There are some male remains and symbols in the shrines but I will not be the first to remark on their overwhelming devotion to femininity. In other words, the shrines may have represented not only the sacred but also the very feminine heart-of-the-home aspects of later harems.

2. Perhaps these suggestions contain too much speculation. There is, for example, the problem that in much of the material culture, prehistoric Anatolia has more in common with the Levant than with Mesopotamia.

3. At first glance, to me, she looks like Lady Justice. Perhaps Justice is not blind after all, but veiled, seeing all and defending separate views of the world.

4. I.e., of the potentate.

5. This represents a neatened version of a document that is in reality full of lacunae and vaguely understood terms. I have used several sources, in the main Driver and Miles (1975).

6. I can recommend three commentaries to this law, Driver and Miles (1975) being the most sober and exhaustive. Jastrow (1921) is not without its usefulness in spite of its age. Lerner's (1986) I deal with in the text.

7. I think a note is in order here to discuss the letter from the archives of Mari, which Lerner quotes (1986:70-71) in support of her theory that the veil marks the pawn. In this letter, thirty of the most attractive women—they are also expected to be *ugbabatum* priestesses—are to be selected out of a shipment of new slaves and given to a man called Warad-ilišu (head eunuch or *rabbin sikkutum*?) to guard. Warad-ilišu is to give these women "the Subarean veil." Another translation offered for this line is "teach them Subarean dancing" (Lerner, 1986:256), but the best translation I find for *šitar* is indeed some sort of garment: if it is related to the Hebrew *str,* then the sense that it conceals or secrets the wearer is indeed implied (i.e., Isaiah 50:6—hiding one's face from shame). Still, the question mark in all translations is warranted.

What is one to do with the adjective *Subarean*? As the source of the most favored slaves in Babylon, probably Mari, too, the land Subartu was composed of a number of ethnic groups and "highlander" may be the best translation. Because of their favor on the slave block, "first-rate" or "light-colored" is also possible. (See Finkelstein, 1955, whom Lerner quotes.) Lerner, however, fails to note—because it would certainly damage her argument—the sense Batto (1974:26) reads into this letter. Being joined to the harem of Mari—with the mark of the veil—denoted some honor. This is not just beauty-contest honor for pretty faces, but "the honor of being attached to the palace and *supported by it.*" The veil was undoubtedly a mark of this protection and support—this honor. The Subarean veil letter and all the letters for which Batto gleaned his impressions belong to female business, the archives of the harem of Queen Shibtu and her *consœurs* who were renowned for their "high status" (p. 5). If this veil were not an honor for them, is it likely they would have given this impression consistently throughout their letters? Obviously, there were worse fates for a slave than to join these women in their harem.

8. In Mesopotamian religious practice, goddesses and their human representatives are associated with certain articles of clothing that suggest precursors to the modern veil. For example, in a hymnal prayer written by Enheduanna, "the Queen of all the *me*" is said to tie these divine powers about her as if they were a garment (Kramer, 1963; see also Falkenstein, 1958). In the Hymn to Enlil (Kramer, 1963:

575), Ninlil, "the holy wife, whose word is gracious," is said to be garbed in something called specifically a "holy *me*-garment" about which all that can be said is that it "has something to do with the *me*." (*Me* are the divine powers that control the universe.) But elsewhere, in the hymn titled "Love in the Gipar," the goddess Inanna prepares for her bridegroom by picking up "that which covers the princely house." We cannot identify for certain what this might be, but the goddess "puts it on her nose"—a strange place for any sort of ornament save a nose ring—or a veil. Rather than as emblems of subservience, Inanna speaks of her "garments as the garments of power" (Kramer, 1969). Jacobsen (1973:294) says that there was a headdress (more descriptive he cannot be) that was originally the one worn by midwives, particularly the goddess Nintur. (Ninmenna, one of her epithets, means "the lady of the headdress.") This divine "midwife of the nation" is praised in two hymns thusly: "[The ability] to give birth to kings, to give birth to high priests is verily in her hand" and "To give birth to kings, tie on the flawless tiara. To give birth to high priests, place the headdress on (their) head. [This ability] is in her hand." The ambitious individuals mentioned in these verses are urged with the symbolism of this garment to remember to whom they owe their life.

Like many female functions, the midwife "goddess appears to have created difficulties for the trend toward anthropomorphism in patriarchal political terms." A goddess as supreme ruler, rather than a God, a midwife rather than a warrior, was difficult to fit into the evermore linear pattern of Mesopotamian thought. "Slowly she had to yield before a male god," Enki/Ea, whose power in both birth and investiture of kings became widely accepted (Jacobsen, 1973:294).

In spite of such changes, it does seem clear that the midwife's headdress remained a symbol of power, both for men and women. Inanna, in the hymnal prayer of Enheduanna, "loves the life-giving tiara, fit for High Priesthood" (Pritchard, 1975). It is a far cry from the symbolism many scholars have seen in the modern descendants of this veil. The modern veil, "despite its forbidding appearance . . . can be considered a liberating invention, since it provides a kind of portable seclusion which enables women to move out of segregated living spaces while still observing purdah" (Papanek, 1971:520). This seems reasonable from an immediate perspective, as it serves the choices of Middle Eastern women today. In a historical perspective, however, it is hard to say which came first, seclusion or the divine represented by the headdress.

9. I follow closely the interpretation of Michael Astour's 1966 article "Tamar the Hierodule."

10. A nice nature-religion name, Tamar. It means the date palm. Like Rachel (Ewe), Deborah (honeybee), and Yael (mountain goat), and very unlike the later Abigail (a name that extols her father) or Bathesheba (extolling her father's foreskin, perhaps?).

11. The Code of Hammurabi #110 reads: "If a *naditum* or an *entum,* who is not living in a *gagum,* has opened (the door of) a beerhouse or has entered a beerhouse for (a drink of) beer, they shall burn that woman."

Astour (1966:193) also cites an Old Babylonian liver model that recommends the same punishment for an *en*-priestess who steals temple property.

12. There are several other words that receive the translation "veil" in the Old Testament. These refer to the "veil" to the holy of holies in the temple and the "veil" that covered Moses's glowing face after his epiphany. These have little to do with

women, and their roots are not connected with the words for items women wear. They do, on the other hand, have much to do with the notion of keeping the sacred out of profane view. There are also a couple of words in the Song of Songs. If one takes these verses to be (as I do) liturgy to accompany ancient fertility rites such as Tamar and her father-in-law were celebrating, then the presence of veils is to be expected and reconfirms this interpretation of both the Song and Genesis 38. On the other hand, the verses of the Song make it clear that these veils are more ornament than veil-as-extension-of-the-harem, for they in no way obscure the beautiful features of the beloved.

13. Interestingly enough, the Umayyad Caliph 'Umar ibn 'Abdul 'Aziz (reigned 717-720 CE) issued a similar proclamation: "Slave girls are not to wear the veil or pretend to be like free women" (Abu Saud, 1984:47). Certainly, slaves and lower-class women were regularly unveiled. The admission must be made that the purdah observance of one class of women usually depends "on the 'purdahlessness' of another" (Nelson, 1974)—the other being the more mobile and visible servants of those in seclusion. And mobility and visibility are seen in our culture, in looking-glass fashion, as the marks of the powerful woman.

First of all, let us remember that a class society is what calls for the remedy of seclusion in the first place, not the other way around. If there were no classes, there would be no need for seclusion. Seclusion cannot do away with inequality, but it does serve a major function of mitigating the inequalities to some degree. It binds all women together in a vertical bond rather than binding them to horizontal loyalties. Consider the protection of a high-class woman able to stand in opposition to the high-class male forces threatening to crush a sister in the lower classes. Consider the guarantees against abandonment in case of divorce or widowhood. I find this more class-crushing than the "charity" demonstrated by the Victorian lady to "her" poor when some form of "deserving" was required of poverty. However well intentioned, such Western women were doing nothing to protect an alternate set of values. They were, indeed, their husbands' best propagandists.

Certainly the Victorian lady felt no dependence on her maid as the wealthy harem occupant feels on hers. The Victorian felt rather that the girl should be glad to have a job. If she wasn't grateful enough, she could always be sacked and replaced with some other more nonindividuated creature, now that money, the lady's having and the maid's not having, had become the major factor in the relationship. Consider in opposition to this the case of the secluded woman and her maid: The girl may be dependent on her mistress for bread and board, but the lady is equally dependent on the girl for news of the outside world and for every errand she wants run. Add to this the occurrence, much more prevalent in the East a hundred years ago, of client families and a maintained tradition of interdependence one did not break for little cause.

Chapter 3

1. For exceptions to these observations, see Blanton, 1994, and Spain, 1992.

2. The Prophet Muhammad's house at Medina is a perfect example of this evolution for which we have historical record. See Watt, 1956.

3. This is the power of the behavioral scientist behind his one-way mirror toward his subject. Or the power Western observers feel and grow hostile to,

the closed houses and cities and veiled women which excluded them . . . which could even reverse the roles of observer and observed. . . . These veiled women are not only an embarrassing enigma to the [Western] photographer, but an outright attack upon him. . . . The womanly gaze is a little like the eye of a camera, like the photographic lens that takes aim at [and possesses] everything [for his own profit]. The photographer makes no mistake about it; it resembles his own when it is extended by the dark chamber or the view finder thrust in the presence of a veiled woman. The photographer feels photographed; having himself become an object-to-be-seen, he loses his initiative; he is dispossessed of his own gaze.

The photographer will respond to this quiet and almost natural challenge by means of a double violation: he will unveil the veiled and give figural representation to the forbidden. [He determines that] if the women are inaccessible to sight (that is veiled), it is because they are imprisoned. (Mabro, 1991: 4-5)

4. See Albenda (1983). I am indebted to David Greenberg for this citation as well as interesting discussion on this point which, I admit, I give but cursory attention.

5. The central courtyard finds a direct descendant in the Spanish patio. Besides being useful for seclusion, it is definitely cooler than other architectural designs and provides a natural air-conditioning in these hot climates.

6. I like to put individual names on this movement as the Bible does, although undoubtedly there was more than one clan involved. Father Abraham came to the Holy Land to escape the corruption of his native Mesopotamia. I imagine him like the early Puritan settlers on New World shores, which they perceived to be empty, pure, of culture. The Puritan forefathers were not so much seeking freedom of religion as the freedom to cleanse their society of the witches becoming tolerated in the "corruption" at home (Bostridge, 1997). Or, I can find a parallel in some fundamentalism in rural Idaho today, seeking "purity" for his "religion." What Abraham and his descendants did not forget to carry with them were the ability (or necessity) of kingship, trade, urbanization and state building, and the harem, as the Bible gives testimony of in the careers of David and Solomon.

Chapter 4

1. Shown by Rivkah Harris (1964) to be etymologically connected to the root meaning "fallow," the "fundamental qualification of the *naditu*" priestess was that she not "marry and bear children."

2. The most exhaustive study on these cones is that of Ellis (1968) and I refer the reader to him. He seems, however, to be unaware of Weidner's (1954-1956) earlier contribution, which appears only in a footnote, after all. The two works do not cancel each other out, but combined, will serve as the basis for my comments. Like these two men, I shall also have to draw heavily on post-Sumerian sources for elucidation.

3. Sellers of clan land were required to pay for a "nail-oil" ceremony as part of the transaction.

4. Although the relationship "remains obscure, especially if one connects the latter with *harāmu*" (Gelb, 1956).

5. *Harimtu* women from the beginning had close connections to taverns—places the holy *naditu* women must not even approach: "When I sit in the entrance of the tavern, I, Ishtar, am a loving *harimtu.*" There is nonetheless something sacred about their occupation, for the most famous *harimtu* in history, she who is sent to tame the wild man Enkidu in *The Epic of Gilgamesh,* performs "a woman's task" for the wild man, leaving him with "wisdom" and "broader understanding." "She possesses," Lerner comments, "a kind of wisdom" that causes the untamed Enkidu to follow "her lead into the city of civilization" (1986:132). Later, when things in the city prove the death of the wild man, he curses the *harimtu*:

> . . . I will curse you with a great curse . . .
> You shall not build a house for your debauch
> You shall not enter the tavern of girls . . .
> May waste places be you couch,
> May the shadow of the town-wall be your stand
> May thorn and bramble skin your feet
> May drunkard and toper alike slap your cheek (p. 133)

"The nature of this curse," Lerner explicates, "tells us that the *harimtu* who mated with [Enkidu] lived an easier and better life than the harlot who has her stand at the town wall and is abused by her drunken customers" (p. 133). It may be something of a "Just So Story" we have here, an explanation of how it is the *harimtu* came to have a more miserable life than her sister the *qadištu* or *naditu,* who seems, on the surface, to have been engaged in the same occupation.

What we may have here is the confusion of cultures and meanings that occurred when the Semitic Akkadian collided with Sumerian. Prostitutes may have been disparaged in the Akkadian cultural system, served as devalued chattel much as they do in modern America. When the Akkadians discovered valued hierodules in the Sumerian culture they overtook but still greatly admired, they were confused as they were at first confused about holy pegs. The holiness may have been translated into their language but not always the holiness of the station into the person of an individual woman. Hence the ambiguities.

6. See the brief articles in either edition of the *Encyclopedia of Islam* (Houtsma, et al., 1927:II:268 or Gibb et al., 1960: III:14.

7. It has been well elucidated by Mary Douglas in her study of *Purity and Danger* (1966).

8. See 1 Chronicles xxiv:8; Ezra ii:32, 39, x:21, 31; Neh. vii:35, 42, x:5, 27, xii:15.

9. The biblical book of Esther is undoubtedly historical fiction, justifying after the fact the acceptance by exilic Jews of a pagan festival, Purim. Even the word "pur" in Purim is Babylonian. Although Mordecai may have been a real personage, along with his niece Esther he makes the Babylonian divine dyad, Marduk and Ishtar. Haman and his wife Zeresh are the Elamite divinities, Humman and Kiririshna, i.e., Seres. These facts, the fact that modern Zoroastrian women are notoriously unsecluded by Muslim standards, and that there are some stories that would indicate that "when the Persians conquered the Greeks, Persian women had nothing

but contempt for *gynaeceum*-bound Athenian women" (Boulding, 1976:344) are still not cause to refute Esther as a demonstration, even fictionalized, of how Persian monarchs, if they were to be accepted as monarchs in the Land Between the Rivers, really had no choice but to take over the refined domestic arrangements of their predecessors. The novelist obviously knew his background well, and the book should not be neglected as a source for information on the state of the harem under the Persians.

What we see in Esther is a palace that is really two palaces in one, arrangements very similar to that which met the first European travelers to these same lands 2,000 years later. Counterbalancing the "king's house," "vizier," "chamberlains" and all, is a complex hierarchy in the "women's house" with its own rules and traditions including a "second harem" (Esther 2:14) where rejects retire. The two houses are mediated by a hierarchy of powerful eunuchs.

Esther's year of preparation to meet the king—(six months with oil of myrrh, six of sweet odors) (Esther 2:12) is reminiscent of the year of preparation the *nin.dingir* underwent, although the indication now seems to be that it is more because King Ahasuerus is divine that such rituals are needed than because his consort is. Is this only the Jewish author's perspective? Surely Herodotos shows us some very powerful Persian women behind the throne in such characters as Atossa and Amestris.

Persian history—such as it is, inscriptions and tablets—is generally silent about the harem—which is why Esther is so valuable. But of course silence is how a system that "writes" dual histories should record the harem. Women's "history" of the time is revealed, to some degree, in the genre called "harem tales" (Cosquin, 1909). In the West, the best known example of the genre is found in the *One Thousand and One Arabian Nights,* in the tales where seclusion provides not only the characters and backdrop for action, but, indeed, propellant for the action as well. If it weren't for seclusion in many cases, there would be no story.

It is commonly noted that the Book of Esther owes at least part of its existence to this literary genre. Vashti may be a real personage—Re'emi (1985) identifies her as Stateira, wife of Artaxerxes II (404-358 BC). But her story has all the high drama and the motifs of the Arabian Nights (not to mention its progeny through Shakespeare—*The Taming of the Shrew*). And isn't Esther, in the parade of female flesh the sovereign has to choose from, much like Scheherazade?

There are, however, important differences that mark the author of Esther as someone looking in on the harem from the outside, one who sees it as an exotic, perhaps even decadent, practice to which those with the Truth need not resort.

When Ahasuerus (perhaps Artaxerxes II), deep in his cups and grown boisterous with his friends, calls for Vashti to appear, she is certainly within her rights to remain hosting her own parallel party in the "women's house." Indeed, I find her modest refusal to appear, even fully clad, the only woman among a group of drunken men, totally understandable. I would go so far as to say that Vashti shows herself to be the only admirable person in the story.

By finding Vashti's will for self-determination worthy of punishment, the biblical author shows himself to be sympathetic with Shakespeare's lines from a beaten Katherine (V:2):

Thy husband is thy lord, thy life, thy
   keeper . . .
And craves no other tribute at thy hands
But love, fair looks, and true obedience—
Too little punishment for so great a debt.
Such duty as the subject owes the prince,
Even such a woman oweth to her husband;
And when she is froward, peevish, sullen,
   sour,
And not obedient to his honest will,
What is she but a foul contending rebel,
And graceless traitor to her loving lord?

Banishment from the royal bed can only seem the ultimate sentence to one who subsumes all power under one majesty—the virile male's. Vashti, if she were a real Persian woman and if she really were queen as the text would have us believe (not just another concubine of a captive people) must have come from one of the seven noble Persian houses. It was customary, even law, for the king of kings to marry into these aristocratic houses. She was probably also mother of the heir—no son of Esther's would be tolerated by the Persian nobility. As such, Vashti maintained all her friends and social contacts, her ties to power and access to resources upon divorce, all but the single, highly overrated avenue of kingly bedsheets. Esther herself would have done better to cultivate other feminine avenues. They would have more permanence. When she does pull off her coup, we learn that it had already been thirty days since Esther had been called for (Esther 4:11). As for Vashti, we can assume she didn't lose much sleep over the break. In fact, she probably slept better, free from erratic erotic interruptions.

Now let us look at the case our author makes for Esther. Like Scheherazade, she wins out over thousands. But Scheherazade wins by her wit and skill as a storyteller. (How gratifying for the inventer of *that* story!) Esther just stands around and looks pretty. Indeed, if she has any wit at all, she uses it to ingratiate herself to the closest "man" around, namely Hegai, the head eunuch, "keeper of the women." Rather than choose the ornaments she likes best, she relies on Hegai's judgment, which, the author tells us, is the proper way to behave. And when it comes to saving her people, she is totally the tool of Mordecai's superior cunning. This is how a woman may hope to advance herself, our biblical storyteller seems to moralize. By being pretty and vacuous, she may ingratiate herself to clever and powerful men and thereby fulfill the will of God.

Indeed it may be said that the author of Esther has twisted the usual "harem tale," which accepts if it does not support the system, and written a tract against seclusion. Make yourself scarce, as Vashti did, from the power world of men, he seems to say, and you will be punished, discarded, and left behind by it. Appear, even uninvited, but appear beautifully according to the male world's criteria, and you shall be rewarded. You shall be rewarded, but by the monolithic system that you have now allowed yourself to join, in which you will never be more than one of the lower rungs.

Chapter 5

1. Counterintuitive as this may appear at first blush. On polygyny correlated with lower fertility rates, see both Page and Reyna and Bouquet in Caldwell, 1975.

2. To be distinguished from "'true' warfare which is carried on for reasons of state and often results in social integration." The ritualized kind results in fragmentation. See D. Harris (1972:257).

3. See Harding (1971) on this important point. Most cultures—except those which environmental stress make particularly misogynic—provide a period after birth when a woman, even a superwoman, is debarred from work. Anthropologist Sarah Hobson (1982) introduces us to the loneliness and boredom of a woman who was ready to leave her cot and go back to work—harsh as it was—long before the time prescribed by her South Indian culture was up. But we can imagine any number of women for whom this period away from the blistering grind of work, time to concentrate on her baby and on healing, might be a godsend.

Indeed, godsend is a good word for it: we recall the biblical injunction that a woman is unclean for forty days after the birth of a boy (fifty for a girl). This led in the Yiddish *shtetl* to the word for new mother, *kimpetorn,* becoming "a byword for indulgence. If a person demands excessive attention, he will be told, 'you are not a kimpetorn.' A hale adult will reject oversolicitude by protesting, 'Why? Am I a kimpetorn?'" (Zborowski and Herzog, 1952:315). This time period is reflected in the traditional European six-week recovery period, which, however, has recently been found to be insufficient in at least half of the cases, particularly after cesarean sections. Oh, for the godsend of uncleanliness today! In light of the fact "that 60 percent of American working women have no rights to any kind of leave when they bear a child" (Hewlett, 1986:174), this biblical six weeks is usually fantasy. Hewlett describes the case of a woman who scrimped and saved on sick leave and vacation time to have a mere two and a half weeks' rest after giving birth by cesarean section. "I don't know how I lived through those first weeks back at work," she told her interviewer (Hewlett, 1986:382).

> "I was exhausted and in pain from the surgery. I could hardly drag myself around. The worst thing was the lack of sleep. Annie woke to be fed at least three times a night, and by midday I was ready to kill for sleep. But somehow I had to work—and to smile and pretend to my boss that I didn't have a family care in the world." [She] is not a masochist. The only reason she did these things to herself and to her child was to keep her job. No other civilized nation makes it so difficult for women to bear children while working.

Some women's problems do not begin with labor, but with conception. Some must stay flat on their backs for seven or eight months. And the stress and environmental hazards of most out-of-the-house jobs can hardly be conducive to optimum health in the next generation.

4. See the descriptions in, for example, Boon, 1977, Liefrinck, 1969, and Ravenholt, 1973.

5. I find this term wonderfully ironic in true looking-glass fashion. It is the "third world" countries that are, or were until colonialism, fully developed to the limits of their environments, and countries of the Western technocracies that continue to be-

lieve in development and which continue to pursue this elusive goal in all corners of the earth—i.e., they are the ones doing the developing.

6. This does not mean drug usage when the drug (or alcohol) is created by the monolith or those interested in the same basic values as the monolith and imported to the natives to (1) extract what little money they have out of them and (2) to keep them tractable, indeed, as an only slightly more pleasant form of genocide than gas chambers. The comparison was strikingly made for me by a pair of travelogues on the Amazon. In the one, natives were shown participating in a "primitive" drug cult in which the harvesting, manufacture, and use of the drug was all done locally and imbued with the sacred and a beautiful sense of local power and nature. The second film presented a picture of horror: the kinsmen of these same natives just down the river where the monolith had penetrated, cutting down the sacred vines of the hallucinogen and attempting to replace them with Jack Daniel's brought about a total collapse of native culture and the complete demoralizing of its people through alcoholism.

Chapter 6

1. Efficiency, efficient, efficiently. These words, in our modern sense of them, are barely 150 years old. This instantly makes them suspect from my point of view, suspect when they are used to label the good pole. Originally, efficient meant what "makes (a thing) be what it is . . . : e.g., 'The efficient cause [of dew] is the temperate cold of the night. Swan *Spec.* M.vii (1643)" as cited in the Second Edition of *The Oxford English Dictionary.* Any number of individualistic ways could be employed to, for example, get supper on the table, all of them, in the end, efficient—in the old sense of the word. Now that efficiency has come to mean "the ratio of useful work performed to the total energy expended," means to an efficient end can be worked into a formula and graded. One single uniform mode of getting dinner on the table comes to be preferred because it is *most* efficient, not more healthful, more enjoyable, more casual, more aesthetically pleasing, more communal, more traditional. Efficiency, in effect (efficiently), is a cultural gradation that allows the fastest means to one value pole to be preferred, and frees more and more energy to attain that pole. Instantly one sees that this is an industrial nation-state definition of energy at play here. As such, it is maladaptive and, in this book, is used always to describe a negative attribute of a process rather than a positive, as the usual use of the modern sense gives it.

2. I cannot leave the dinosaurs without a nod to Psittacosaurus, Maiasaura ("good mother lizard"), and other species recent excavations have revealed to show better-than-suspected, even charming parenting skills. I feel safe in maintaining, nonetheless, that none approached mammalian levels.

3. Even when she is not interested, which opens the way to rape, impossible among other animals.

4. See Conkey and Spector (1984) for more literature on this topic—and for an argument against it.

5. Johanson's discoveries (Johanson and Edey, 1981) push the date back beyond tools and Olduvai.

6. See Johanson and Shreeve, 1989, as well as, in a more scholarly vein, Hay and Leakey, 1982, and White and Suwa, 1987.

Chapter 7

1. Or himself, I would suggest, when the future of genes is allowed, by the loss of instinct, to be forgotten.

2. Most societies in the world make some attempt at this indoctrination. Unfortunately, what our society teaches only helps the exploitation of the one side. Never before have males been so free to move about, never have other "virtues"—success, personal happiness—been allowed to supplant this teaching. Is it any wonder that Cassetty and McRoy could write in 1983, "While the past decade has witnessed the 'liberation' of women, it belies the attendant fact that women and their children now compromise the largest portion of America's poor" (p. 36)? The few years since have compounded the problem.

3. See Weinbaum (1977:58-59):

> When the [Nazi] party had no power, when it was in fact a legal risk to become a member, women formed a considerable proportion; as the party became more powerful, the internal position of women diminished. Similarly, in China, before the [Communist] party's actual seizure of state power. . . . For as male socialist leaders concentrate on the consolidation of power, women would-be leaders find themselves marginalized as an unheeded voice of revolutionary consciousness, (or, it might be said, conscience). . . . So, contrary to the opinion of many left men—that [Rosa] Luxenburg was one of them—she *was* "acting like a woman," by her insistence on revolutionary purity of the left. For it didn't make sense to many women to put faith in parliamentary or trade union accomplishments. After all, being female, they could neither vote (let alone get elected to parliamentary seats) nor have a base for power in the mostly male trade unions. So, unlike the leading socialist men, they did not have the option of stepping in to redirect bourgeois institutions toward socialist ends.

The same trend has been noted in many a revolution, from early Christianity and Islam to Mormonism. As a revolution becomes respectable and powerful, opportunities for women wither; women are supplanted and (although not verbally, perhaps) disenchanted. Women, by definition, should always be subversive, whatever party comes to power in a monolithic world.

Chapter 8

1. I am perfectly aware that there is much debate concerning the validity of the historical progression Marvin Harris (1979), Harner (1970), and Divale (1973) present and which I am rattling off as a given. I am doing this in the interest of simplicity. The reader who has doubts may consult either of the last two sources for references that bolster other views. This point seems to be the most controversial one I ask the reader to take on faith, so I have decided, with the encouragement particularly of Da-

vid Greenberg, to put this note here. It could occur at numerous other points throughout the book. In all cases of doubt, please refer to the references cited for differing opinions. I do limit my immediate references to those that come closest to my own vision of the facts.

2. Witchcraft, it may be noted, serves a number of purposes in different cultures. In many societies it serves the purpose taken in ours by lawsuits: someone is surely to blame and someone must surely pay. We will return to the topic of witchcraft in a later chapter.

3. See Chapter 4.

Chapter 9

1. "Virgin" and "empty," of course, only to their level of exploitation. The fate of the American Indians is better documented and may give some inclination of the unsung fates of vanished peoples all across both Europe and Asia before the first pioneers of the Neolithic.

2. This pioneering mode of agriculture—what any agriculture, unstable system that it is, would be if it had the luxury—has been aptly described by D. Harris (1972:249) as "involving progressive *linear* rather than *cyclic* shifts of clearings"(my italics).

3. This is, of course, an echo of Carneiro's circumscribed agricultural land theory (1970). Since Japan will provide important parallels further on, it might be pointed out that those farmers who moved eastward from China eventually found themselves in Japan in a similar cul-de-sac.

4. This type of soil is common in the tropics and is best served by a swidden or slash-and-burn agriculture.

5. Although for some braver souls this route remained a possibility, particularly after the domestication of the camel, c. 2000 BCE.

6. I'm taking the liberty of calling them this at the risk of coming down heavily on one side of the "Sumerian Question," a conflict whose resolution I hope will not influence my argument one way or the other in the long run.

7. Argument concerning not only irrigation, but all domestication of plants and animals. See Jacobs, 1969.

8. There is a bit of a paradox in the nature of charity here, but since religions appeal to it again and again, we can't let that stop the logic.

Chapter 10

1. Also witness the position in which women find themselves when sex is added to the tour package. See Morgan, 1984, on "Prostitution, Sex Tourism and the Traffick in Women."

Chapter 11

1. Or of the manufacturing enterprise which, as we have seen, is at the base the same thing: "industrialization—the traditional expedient for nations with too many people and too little land" (Bray, 1972:921).

2. Bushaway (1982:50) calls gleaning "this annual suspension of property rights."

3. Finding hard facts to actually pin a similar "enclosure" movement into ancient Mesopotamia is difficult, but possible. We might begin with the famous roller seals, evidenced from as early as the late Chalcolithic, whose purpose was clearly to limit legitimate access to the fruits of the land (Zagarell, 1986b).* Of particular interest to our subject is the fact that "the late Neolithic/early Chalcolithic sealings are often geometric in design, those of the later Chalcolithic phases are typically zoomorphic and anthropomorphic." As the seals evolve through time, "by the Late Uruk and Jamdet Nasr periods . . . a very common type of seal represents *women* performing" numerous activities, including "herding of goats and sheep, raising of cattle, storage of grains, working of fields and orchards, fishing, potting, weaving and spinning" (p. 418).

Very important evidence for the shift from communal or clan-based land ownership to ownership by individuals (usually powerful males) in Mesopotamia is gathered from *kudurrus*. These are large columns of rock or baked clay on which important land transactions were recorded. Accompanied by the *kag-i* rite, the expense of which was borne by the seller, these columns were set up either out in the fields described in the deed or in central places in town. Here they served as a constant reminder to any descendant of the sellers, even if she worked that land every day, that she no longer had any direct claim to the produce of that land. On the earliest *kudurrus,* the number of sellers is large—up to nine. Their genealogies are given in some detail and we can usually see that they were kinsmen of a single lineage.The land thus sold was clan land, but the interests of women are rarely addressed in these alienations of property, the interests of children never. It is also very telling that in the most scandalously low exchange (recorded on the Obelisk of Maništusu), even a majority of the male members of the clan could not be counted on to acquiesce and their names are replaced by those of forty-nine royal courtiers—who in other similar cases had the added attraction of being happy to fulfill this duty for free. It is always the head of the clan who gets the most gifts and the lion's share of the payment; generally other (usually male) clan members were given a (nominal) fee to witness the deed, thereby theoretically acknowledging their approval.

By the time of Sargon the Great (c. 2300 BCE), secondary sellers all but vanish from the *kudurrus*. "Almost all the land sales reported are to leading officials" (p. 416) from smaller landholders, and this is not just a function of the fact that the scribes whose handiwork we have were employed by urban institutions and the large landowners. The clan as communal landholder had vanished—sold to the highest bidder—and all transactions of land, that most vital of means of production, were now between powerful individual male wheelers and dealers (Gelb, 1979). It is an easy guess to make that such persons could bring political or economic pressure to bear on the seller, either to sell in the first place, or to bring the price down ridiculously low.

There are interesting terms for different types of land that can be gleaned from the texts, but only two have great attraction for our subject here. The first is *gán.bar,* literally "open fields." It is vaguely understood, but the equation of term and similar social circumstance with that found in post-medieval England is too blatant to pass without comment. The second is *im-ru-a.* In other contexts, *im-ru-a* can be translated simply as "family" or "clan." In some contexts, however, it has particular reference to some sort of land. By exploring what was grown on this land, it has been determined that it was "probably a common name for all tracts of land not used for farming and gardening, including swamps, pastures, woods and steppe land." These lands were important for the grazing of animals, for the gathering of fuel and other wild products, perhaps hunting, too. If the connection with clans is true, as seems likely, then this land served as did the commons and wastes of medieval England.

The reforms of Urukagina sought to stop this hemorrhaging of the means of production away from the worker. Under these reforms, people had only "the right to sell their house and moveable property," and "the right of undisturbed possession of water on their plot, but not the right to sell the plot itself" (Diakonoff, 1954:8). On the other hand, there is even a technical term for clan land that had become alienable: *gán-sám.* That such sales were closely connected to the prevailing trade market can be seen by the fact

> that the prices of land are governed by the average ratio of profit which in the Ancient East can for practical reasons be conventionally equated to the average interest on loans. Thus, an average profit of 33 percent means that the average price of land will not exceed the price of three yearly crops. Therefore the price of land in Sumer was extremely low, not exceeding three to four yearly crops (p. 8).

One final note: as time progressed, it can be seen that the disinherited became more and more willing to accept allotments of (often finished) goods rather than their ancient allotments (although alienable) of land in return for their service to temple or king. Often it seems such people began their service as refugees. (From infertile land? From land they'd been forced to sell? In effect it is the same.) But a single generation is all that would be needed to make their removal from the land permanent and handouts of loaves of bread and bolts of cloth as good and free a life as any, for they knew no other but starvation.

4. My source research was carried out in the 1950s; the present Iraqi crisis is ignored.

Chapter 12

1. The psychiatrist Julian Jaynes in his book *The Origin of the Consciousness in the Breakdown of the Bicameral Mind* has some very enlightening things to say on the subject, and the Introduction gives exercises to help the highly individuated brain admit its own individuation; still, it isn't easy.

2. The text is unclear at this point.

3. See Talcott Parsons (1960:2), who writes:

> One of the most salient structural characteristics [of our society] . . . is the prominence . . . of relatively large-scale organizations with specialized functions, what rather loosely tend to be called "bureaucracies." At the role level these organizations are composed of relatively pure-type "Occupational" roles where the status and responsibilities of the incumbents are relatively fully segregated from their "private" affairs in terms of premises, kinship relations, property, and the like.

4. Not coincidentally, the North African historian and father of social sciences Ibn Khaldun saw the phenomenon in his own medieval century. "Genealogies became confused," he said as a corollary to urban settlement.

5. Sumerian grandfathers from both sides of the family seem to have shared a single term, as did cousins, but this may be due to the imperfection of our knowledge of the language. As an interesting sidelight, it may be mentioned that some greater intricacy can be found among in-laws, the man married to a woman claiming a different term than that he uses to refer to her brother.

6. Note the male emphasis of this development. The poetry aspect of the heroics is minimal, but I would maintain that modern America has a parallel period in the highly individuated, shoot-'em-up days of the cowboys.

7. According to Robin Morgan's definition, religion, from the Latin "bound by rules," is linear religion, and "religion is terror" (1989:88). She and I disagree only as to which pole is to be called religious, not in our definition of what is good and what is bad.

8. The tablets on which these proverbs were found date to a later period but they are written in Sumerian and were no doubt preserved from earlier times.

9. Think linearly, in our terminology.

10. My translation.

Chapter 13

1. His use of the word "unstable" contradicts mine, but we get the picture.

2. Such a scale, minus the monocropping, was devised by Esther Boserup, 1965.

3. One can take a child mushroom hunting, but not to the factory, for the factory owner demands 100 percent of one's time for the privilege of working for him: he owns all the resources.

4. The quote continues:

> In parenthesis it should be noted that the flat roof today in a large part of the Middle East is regarded as a mark of poverty, and that the pitched tiled roof has become virtually a status symbol. In some instances house owners have even been prepared to suffer the inconvenience of having no clear space in which to work in order to demonstrate their "superiority" by giving their dwellings pitched roofs.

There are, of course, large areas where pitched roofs today remain the norm. Most often these are in unusually high rainfall areas where any surface of mud plaster on which pools of water could collect would be inviting disaster.

5. A view of the skyline of any traditional Middle Eastern city that discloses tightly-packed grape arbors there two and three stories above the soil they are growing in, and the coffee cans of pepper and tomato plants, will emphasize this "shade of one's own fig tree" nature of the flat roof. "To sleep on when it gets hot" is but a very limited explanation of the phenomenon.

6. By Elizabeth Warnock Fernea in her book *A Street in Marrakesh* (1976a) and Joseph, 1978, among others.

Chapter 14

1. For a bibliography and discussion from a "traditional" feminist perspective (one that frowns on dichotomy as a general rule), see Conkey and Spector, 1984.

2. See J. Brown (1973, 1982) for famous and important discussions of this point.

3. Lee, *The !Kung San* quoted in Woolfson 1982:29.

4. Valued because they are required to gain one's "fair" share of the limited resources available.

Chapter 15

1. Uchitel (1984b:262) counters that "the whole theory about the slaughter of male captives is founded on a misunderstanding" of texts. This has no significant effect on the thrust of my argument, I don't think.

2. There are also lists of women consigned to temple grain mills, which is as close to the industrialization of food production that Mesopotamia attained.

3. Zagarell actually says "public/communal" here.

4. Although he fails to mention it here, elsewhere he shows that these "slaves" were mostly women.

5. This barrier to the keeping of male slaves must not be underestimated, as the rapid rise and spread of the creation of eunuchs to circumvent the problem testifies.

Chapter 16

1. In the traditional society of Dwyer (1978) as opposed to the lower levels of a society now heavily taken under the Western monolith as described by Rausch (2000).

2. It may be argued that modern democracy is to blame for the Palestinian birth rate: they are in a battle to the death for the land called Israel, a battle where, yes, tanks, guns, and masses of willing martyrs count, but where numbers pressing to the ballot box or at least to United Nations charity concerns might count even more.

3. A recent estimate. See Morgan, 1989.

Chapter 17

1. Under seclusion, certain vital areas of information are the preserve of women alone and men have access through this information only through their women.

2. Note Lerner's use of "revolution" as the cultural parallel to biological evolution and the necessity of having adaptability maintained in alternatives for revolution to turn to. This may be true of political ideas, but, unfortunately, I doubt it is true of other values, as most revolutions only tend to replace one group wielding male-type political power by another group wielding the same type of power in which only the politics has changed, become more efficient. Although their stated philosophies may indeed be those of the supressed, I cannot think of one historical event termed "revolution" where this actually happened for any longer than it took a new opposition to gain some strength.

3. Alas, even we female historians cannot get our symbols together; we have been most fiercely undermined.

4. The better to exploit you with, my dear.

5. Humphreys (1977:362, 366) also makes comparison of simple and complex societies in a similar vein, finding that "it is differentiation into hierarchically organized structures and not the mere multiplication of options which marks the elaborated code."

Chapter 18

1. Likewise it was a great puzzle to J. Pierce (1964b) that his Turks had "almost no sex gender differentiation in the language" although "there is a sharp dichotomy between males and females in all walks of village life" (p. 75). For Turkish sexual dialects, see later in this chapter.

2. I prefer to call both Emegir and Emesal "languages" instead of "dialects." I have failed to find a better word to convey the sense of their independence. "Dialect," which many writers—like those I quote here—prefer, makes the languages, particularly the female, seem lesser and dependent. Illich aptly says that "gender-specific speech is not a variety of 'the' language, but one of its two fundamental, constitutive complements" (1982:133). American men can go through life and never use the word "mauve"—but English is a richer language for it.

3. I've consulted seven works for my understanding of Emesal: Krecher's 1967 "Zum Emesal-Dialekt des Sumerischen," Diakonoff's 1975 "Ancient Writing and Ancient Written Language," Silvestri's 1976 "Appunti sulla eme.sal sumerica," Schretter's 1990 *Emesal Studien: Sprach- und literaturgeschichtliche Untersuchungen zur sogenannten Frauensprache des Sumerischen,* Sefati's 1998 *Love Songs in Sumerian Literature,* Hayes' 2000 *A Manual of Sumerian Grammar and Texts,* and Whittaker's 2002 "Linguistic Anthropology and the Study of Emesal as (a) Women's Language." That seven men reached such different conclusions is testimony to how unstable our knowledge on the matter really is. I owe my translation of Silvestri to Giovanni Tata, to whom I am most grateful.

The exact meaning of the word "Emesal" is still under discussion. Whittaker (2002) cites seven disparate explanations as to the nature of the tongue. The first part of this compound word, "eme," meaning "language," seems clear enough, but the second part is more difficult. Popular translations at present are "fine," "twisted," or "quaint" language. It derives, however, "from an Uruk IV depiction of the pubic triangle" (p. 634). Much later (about 1750 BCE), in the Hittite language, not the Sumerian, that "SAL" becomes the determinative par excellence for all things feminine, proper names of women and goddesses as well as in such words as SAL.LUGAL "queen," SAL.SIR "female singer" and SAL.SU.GI "witch" (Silvestri, 1976:221). SAL is equated also with *galla,* "eunuch, man who sings in a fine, feminine or birdlike voice." We shall have more to say about eunuchs in the next chapter.

I must accept Diakonoff's (1975) explanation of why it is that the Emesal language does not appear spelled out in the texts until the Old Babylonian period (c. 1900 BCE) at the earliest. As Diakonoff explains, cuneiform, Egyptian hieroglyphics, and even early alphabets were only elaborate mnemonic devices. It is only after Sumerian was dead as a spoken, native language that a more complete writing system was called for than the mere one-character symbol that a native speaker would have known with second nature whether he must pronounce in Emegir or she must say in Emesal. Just so did Hebrew cry out for the addition of "points" representing vowels once the language died out as a living language around 200 BCE. The sacred text had not needed such precise clues to pronunciation until then, and modern native-speaking Israelis manage very well without vowels in their books and newspapers again today.

Emesal was not originally the language of divine females only. I believe that Emesal became attached to the divine in particular when Emegir did so as well: i.e., when Sumerian ceased to be spoken anywhere but in the temples as a sacred language much as Catholic Latin until recently or Hindu Sanskrit today. This usage continued almost to the time of Christ, whereas Sumerian as a native tongue died out surely by 2000 BCE. We have so little preserved in this language from the time it was alive and, as we have seen, while it lived it was only written in a very brief shorthand that would not distinguish the two dialects. Fortunately, the inheritors of the Sumerian cult, the Old Babylonians, thought it worthwhile to preserve and write out in a longer notation not only hymns and religious poems, but a number of proverbs in Emesal as well dealing with very mundane household women's matters (all from Gordon, 1959). It is a stretch to conceive of the speakers as being goddesses.

> My spouse heaps things up for me;
> My child measures things out for me.
> Let my spouse remove the bones from the fish for me. (p. 107)

(Note that, if it were not for the fact that this was written in Emesal, we would have no reason not to think it might be a husband and a father who is speaking: such is Sumerian's lack of grammatical and vocabularic sexing.)

> How the merchant has reduced the amount of silver!
> How the grain merchant has reduced the amount of barley! (p. 128)

(This, as Gordon indicates, is "the complaint of a housewife . . . over being cheated in the marketplace.")

> Sons-in-law: what they have brought! (i.e., the brideprice)
> Fathers-in-law (i.e., the brides' fathers): what they have had to dispose of!
>   (p. 130)

> Meat with fat is too good! Meat with suet is too good!
> What shall we give the slave girl to eat? (p. 143)

("The words of the mistress . . . to her husband or to a housekeeper or steward," Gordon tells us of this latter one.)

> "You are pouring off the fat from the meat.
>   (Note: "The fat was not to have been
>   poured off since it was believed to make
>   the meat more tasty.")
> You are ruining the roasted barley!
> You fellow, when I lift up the soup-cauldron,
>   watch out for your feet," she says. (p. 145)

("The words of the mistress of a household . . . who stands over the kitchen servants, nagging them at every turn.")

It is important to note that the knowledge that these words were spoken in Emesal, hence by a woman, gives the proverbs their meaning. Second, a technical study of these proverbs discloses that, as in the case of numerous hymns, only a few words are written out in the dialect, just enough to give the reader the necessary clues to complete pronunciation.

4. As is much of Sumerian, due to its agglutinative nature. Agglutination is a technical linguistic term meaning that the language is based on numerous particles that are combined to form words. These particles tend to be monosyllabic. Chinese is another example of a language heavy in monosyllabic atoms of meaning. Interestingly, it might be this trait that led both of these languages to be the originators of writing systems since monosyllabic particles rendered by pictographs using lots of rebus and homonyms seems a logical step.

5. Examples from Falkenstein and von Soden, 1953, my translations.

6. It is possible that agglutinative languages (such as Sumerian) tend to phonetic, hence dialectical dichotomy, while nonagglutinative languages (say, French or German) favor morphological. Hence gender differences when their culture calls for more linguistic sexual distinction.

7. This is the word used by the translator on page 8 of the Introduction in Ki, 1981.

8. Another acquaintance (Mentley, 1988) whose work was confined to Istanbul declared that women there cultivated a higher, more "feminine" tone, like Wasilewska's discovery in rural Anatolia, but not a true dialect per se.

9. I am asked why this period, if so named, did not produce writing that we can study for evidences of a women's dialect. Although women were definitely the power behind the throne, written political communication and the tedium of the records office were formulaically male.

10. Some suggest Emesal clung to older linguistic forms while the "main" language moved forward, leaving them in the harem. In contrast to this is the parallel Whittaker (2002) draws between Emegir/Emesal and

the Old Indic languages, Vedic and Sanskrit[/]numerous vernaculars called Prakrits [which] evolved in the course of the 1st millennium B.C. . . . [and] eventually developed into the modern Indic languages of today. . . . In . . . classical dramas high-ranking male characters, such as the king and the brahmins, speak and sing Sanskrit (pp. 638-639)

whereas in a stylized fashion, Prakrits are found in the mouths of women characters (Falkenstein and von Soden, 1953).

11. Fontaine (1989:75) credits Enheduanna with "one of the world's first efforts at a 'systematic theology.'" Well as this speaks for Enheduanna's intelligence, she was not wise enough to realize that attempts in this direction were steps toward "syncretic" or imperialistic religion.

12. Farrokhzād's "Frontier Walls," translated 1982:40-42.

13. "In the Cold Streets of Night," translated 1981:42-50

14. "Green Delusion," translated 1982:67-69.

15. "Born Again," Ibid., pp. 90-92.

16. "The Voice Alone Is Left," Ibid., pp. 116-118.

Chapter 19

1. Not that America was unpeopled before Europeans came; European settlers just treated it that way.

2. Shown by Diakonoff (1975). To this Sumerian word Silvestri (1976) has given the etymology of an original *lu-uru,* or "man-woman." A likely relationship, particularly because of this priesthood's connection with dirges and songs of mourning, may be found with the *gallas,* "the underworld's inhuman, loveless and cruel demons" (Kramer, 1963:257). We have two little poems from the Sumerian describing these netherworld beings: They

> Take away the wife from the man's lap,
> Take away the child from the nursemaid's breast;

and they

> Sate not with pleasure the wife's lap,
> Kiss not the well-fed children,
> Take away the man's son from his knee,
> Carry off the daughter-in-law from the house of the father-in-law.

(Kramer, 1963:257)

Other, to my mind less likely, etymologies are offered by comparison with the Hebrew root *gll,* "to turn oneself" (Cumont et al., 1933) or *klh,* "bride."

The *galas'* castrated state—or lack of it—has been the topic of much debate. For many years it was thought that castration, if it existed in Sumer, was never commented upon by the scribes. Some insisted it didn't exist, others that no Sumerian thought to turn the anthropological eye or voice of prophetic doom upon it: it was normal practice which everyone understood and accepted. Or perhaps it was too sacred to commit to dirty clay. Maekawa (1980) has interpreted the word amar-KUD as "young castrated animal/man," the sons of the slave women who worked in the textile factories.

3. Cumont et al. (1933:675). My translation.

4. Perhaps she was a *naditu* who was forbidden to have children? This would be a perfect match in that case.

5. Isn't that an interesting contradiction, eunuch patriarch?

6. Another transcultural parallel to the *galu* is found in the berdache of the American Plains Indians. "The berdache fundamentally represents a social adaptation of unacceptable inclinations and desires by means of certain institutional elaborations whereby these deviants could find an acceptable social niche" (Thayer, 1980:287). Certainly one can sympathize with the lad whom the strongest socialization failed to turn into a scalp-taking warrior. Childhood games for these Native Americans included placing burning sunflower seeds on the insides of the wrists without flinching. The Plains Indians granted divinity to the products of the berdache quilling circles. Evidence seems to indicate that berdache was not always a voluntary calling. Helpful as a dread of the braves' bloodthirsty life might have been in inducing the necessary visions of calling, there are on record the stories of plenty of men who fought all the divine proddings, all the manipulations of family and friends urging them to don women's garb. In some cases, suicide was preferable. No doubt life on the western plains went smoother with the berdache fulfilling his office as respected go-between for marriage partners or as nurse to the fallen members of a war party.

7. One of her critics, Gill Shepherd (Shepherd et al., 1978), on the other hand, refuses to believe that economics isn't at the base of it all. *Xaniths,* Shepherd insists, must be from the lower, exploited strata whose lack of success on the wedding night is due more to the inability to raise the bride-price than the phallus. Underneath it all, Shepherd seems to be pressing for the ideal socialist state in which each man would have equal access to the resources for bride-price (if this "primitive" means of extortion is not done away with altogether), and hence this aberrant social class would disappear. Wikan (1978) effectively counters with descriptions of wealthy aging *xaniths* who cease prostitution and pay men ("real" men, in Omani terms) to come to them. Although I can see the flaws in Shepherd's argument, I do think economics is part of the male Omani's terrors, as I expound in the text.

8. These bazaars probably date to ancient Mesopotamia's early searches for resources.

9. Like the berdache of the Plains tribes. See Longman, 2002, and Callender and Kochems, 1993.

10. And on the American Plains. Transsexuals also serve as the holiest of shamans among the sexual-dialected Chuckchee.

Chapter 20

1. I am alluding, of course, to the case of Frederick the Great penitent before Pope Gregory VII during the Investiture Controversy in the latter part of the eleventh century. See, e.g., Tellenbach, 1959.

2. This division seems to be part of the original Indo-European social structure (Mallory, 1989), which used other means to create vernacular gender.

3. It is a two-sided arrangement, of course, and it is a cruel and unnatural mother who is not thinking of her daughter's happiness when she meets with prospective mothers-in-law.

4. Divorce statistics vary wildly throughout the traditional Arab world from almost none to 40 percent and higher in Morocco, rates that rival those of the United States.

5. Virginity is only prized in a woman's first marriage. After that the pressure is off, and in many more ways than just proving sexual purity.

6. Modern witches like to put the figure at nine million but there seems no hard evidence for this but a tradition—and a recent one started perhaps by Gardner (2004), who may have, in the tradition of traditionalists, added a zero to the real figure. Even Hoyt (1981) can justify, however, the conservative estimate of one million.

7. This is the trial of Johann Schüler, his wife, and many more inhabitants of Lindheim, Germany, in 1663-1664 (Hoyt, 1981:75). The Germanic locus and absolute horror of the witch trials can lead the reader to the impression that Hitler was merely carrying on a time-worn tradition with modern equipment in his death camps. Abstracting one portion of humanity into inhumanity is, of course, a necessary prerequisite to atrocities of this sort, whether the group be Jews and gypsies or whether they be women (the great witch-hunters Kramer and Sprenger gave the etymology of "feminine" as *Fe* plus *Minus,* i.e., "less faith" (Hoyt, 1981:51). Such abstractions are not the aberration of a particular people at a particular time but a necessary corollary when the culture begins to move first into urbanism (Reformation Germany), then imperialism (Nazi Germany), and finally the world corporate mode. Italy was failing to keep up with Germany in reaching the bourgeoisie mode; that is as good a one-sentence reason why Rome, where the Pope was the strongest (hence should have had more burnings, according to the unfounded anti-Catholic theory), singularly lagged behind in the witch-hunt method of appropriating someone else's resources to bolster one's own. The world corporate mode seems to be making one final abstraction, now that witches and Jews are too close for comfort and we have grown more "civilized" than to persecute them. Now the "third world" is a vague and general enough term to allow us to exploit, torture, and kill thousands, confiscate their lands and goods all with no twinge of personal guilt. I'll confess the abstraction is great—the greatest of all. The connection between our bananas, so healthy and nonfattening, and Central American death squads is very hard to see from our breakfast table—probably about as hard as it was for the witch-hunters to see the connection between the system that supported their ease and the suffering of their victims. But the connection is not one wit more tenuous, and to raise no voice of objection against what we watch with nightly fascination on the tube (even if that little voice is all we have) deserves equal condemnation to that we like to heap upon the silent German majority in the 1930s and 1940s or on the curious, stupefied populace drawn by the flames of a witch burning in the seventeenth century.

8. See the first note for this chapter.

Chapter 21

1. In all fairness, it must be reported than the husbands of some agoraphobes began to "go crazy" when their wives showed improvement (Sidenberg and DeCrow, 1983), so divorce is not the universal reaction and there may be more to family politics here than I am suggesting.

Bibliography

Abel, Ludwig (1891). *Die Sieben Mu`allakât.* Berlin: Verlag von W. Spemann.

Abu-Lughod, Lila (1986). *Veiled Sentiments: Honor and Poetry in a Bedouin Society.* Berkeley and Los Angeles: University of California Press.

Abu Saud, Abeer (1984). *Qatari Women, Past and Present.* London: Longman.

Adams, Robert McCormick (1965). *The Evolution of Urban Society: Early Mesopotamia and PreHispanic Mexico.* Chicago: Aldine Publishing Co.

———.1972 "Patterns of urbanization in early southern Mesopotamia." In P. J. Ucko, R. Tringham, and G. W. Dimbleby, *Man, Settlement and Urbanism* (pp. 735-749). Proceedings of a meeting of the Research Seminar in Arcaeology and Related Subjects held at the Institute of Archaeology, London University. London: Duckworth.

Adler, Margot (1986). *Drawing Down the Moon,* rev. ed. Boston: Beacon Press.

Ahmed, Leila (1982). "Western ethnocentrism and perceptions of the harem." *Feminist Studies* 8:3 (Fall), pp. 521-534.

Albenda, Pauline (1983). "Western Asiatic women in the Iron Age: Their image revealed." *Biblical Archaeologist* 46:2, pp. 83-88.

Allan, W. (1972). "Ecology, techniques and settlement patterns." In P. J. Ucko, R. Tringham, and G .W. Dimbleby, *Man, Settlement and Urbanism* (pp. 211-226). Proceedings of a meeting of the Research Seminar in Arcaeology and Related Subjects held at the Institute of Archaeology, London University. London: Duckworth.

Altorki, Soraya (1977). "Family organization and women's power in urban Saudi Arabian society." *Journal of Anthropological Research* 33:3 (Fall), p. 277.

Arden, Harvey and Bruno Barbery (1986). "Morocco's ancient city of Fez." *National Geographic* 169, pp. 330-353.

Armstrong, Sally (2002). *Veiled Threat: The Hidden Power of the Women of Afghanistan.* New York: Four Walls Eight Windows.

Arnott, Peter D. (1961). "Introduction to *Medea.*" In *Three Greek Plays for the Theatre.* Indiana University Press.

Aro, Jussi (1964). "Gemeinsemitische Ackerbauterminologie." *Zeitschrift der Deutscher Morganländischer Gesellschaft* 113, pp. 474-480.

Astour, Michael C. (1966). "Tamar the Hierodule: An essay in the method of vestigial motifs." *Journal of Biblical Literature* LXXXV:2, pp. 185-196.

Atwood, Margaret (2003). "A book lover's tale: A literary life raft on Iran's fundamentalist sea." *Amnesty Now* (Fall), pp. 4-7, 26.

A History of Women's Seclusion in the Middle East
Published by the Haworth Press, Inc., 2006. All rights reserved.
doi:10.1300/5666_24

Avi-Yonah, Michael (1961). "Oriental art in Roman Palestine." *Studi Semitici* 5.

Ayala, Francisco J. (1978). "The mechanisms of evolution." *Scientific American* 239:3 (September), pp. 56-65.

Ayalon, David (1979). "On the eunuchs in Islam." In *Jerusalem Studies in Arabic and Islam, Vol 1* (pp. 68-87). Jerusalem: Magnes Press, the Hebrew University.

———. (1988). *Outsiders in the Lands of Islam: Mamluks, Mongols and Eunuchs.* London: Variorum Reprints.

Bahrani, Zainab (2001). *Women of Babylon: Gender and Representation in Mesopotamia.* London and New York: Routledge.

Barstow, Anne (1978). "The uses of archeology for women's history: James Mellaart's work on the neolithic goddess at Çatal Hüyük." *Feminist Studies* 4:3 (October), pp. 7-18.

Bateson, Mary Catherine (1984). *With a Daughter's Eye.* New York: Morrow.

Batto, Bernard (1974). *Studies on Women at Mari.* Baltimore: Johns Hopkins University Press.

Beck, Lois and Nikki Keddie (1978). *Women in the Muslim World.* Cambridge, MA: Harvard University Press.

Beit-Hallahmi, Benjamin et al. (1974). "Grammatical gender and gender identity development: Cross cultural and cross lingual implications." *American Journal of Orthopsychiatry* 44:3, pp. 424-431.

Bell, Sir Harold Idris (1957). *Cults and Creeds in Graeco-Roman Egypt.* Liverpool: University Press.

Bergson, Henri (1977). *The Two Sources of Morality and Religion.* Notre Dame, IN: University of Notre Dame Press.

Berry, Wendell (1987). *Home Economics.* San Francisco: North Point Press.

Bierce, Ambrose (1911). *The Devil's Dictionary.* New York: Albert and Charles Boni, Inc.

Binford, Lewis R. and Sally R. Binford (1966). "A preliminary analysis of functional variability in the Mousterian of Levallois Glacies." *American Anthropologist/Special Publications,* pp. 238-295.

Birdsell, Joseph (1968). "Some predictions for the pleistocene based on equilibrium systems among recent hunter-gatherers." In R. Lee and Il De Vore, *Man the Hunter* (pp. 229-449). Chicago: Aldine.

Black, Jeremy A. (1991). "Eme-sal cult songs and prayers." *Aula Orientalis* 9, pp. 23-36.

Blanton, Richard E. (1994). *Houses and Households: A Comparative Study.* New York: Plenum Press.

Blau, P. (1964). *Exchange and Power in Social Life.* New York: John Wiley.

Bledstein, Burton J. (1976). *The Culture of Professionalism: The Middle Class and the Development of Higher Education in America.* New York: Norton.

Bloch, R. Howard (1991). *Medieval Misogyny and the Invention of Western Romantic Love.* Chicago: University of Chicago Press.

Boak, A. E. R. (1955). *Manpower Shortage and the Fall of the Roman Empire in the West*. Ann Arbor, MI: University of Michigan Press.

Bodine, Ann (1975). "Sex differentiation in language." In Barrie Thorne and Nancy Henley, *Language and Sex: Difference and Dominance* (pp. 130-151). Rowley, MA: Newbury House Publishers.

Bodmer, Frederick (1944). *The Loom of Language*. Ed. by Lancelot Hogben. New York: W. W. Norton and Company, Inc.

Bohr, Neils (1939). "Natural philosophy and human cultures." *Nature* 143 (February 18), pp. 268-272.

Boon, James A. (1977). *The Anthropological Romance of Bali 1597-1972*. Cambridge: Cambridge University Press.

Boserup, Esther (1965). *The Conditions of Agricultural Growth*. Chicago: Aldine.

———. (1974). *Women's Role in Economic Development*. New York: St. Martin's Press.

Bossen, Laurel (1975). "Women in modernizing societies." *American Ethnologist* 2:4 (November), pp. 587-591.

Bostridge, Ian (1997). *Witchcraft and Its Transformations c. 1650-c. 1750*. Oxford: Clarendon Press.

Boulding, Elise (1976). *The Underside of History*. Boulder, CO: Westview Press.

Boyd, R. (1972). "Urbanization, morbidity and mortality." In P. J. Ucko, R. Tringham, and G. W. Dimbleby, *Man, Settlement and Urbanism* (pp. 345-352). Proceedings of a meeting of the Research Seminar in Arcaeology and Related Subjects held at the Institute of Archaeology, London University. London: Duckworth.

Bray, Warwick (1972). "Land-use, settlement patterns and politics in preHispanic Middle America: A review." In P. J. Ucko, R. Tringham, and G. W. Dimbleby, *Man, Settlement and Urbanism* (pp. 909-926). Proceedings of a meeting of the Research Seminar in Arcaeology and Related Subjects held at the Institute of Archaeology, London University. London: Duckworth.

———. (1977). "Civilising the Aztecs." In J. Friedman and M. J. Rowlands, *The Evolution of Social Systems* (pp. 373-398). London: Duckworth.

Bridenthal, Renate and Claudia Koonz (1977). *Becoming Visible: Women in European History*. Boston: Houghton Mifflin.

Bridge, Anthony (1978). *Theodora, Portrait in a Byzantine Landscape*. London: Cassell, Ltd.

Brinkman, J.A. (ed.) (1964). *Studies Presented to A. L. Oppenheim*. Chicago: University of Chicago, Oriental Institute.

Brothwell, Don (1972). "Community health as a factor in urban cultural evolution." In P. J. Ucko, R. Tringham, and G. W. Dimbleby, *Man, Settlement and Urbanism* (pp. 353-361). Proceedings of a meeting of the Research Seminar in Arcaeology and Related Subjects held at the Institute of Archaeology, London University. London: Duckworth.

Brown, Francis et al. (1906). *A Hebrew and English Lexicon of the Old Testament.* Boston: Houghton Mifflin, Co.

Brown, Judith K. (1973). "The subsistence activities of women and the socialization of children." *Ethos* 1:4, pp. 413-423.

―――. (1982) "Cross-cultural perspectives on middle-aged women." *Current Anthropology* 23:2 (April), pp.143-165.

Buckley, William F., Jr. (1978). "Up from liberalism." Quoted in *Yale Alumni Magazine* (April), p. 37.

Burn, Andrew Robert (1984). *Persia and the Greeks: The Defense of the West, c. 546-478 BC,* Second Edition. London: Duckworth.

Bushaway, Bob (1982). *By Rite: Custom, Ceremony and Community in England 1700-1880.* London: Junction Books.

Buttrick, George Arthur et al. (1962). *The Interpreter's Dictionary of the Bible.* New York: Abingdon Press.

Butz, K. (1978-1979). "Fischabgabe und Feldabgabe in Fischen und Vögeln an den Nana-Tempel in Ur in altbabylonischer Zeit: Ein Versuch." *Archiv für Orientforschung* 26, pp. 30-44.

―――. (1984). "On salt again . . . Lexikalische Randbemerkungen." *Journal of the Economic and Social History of the Orient* 27, pp. 272-316.

Caldwell, John C. (ed.) (1975). *Population Growth and Socioeconomic Change in West Africa.* New York: Columbia University Press.

Callender, Charles and Lee M. Kochems (1993). "The North American berdache." In D.N. Suggs and A.W. Miracle, *Culture and Human Sexuality: A Reader* (pp. 367-397). Pacific Grove, CA: Brooks/Cole.

Campbell, Joseph (1949). *The Hero with a Thousand Faces.* Princeton, NJ: Princeton University Press.

Campbell, Rex R. (1985). "Crisis on the farm." *American Deomographics* (October), pp. 30-33.

Carneiro, Robert (1970). "A theory of the origin of the state." *Science* 169, pp. 733-738.

Carroll, Lewis (1871). *Through the Looking Glass.* London: Macmillan and Co.

―――. (1879). *Euclid and His Modern Rivals.* London: Macmillan and Co. (Usually listed under his real name, Charles Lutwidge Dodgson.)

Cassetty, Judith H. and Ruth McRoy (1983). "Gender, race, and the shrinking welfare dollar." *Public Welfare* (Summer), pp. 36-39.

Chadwick, H. Munro (1912). *The Heroic Age.* Cambridge: University Press.

Cherfas, Jeremy and John Gribbin (1984). *The Redundant Male.* London: Bodley Head.

Chicago, Judy (1979). *Dinner Party.* Garden City, NY: Anchor Press/Doubleday.

Chughtai, Ismat (1987). "Tiny's granny." In Kali for Women (eds.), *True Tales: Contemporary Writing by Indian Women* (pp. 167-184). New Dehli, India: Kali for Women.

Coggins, R. J. (1985). *Israel Among the Nations: A Commentary on the Books of Nahum, Obadiah and Esther by S. Paul Re'emi*. Edinburgh: Handsel Press.

Cohen, M. N. and George Armelagos (eds.) (1984). *Paleopathology at the Origins of Agriculture*. Orlando, FL: Academic Press.

Cohen, Mark E. (1981). *Sumerian Hymnology: The Eršemma*. Cincinnati: Hebrew Union College.

Cohn, Samuel K. and Steven A. Epstein (1996). *Portraits in Medieval and Renaissance Living: Essays in Memory of David Herlihy*. Ann Arbor: University of Michigan Press.

Conkey, Margaret W. and Janet D. Spector (1984). "Archaeology and the study of gender." In M. B. Schiffer, *Advances in Archaeological Method and Theory*, Volume 7 (pp. 1-38). Orlando, FL: Academic Press.

Conlin, Michelle (2003). "The new gender gap." *Business Week Online,* May 26. Available at www.businessweek.com/print/magazine/content/03_21/b3834001 _mz001.htm?mz.

Cook, John Manuel (1962). *The Greeks in Ionia and the East*. London: Thames and Hudson.

Cooley, John (1982). *Libyan Sandstorm*. New York: Holt, Rinehart and Winston.

Cooper, Elizabeth (1915). *The Harim and the Purdah*. London: T. Fisher Unwin.

Corkran, David H. (1967). *The Creek Frontier, 1540-1783*. Norman: University of Oklahoma Press.

Cosquin, Emmanuel (1909). "Le Prologue-Cadre des Mille et une Nuits: Les Légendes Perses et le Livre d'Esther." *Revue biblique,* 18.

Cowan, J. M. (1976). *Arabic-English Dictionary*. Ithaca, NY: Spoken Language Services, Inc.

Crossan, John Dominic and Jonathan L. Reed (2004). *In Search of Paul*. San Francisco: Harper Collins.

Croutier, Alev Lytle (1989). *Harem: The World Behind the Veil*. New York: Abbeville Press.

Cumont, F. et al. (1933). *L'Antiquité Classique*. Bruzelles, Louvain: Marcel Istas.

Dando, Wiliam A. (1980). *The Geography of Famine*. London: V. H. Winston.

David, Elizabeth (1977). *English Bread and Yeast Cookery*. London: Allen Lane.

David, Martin (1933). "Beiträge zu den altassyrischen Briefen aus Kappadokien." *Orientalistische Literaturzeitung* 4, pp. 209-220.

Dawkins, Richard (1976). *The Selfish Gene*. New York: Oxford University Press.

Delougaz, Pinhas (1967). "Concluding remarks." In P. Delougaz, H. D. Hill, and S. Lloyd, *Private Houses and Graves in the Diyala Region* (pp. 274-278). The University of Chicago, Oriental Institute Publications, Vol. LXXXVIII. Chicago, IL: The University of Chicago Press.

Delougaz, Pinhas, Harold D. Hill, and Seton Lloyd (1967). *Private Houses and Graves in the Diyala Region*. The University of Chicago, Oriental Institute Publications, Vol. LXXXVIII. Chicago, IL: The University of Chicago Press.

Democracy Now (2004, December 16). "Unocal settles landmark human rights case with Burmese villagers." *Democracy Now.* Available at www.democracynow .org/article.pl?sid=04/12/16/1444238.

Devall, Bill and George Sessions (1985). *Deep Ecology.* Salt Lake City: Gibbs M. Smith, Inc. Peregrine Smith Books.

de Vaux, Roland (1935). "Sur le voile des femmes dans l'orient ancien." *Revue Biblique* XLIV, pp. 397-412.

Dewald, Carolyn (1981). "Women and culture in Herodotus' *Histories.*" In H.P. Foley, *Reflections of Women in Antiquity* (pp. 91-125). New York: Gordon and Breach Science Publishers.

Diakonoff, Igor Mikhailovich (1954). "Sale of land in pre-Sargonic Sumer." In *Papers Presented by the Soviet Delegation at the XXIII International Congress of Orientalists, Assyriology* (pp. 19-29). Moscow: USSR Academy of Science.

———. (1958). "Some remarks on the 'reforms' of Urugakina." *Revue d'Assyriologie et d'Archéologie Orientale,* LII:1.

———. (1965). *Semito-Hamitic Languages: An Essay in Classification.* Moscow: Nauka, Central Department of Oriental Literature.

———. (1971). *Hurrisch und Urartäisch.* Münchener Studien zur Sprachwissenschaft, Beiheft 6, Neue Folge, München: R. Kitzinger.

———. (1972). "Socio-economic classes in Babylonia and the Babylonian concept of social stratification." In *Compte Rendu, Recontre Assyriologique Internationale* 18 (Munich 1972), pp. 41-52.

———. (1975). "Ancient writing and ancient written language: Pitfalls and peculiarities in the study of Sumerian." In *Sumerological Studies in Honor of Thorkild Jacobsen on his Seventieth Birthday, June 7, 1974.* The Oriental Institute of the University of Chicago, Assyriological Studies, No. 20. Chicago: University of Chicago Press.

Diamond, Stanley (1974). *In Search of the Primitive: A Critique of Civilization.* New Brunswick, NJ: Transaction Books.

Dickerson, William Edwin Shapard (1965). *The White Path.* San Antonio: Naylor Co.

Dickson, H. R. P. (1949). *The Arab of the Desert.* London: George Allen and Unwin, Ltd.

Dietze, Gottfried (1960). *The Federalist: A Classic on Federalism and Free Government.* Baltimore: The Johns Hopkins Press.

Divale, William T. (1973). "Systematic population control in the Middle and Upper Paleolithic: Inferences based on contemporary hunter-gatherers." *World Archaeology* 4, pp. 222-243.

Dorsky, Susan (1986). *Women of Amran: A Middle Eastern Ethnographic Study.* Salt Lake City: University of Utah Press.

Douglas, Ann (1977). *The Feminization of American Culture.* New York: Avon Books.

Douglas, Mary (1966). *Purity and Danger: An Analysis of Concepts of Pollution and Taboo.* London: Routledge and K. Paul.

———. (1972). "Symbolic orders in the use of domestic space." In P. J. Ucko, R. Tringham, and G. W. Dimbleby, *Man, Settlement and Urbanism* (pp. 513-521). Proceedings of a meeting of the Research Seminar in Archaeology and Related Subjects held at the Institute of Archaeology, London University. London: Duckworth.

Draper, Patricia (1975). "!Kung Women: Contrasts in sexual egalitarianism in foraging and sedentary contexts." In R. R. Reiter, *Toward an Anthropology of Women* (pp. 77-109). New York and London: Monthly Review Press.

Driver, Godfrey Rolles and John C. Miles (1975). *The Assyrian Laws.* Edited with translation and commentary by Godfrey Rolles Driver and John C. Miles. Darmstadt: Scientia Verlag Aalen.

Dumond, D. E. (1972). "Population growth and political centralisation." In B. Spooner, *Population Growth: Anthropological Implications* (pp. 286-310). Cambridge, MA: University Press.

Dunton-Downer, Leslie (1989). "Feminist writing and the vulgar tongue: Kathy Acker's *Obscenics.*" *Harvard Graduate Society Newsletter* (Winter), pp. 7-10.

Durant, Will (1966). *The Life of Greece, The Story of Civilization: II.* New York: Simon and Schuster.

Dwyer, Daisy H. (1978). *Images and Self-Images: Male and Female in Morocco.* New York: Columbia University Press.

Dyckhoff, Christian B. (2002). "Priester und Priesterinnen im altbabylonischen Larsa. Das Amtsarchiv als Grundlage für prosopographische Forschung." In S. Parpola and R. M. Whiting, *Sex and Gender in the Ancient Near East: Proceedings of the 47th Rencontre Assyriologique Internationale, Helsinki, July 2-6, 2001,* Volume 1 (pp. 123-127). Helsinki: the Neo-Assyrian Text Corpus Project, two volumes.

Eisler, Riane (1987). *The Chalice and the Blade.* San Francisco: Harper and Row.

Ellis, Richard S. (1968). *Foundation Deposits in Ancient Mesopotamia.* New Haven, CT: Yale University Press.

el-Saadawi, Nawal (1980). *The Hidden Face of Eve: Women in the Arab World.* Boston: Beacon Press.

Emery, Theo (2003). "Female med school applicants surpass men." The Associated Press, December 5. Available at www.elisesutton.homestead.com/articles8 .html-75k.

Engels, Friedrich (1902). *The Origin of the Family, Private Property and the State.* Translated by Ernest Untermann. Chicago: H. Kerr and Co.

Epstein, David F. (1984). *The Political Theory of the Federalist.* Chicago: University of Chicago Press.

Ericksen, Anne Baye (2001). "Women of the Valley." *Graduating Engineer and Computer Careers Online.* Available at www.graduatingengineer.com/articles/ women/11-14-01.html.

Evans-Pritchard, E. E. (1973). "Foreword." In R. Needham, *Right and Left: Essays on Dual Symbolic Classification* (pp. ix-x) Chicago: University of Chicago Press.

Faegre, Torvald (1979). *Tents: Architecture of the Nomads.* Garden City, NY: Anchor Books.

Falkenstein, Adam (1958). "Enhedu'anna, die Tochter Sargons von Akkade." *Revue d'Assyriologie et d'Archéologie Orientale* 52:2, pp. 129-131.

———. (1974). *The Sumerian Temple City.* Los Angeles: Undena Publications.

Falkenstein, Adam and Wolfram von Soden (1953). *Sumerische und Akkadische Hymnen und Gebete.* Zürich: Artemis-Verlag.

Farrokhzād, Forūgh (1981). *Another Birth: Selected Poems of Forugh Farrokhzad.* Translated by Hassan Javadi and Susan Sallée. Emeryville, CA: Albany Press.

———. (1982). *Bride of the Acacias,* translated by Jascha Kessler with Amin Banani. Delmar, NY: Caravan Books.

Fernea, Elizabeth Warnock (1969). *Guests of the Sheik: An Ethnography of an Iraqi Village.* New York: Anchor Books.

———. (1976a). *A Street in Marrakesh.* New York: Anchor Books.

———. (1976b). *Women of Marrakesh.* Icarus Films.

Fernea, Elizabeth and Basima Qattan Bezirgan (1977). *Middle Eastern Muslim Women Speak.* Austin: University of Texas Press.

Fernea, Robert A. (1970). *Shaykh and Effendi: Changing Patterns of Authority Among the El Shabana of Southern Iraq.* Cambridge, MA: Harvard University Press.

Finkelstein, J.J. (1955). "Subartu and Subarians in old Babylonian sources." *Journal of Cuneiform Studies* 9, pp. 1-7.

———. (1966). "Sex offenses in Babylonian laws." *Journal of the American Oriental Society* 86, pp. 355-372.

Flannery, K. (1972). "The origins of the village as a settlement type in Mesoamerica and the Near East: A comparative study." In P. J. Ucko, R. Tringham, and G. W. Dimbleby, *Man, Settlement and Urbanism* (pp. 23-54). Proceedings of a meeting of the Research Seminar in Archaeology and Related Subjects held at the Institute of Archaeology, London University. London: Duckworth.

Flannery, Regina (1953-1957). *The Gros Ventres of Montana.* Washington: Catholic University of America Press, two volumes.

Foley, Helene P. (ed.) (1981). *Reflections of Women in Antiquity.* New York: Gordon and Breach Science Publishers.

Fontaine, C. (1989). "A heifer from thy stable: On goddesses and the status of women in the ancient Near East." *Union Seminary Quarterly Review* 43, pp. 67-91.

Forge, Anthony (1972). "Normative factors in the settlement size of Neolithic cultivators (New Guniea)." In P. J. Ucko, R. Tringham, and G. W. Dimbleby, *Man, Settlement and Urbanism* (pp. 365-376). Proceedings of a meeting of the Research Seminar in Archaeology and Related Subjects held at the Institute of Archaeology, London University. London: Duckworth.

Foster, Joseph Frederick (1969). *On Some Phonological Rules of Turkish.* Ann Arbor: University Microfilms International.

Frankfort, H. et al. (1949). *Before Philosophy: The Intellectual Adventure of Ancient Man.* Baltimore, MD: Penguin Books.

Freeman, Derek (1983). *Margaret Mead and Samoa: The Making and Unmaking of an Anthropological Myth.* Cambridge, MA: Harvard University Press.

Friedberg, Claudine (1977). "The development of traditional agricultural practices in Western Timor." In J. Friedman and M. J. Rowlands, *The Evolution of Social Systems* (pp. 137-171). London: Duckworth.

Friedl, Ernestine (1967). "The position of women: Appearance and reality." *Anthropological Quarterly* 40, p. 97.

Friedman, J. and M.J. Rowlands (1977). *The Evolution of Social Systems.* London: Duckworth.

Frisch, Rose and J. McArthur (1974). "Menstrual cycles: Fatness as a determinant of minimum weight for height necessary for their maintenance or onset." *Science* 185, pp. 949-951.

Fromm, Erich (1941 [1969]). *Escape from Freedom.* New York: Avon Books.

Gadd, C. J. (1954). "Inscribed prisms of Sargon II from Nimrud." *Iraq* XVI, p. 179.

Gardiner, Sir Alan (1957). *Egyptian Grammer,* Third Edition. Oxford: Griffith Institute, Ashmolean Museum.

Gardner, Gerald B. (2004). *Witchcraft Today.* Secaucus, NJ: Citadel Press.

Garnett, Lucy Mary Jane (1890-1891) *The Women of Turkey and Their Folklore.* London: D. Nutt, two volumes.

Gelb, Ignace J. (1956-). *Assyrian Dictionary.* Chicago: University of Chicago, Oriental Institute.

———. (1979). "Definition and discussion of slavery and serfdom." *Ugarit-Forschungen* 11, pp. 283-297.

Gibb, H.A.R. et. al (1960-). *The Encyclopaedia of Islam.* Leiden: Brill.

Gilbert, Alan E. (1976). *Religion and Society in Industrial England: Church, Chapel and Social Change 1740-1914.* London and New York: Longman.

Githongo, John (2001). "Iran is already fighting America's battle for it." *The East African.* September 17-September 24.

Glover, I. C. (1972). "Settlements and mobility among the hunter-gatherers of south-east Asia." In P. J. Ucko, R. Tringham, and G. W. Dimbleby, *Man, Settlement and Urbanism* (pp. 157-164). Proceedings of a meeting of the Research Seminar in Archaeology and Related Subjects held at the Institute of Archaeology, London University. London: Duckworth.

Godelier, Maurice (1977). "Politics as 'infrastructure': An anthropologist's thoughts on the example of classical Greece and the notions of relations of production and economic determination." In J. Friedman and M. J. Rowlands, *The Evolution of Social Systems* (pp. 13-28). London: Duckworth.

Goldberg, Steven (1973). *The Inevitability of Patriarchy.* New York: Morrow.

Goodman, Robert F. (1994). "Introduction." In R. F. Goodman and A. Ben-Ze'ev, *Good Gossip*. Lawrence, KS: University Press of Kansas.

Goodman, Robert F. and Aaron Ben-Ze'ev (1994). *Good Gossip*. Lawrence, KS: University Press of Kansas.

Gordon, Edmund Irwin (1959). *Sumerian Proverbs: Glimpses of Everyday Life in Ancient Mesopotamia*. Philadelphia: University Museum, University of Pennsylvania.

Graham, J. Walter (1966). "Origins and interrelations of the Greek house and the Roman house." *Phoenix* 20, p. 1.

Greenberg, David (1984). Personal communication.

Greer, Thomas H. (1977). *A Brief History of Western Man*. New York: Harcourt Brace Jovanovich.

Gribbin, John (1984). *In Search of Schrödinger's Cat: Quantum Physics and Reality*. Toronto: Bantam Books.

Griffin, Susan (1978). *Woman and Nature: The Roaring Inside Her*. New York: Harper and Row Publishers.

Gruppe, Otto (1906). *Griechische mythologie und religionsgeschichte*. München: Beck, two volumes.

Gwyn, W. B. (1965). *The Meaning of the Separation of Powers: An Analysis of the Doctrine from Its Origin to the Adoption of the United States Constitution*. Tulane Studies in Political Science, Vol. IX. New Orleans: Tulane University Press.

Haas, Mary (1944). "Men's and women's speech in Koasati." Reprinted in Haas, *Language Culture and History* (1978). Stanford, CA: Stanford University Press.

————. (1978). *Language, Culture and History*. Stanford: Stanford University Press.

Hallo, William W. (2002). "Love and marriage in Ashtata." In S. Parpola and R. M. Whiting, *Sex and Gender in the Ancient Near East: Proceedings of the 47th Recontre Assyriologique Internationale, Helsinki, July 2-6, 2001*, Volume 1 (pp. 203-216). Helsinki: the Neo-Assyrian Text Corpus Project, two volumes.

Hamblin, Dora Jane and the editors of Time-Life (1973). *The First Cities*. New York: Time-Life Books.

Harding, M. Esther (1971). *Women's Mysteries: Ancient and Modern*. New York: Harper and Row.

Hardy, Thomas (1978a). *Far from the Madding Crowd*. New York: Penguin.

————. (1978b). *Tess of the d'Urbervilles: A Pure Woman*. New York: Penguin.

Harner, Michael (1970). "Population pressure and the social evolution of agriculturalists." *Southwestern Journal of Anthropology* 26, pp. 67-86.

Harris, David R. (1972). "Swidden systems and settlement." In P. J. Ucko, R. Tringham, and G. W. Dimbleby, *Man, Settlement and Urbanism* (pp. 245-262). Proceedings of a meeting of the Research Seminar in Archaeology and Related Subjects held at the Institute of Archaeology, London University. London: Duckworth.

————. (1977). "Settling down: An evolutionary model for the transformation of mobile bands into sedentary communities." In J. Friedman and M.J. Rowlands, *The Evolution of Social Systems* (pp. 401-417). London: Duckworth.

Harris, Marvin (1974). *Cows, Pigs, Wars and Witches: The Riddles of Culture.* New York: Random House.

————. (1977). *Cannibals and Kings: The Origins of Cultures.* New York: Random House.

————. (1979). *Cultural Materialism: The Struggle for a Science of Culture.* New York: Random House.

————. (1985). *Good to Eat: Riddles of Food and Culture.* New York: Simon and Schuster.

————. (1989). *Our Kind.* New York: Harper and Row.

Harris, Rivkah (1962). "Biographical notes on the *Naditu* women of Nippur." *Journal of Cuneiform Studies* XVI, pp. 1-12.

————. (1963). "The organization and administration of the cloister in ancient Babylonia." *Journal of the Economic and Social History of the Orient* VI, pp. 121-157.

————. (1964). "The *Naditu* woman." In J.A., Brinkman, *Studies Presented to A.L. Oppenheim* (pp. 106-135). Chicago: University of Chicago, Oriental Institute.

————. (1975). *Ancient Sippar: A Demographic Study of an Old Babylonian City (1894-1595 BC).* Istanbul: Historisch-Archeologisch Institut.

Harrison, Dick (1998). *The Age of Abbesses and Queens: Gender and Political Culture in Early Medieval Europe.* Lund, Sweden: Nordic Academic Press.

Hart, John, Rita Sloan Berndt, and Alfonso Caramazza (1985). "Category-specific naming deficit following cerebral infarction." *Nature* 316 (August), pp. 439-440.

Hassall, M. C. W. (1972). "Roman urbanization in Western Europe." In P. J. Ucko, R. Tringham, and G. W. Dimbleby, *Man, Settlement and Urbanism* (pp. 857-861). Proceedings of a meeting of the Research Seminar in Archaeology and Related Subjects held at the Institute of Archaeology, London University. London: Duckworth.

Hay, Richard L. and Mary D. Leakey (1982). "The fossil footprints of Laetoli." *Scientific American* (February), pp. 50-57.

Hayden, Brian (1973). "Population control among hunter/gatherers." *World Archaeology* 4, pp. 205-221.

Hayes, John L. (2000). *A Manual of Sumerian Grammar and Texts,* Second Edition. Malibu: Undena Publications.

Hegel, G. W. F. (1929). *Selections.* New York: Charles Scribner's Sons.

Heinrich, Ernst (1931). *Fara.* Berlin: Walter Andrea.

Herodotus (1954). *The Histories,* translated by Aubrey de Sélincourt. Harmondsworth, UK: Penguin Books Inc.

Herzen, Alexander (1979). *From the Other Shore.* Oxford: Oxford University Press.

Hewlett, Sylvia Ann (1986). *A Lesser Life: The Myth of Women's Liberation in America.* New York: William Morrow and Company, Inc.

————. (1987). "When a husband walks out." *Parade Magazine* (June 7), pp. 4-5.

Hill, Harold D. (1967). "Tell Asmar: The private house area." In P. Delougaz, H. D. Hill, and S. Lloyd, *Private Houses and Graves in the Diyala Region* (pp. 143-181). The University of Chicago, Oriental Institute Publications, Vol. LXXXVIII. Chicago, IL: The University of Chicago Press.

Hillman, James (1983). *Interviews.* New York: Harper and Row.

Hirsch, Fred (1976). *Social Limits to Growth.* Cambridge, MA: Harvard University Press.

Hobhouse, Henry (1986). *Seeds of Change: Five Plants That Changed the World.* New York: Harper and Row.

Hobson, Sarah (1982). *Family Web: A Story of India.* Chicago: Academy Press.

Hodder, Ian (1998). "Discussion with the goddess community." Available at http://catalhoyuk.com/library/goddess.html.

Hodges, H. W. M. (1972). "Domestic building materials and ancient settlements." In P. J. Ucko, R. Tringham, and G. W. Dimbleby, *Man, Settlement and Urbanism* (pp. 523-530). Proceedings of a meeting of the Research Seminar in Archaeology and Related Subjects held at the Institute of Archaeology, London University, London: Duckworth.

Hofstadter, Douglas R. (1979). *Gödel, Escher, Bach: An Eternal Golden Braid.* New York: Vintage Books.

Honigmann, John J. (1957). "Women in West Pakistan." In S. Maron, *Pakistan: Society and Culture* (pp. 154-176). New Haven, CT: HRAF.

Houtsma, M. Th. et al. (1927). *The Encyclopedia of Islam.* Leyden: E. J. Brill.

Hoyt, Charles Alva (1981). *Witchcraft.* Carbondale and Edwardsville: Southern Illinois University Press.

Hughes, Muriel Joy (1943). *Women Healers in Medieval Life and Literature.* Freeport, NY: Books for Libraries Press.

Humphreys, S. C. (1977). "Evolution and history: Approaches to the study of structural differentiation." In J. Friedman and M. J. Rowlands, *The Evolution of Social Systems* (pp. 341-371). London: Duckworth.

Humphries, Jane (1977). "The working class family, women's liberation, and class struggle: The case of nineteenth century British history." *Review of Radical Political Economics* 9, pp. 25-41.

Hurgronje, C. Snouck (1931). *Mekka in the Latter Part of the 19th Century.* Leyden: E. J. Brill.

Ibn Khaldûn, (1958). *The Muqaddimah.* Translated by Franz Rosenthal. Princeton, NJ: Princeton University Press.

Illich, Ivan (1982). *Gender.* New York: Pantheon Books.

Isaac, Glynn L. (1972). "Comparative studies of Pleistocene site locations in East Africa." In P. J. Ucko, R. Tringham, and G. W. Dimbleby, *Man, Settlement and Urbanism* (pp. 165-176). Proceedings of a meeting of the Research Seminar in

Archaeology and Related Subjects held at the Institute of Archaeology, London University. London: Duckworth.

Jacobs, Jane (1969). *The Economy of Cities.* New York: Random House.

Jacobsen, Thorkild (1949). "Mesopotamia." In H. Frankfort et al., *Before Philosophy: The Intellectual Adventure of Ancient Man* (pp. 185-234). Baltimore, MD: Penquin Books.

―――. (1959). "Notes of selected sayings." In E. I. Gordon, *Sumerian Proverbs: Glimpses of Everyday Life in Ancient Mesopotamia* (pp. 447-487). Philadelphia: University Museum, University of Pennsylvania.

―――. (1973). "Notes on Nintun." *Orientalia* 42, p. 274.

Jacobsen, Thorkild and R. M. Adams (1958). "Salt and silt in ancient Mesopotamian agriculture." *Science* 128, pp. 1251-1258.

Jahan, Roushan (1988a). "Rokeya: An introduction to her life." In B. Rokeya, *"Sultana's Dream" and Selections from "The Secluded Ones"* (pp. 27-57). Edited and translated by Roushan Jahan. New York: The Feminist Press at The City University of New York.

Jahan, Roushan (1988b). *"The Secluded Ones:* Purdah observed" In B. Rokeya, *"Sultana's Dream" and Selections from "The Secluded Ones"* (pp. 19-23). Edited and translated by Roushan Jahan. New York: The Feminist Press at The City University of New York.

Jastrow, Morris (1921). "Veiling in ancient Assyria." *Revue Archeologique* 14 (Fifth Series), pp. 209-238.

Jaynes, Julian (1976). *The Origin of Consciousness in the Breakdown of the Bicameral Mind.* Boston: Houghton Mifflin.

Jean, Cynthia (2002). "Male and female supernatural assistants in Mesopotamian Magic." In S. Parpola and R. M. Whiting, *Sex and Gender in the Ancient Near East: Proceedings of the 47th Recontre Assyriologique International, Helsinki, July 2-6, 2001,* Volume 1 (pp. 255-261). Helsinki: the Neo-Assyrian Text Corpus Project, two volumes.

Jeremias, A. (1931). "Der Schleier von Sumer bis heute." *Der Alte Orient* 31, 1/2, pp. 1-70.

Johanson, Donald C. and Maitland A. Edey (1981). *Lucy: The Beginnings of Humankind.* New York: Simon and Schuster.

Johanson, Donald C. and James Shreeve (1989). *Lucy's Child: The Discovery of a Human Ancestor.* New York: William Morrow and Company, Inc.

Johnson, Allan Chester (1951). *Egypt and the Roman Empire.* Ann Arbor, MI: University of Michigan Press.

Johnson, Bobby H. (1976). *The Coushatta People.* Phoenix: Indian Tribal Series.

Johnson, Penelope D. (1991). *Equal in Monastic Profession: Religious Women in Medieval France.* Chicago: University of Chicago Press.

Jonas, Hans (1958). *The Gnostic Religion: The Message of the Alien God and the Beginings of Christianity,* Second Edition. Boston: Beacon Press.

Jones, A. H. M. (1964). *The Later Roman Empire, 284-602: A Social, Economic and Administrative Survey.* Norman, OK: University of Oklahoma Press.

Joseph, Suad (1978). "Women and the neighborhood street in Borj Hammoud, Lebanon." In L. Beck and N. Keddie, *Women in the Muslim World* (pp. 541-557). Cambridge, MA: Harvard University Press.

Kali for Women (eds.) (1987). *Truth Tales: Contemporary Writing by Indian Women.* New Dehli: Kali for Women.

Kassis, Hanna E. (1983). *A Concordance of the Qur'an.* Los Angeles: University of California Press.

Kaupp, P. Ann (1986). Personal communication.

Keddie, Nikki R. (1980). "Iran: Change in Islam; Islam in change." *International Journal of Middle Eastern Studies* II, pp. 527-542.

Keller, Werner (1956). *The Bible As History,* Second Edition. New York: William Morrow and Company, Inc.

Ki, Tsurayuki (1981). *The Tosa Diary.* Translated from the Japanese by William N. Porter. Rutland, VT: C. E. Tuttle.

Kirkbride, Diana (1966). "Five seasons at the pre-pottery neolithic village of Beidha in Jordan." *Palestine Exploration Quarterly* 98 (January-June), pp. 8-61.

———. (1967). "Beidha 1965: An interim report." *Palestine Exploration Quarterly* 99 (January-June), pp. 5-13.

Kitagawa, Chisato (1977). "A source of femininity in Japanese: In defense of Robin Lakoff's 'Language and Woman's Place.'" *Papers in Linguistics* 10, pp. 275-298.

Koch-Westenholz, Ulla (2002). "Everyday life of women according to first millennium omen apodoses." In S. Parpola and R. M. Whiting, *Sex and Gender in the Ancient Near East: Proceedings of the 47th Recontre Assyriologique International, Helsinki, July 2-6, 2001,* Volume 1 (pp. 301-309). Helsinki: the Neo-Assyrian Text Corpus Project, two volumes.

Kohl, Larry (1989). "Above China." *National Geographic* 175:3, pp. 278-311.

Kotker, Norman (1967). *The Holy Land in the Time of Jesus.* London: Cassell.

Kraeling, Carl Hermann (1967). *The Christian Building.* New Haven: Dura Europas Publications.

Kramer, Samuel Noah (1963). *Sumerians.* Chicago: University of Chicago Press.

———. (1969). *The Sacred Marriage Rite: Aspects of Faith, Myth and Ritual in Ancient Sumer.* Bloomington, IN: Indiana University Press.

Krecher, J. (1967). "Zum Emesal-Dialekt des Sumerischen." *Heidelberger Studier zum Alten Orient. Adam Falkenstein zum 17. September, 1966.* Wiesbaden, pp. 87-110.

Kundera, Milan (1980). *The Book of Laughter and Forgetting.* New York: A. A. Knopf.

———. (1984). *The Unbearable Lightness of Being.* New York: Harper and Row.

Labov, W. (1966). *The Social Stratification of English in New York City.* Washington, DC: Center for Applied Linguistics.

Lambert, Maurice (1956). "Les 'Réformes' d'Urukagina." *Revue d'Assyriologie et d'Archéologie Orientale* L:4, pp. 172-183.

Lambert, Wilfred G. (1969). "A Middle Assyrian Medical Text." *Iraq* 31, pp. 28-38.

Lao Tzu (1963). *Tao Te Ching*. Translated by D. C. Lau. Harmondsworth, Middlesex, England: Penguin Books.

Lapinkivi, Pirjo (2002). "The adorning of the bride: Providing her with wisdom." In S. Parpola and R. M. Whiting, *Sex and Gender in the Ancient Near East: Proceedings of the 47th Recontre Assyriologique International, Helsinki, July 2-6, 2001,* Volume 1 (pp. 327-335). Helsinki: the Neo-Assyrian Text Corpus Project, two volumes.

Layton, Robert (1972). "Settlement and community." In P. J. Ucko, R. Tringham, and G. W. Dimbleby, *Man, Settlement and Urbanism* (pp. 377-382). Proceedings of a meeting of the Research Seminar in Archaeology and Related Subjects held at the Institute of Archaeology, London University. London: Duckworth.

Leacock, Eleanor (1972). "Introduction" to F. Engels, *The Origin of the Family, Private Property and the State* (pp. 7-67). Chicago: H. Kerr and Co.

Lee, R. B. (1972). "Work effort, group structure and land use in contemporary hunter-gatherers." In P. J. Ucko, R. Tringham, and G. W. Dimbleby, *Man, Settlement and Urbanism* (pp. 177-185). Proceedings of a meeting of the Research Seminar in Archaeology and Related Subjects held at the Institute of Archaeology, London University. London: Duckworth.

———. (1979). *The !Kung San*. Cambridge: Cambridge University Press.

Lee, Richard and I. De Vore (eds.) (1968). *Man the Hunter*. Chicago: Aldine.

Lerner, Gerda (1986). *The Creation of Patriarchy*. New York: Oxford University Press.

Lévi-Strauss, Claude (1963). *Structural Anthropology*. New York: Basic Books, Inc.

Levy, Reuben (1957). *The Social Structure of Islam*. Cambridge: Cambridge University Press.

Lewin, Bernhard (1978). *A Vocabulary of the Hudailian Poems*. Göteberg: Kungl. Vetenskaps- och Vitterhets-Samhället.

Lewis, Naphtali (1968). *Inventory of Compulsory Services in Ptolomaic and Roman Egypt*. New Haven, CT: American Society of Papyrologists.

Liefrinck, F. A. (1969). "Rice cultivation in northern Bali." In *Bali, Further Studies in Life, Thought and Ritual*. The Hague: Van Hoeve.

Lindsay, Jack (1963). *Daily Life in Roman Egypt*. London: Frederick Muller.

Lipinski, E. (1975). *Studies in Aramaic Inscriptions and Onomastics*. Leuven: Leuven University Press.

Lloyd, Seton (1967). "The Northern Palace area." In P. Delougaz, H. D. Hill, and S. Lloyd, *Private Houses and Graves in the Diyala Region* (pp. 181-195). The University of Chicago, Oriental Institute Publications, Vol. LXXXVIII. Chicago, IL: The University of Chicago Press.

Lloyd, Seton and Fuad Safar (1945). "Tell Hassuna: Excavations by the Iraq government Directorate General of Antiquities in 1943 and 1944." *Journal of Near Eastern Studies* 4:4 pp. 255-289.

Locke, John (1952). *The Second Treatise of Government.* New York: The Liberal Arts Press.

Loewenberg, J. (1929). "Introduction." In G. W. F. Hegel, *Selections* (pp. ix-xliii). New York: Charles Scribner's Sons.

Longman, Chia (2002). "Dynamics of sex, gender and culture: The Native American Berdache or 'two-spirit people' in discourse and context." In B. Saunders and M.-C. Foblets, *Changing Genders in Intercultural Perspectives* (pp. 121-153). Leuven: Leuven University Press

Lovejoy, C. O. (1974). "The gait of Australopithecines." *Yearbook of Physical Anthropology* 17, pp. 147-161.

———. (1980). "Hominid origins: The role of bipedalism." *American Journal of Physical Anthropology* 52 (February), p. 250.

Lucian (1976). *The Syrian Goddess.* Translated by Harold W. Attridge and Robert A. Oden. Missoula, MT: Scholars Press for the Society of Biblical Literature.

Mabro, Judy (1991). *Veiled Half-Truths: Western Travellers' Perceptions of Middle Eastern Women.* London and New York: I.B. Tauris and Co., Ltd.

Macfarlane, Alan (1970). *Witchcraft in Tudor and Stuart England.* London: Routledge and Kegan Paul.

MacMullen, R. (1976). *The Roman Government's Response to Crisis, A.D. 235-337.* New Haven, CT: Yale University Press.

Madison, James, Alexander Hamilton, and John Jay (1976). *The Federalist.* Introduction by Edward Mead Earle. Washington, New York: Robert B. Luce, Inc.

Maekawa, K. (1980). "Female weavers and their children." *Acta Sumerologica* 2, pp. 81-125.

Mahfouz, Naguib (1990). *Palace Walk.* Translated by William Maynard Hutchins and Olive E. Kenny. New York: Anchor Books.

Malcolm, Andrew H. (1986). *Final Harvest: An American Tragedy.* New York: New American Library.

Mallory, J. P. (1989). *In Search of the Indo-Europeans: Language, Archaeology and Myth.* London: Thames and Hudson, Ltd.

Marmon, Shaun Elizabeth (1995). *Eunuchs and Sacred Boundaries in Islamic Society.* New York: Oxford University Press.

Maron, S. (1957). *Pakistan: Society and Culture.* New Haven, CT: HRAF.

Marshall, Susan Elaine (1980). *The Power of the Veil: The Politics of Female Status in North Africa.* Dissertation from the University of Massachusetts.

Martiny, Günter (1966). "Die Gegensätze im Babylonischer und Assyrischer Tempelbau." *Abhandlungen für die Kunde des Morgenlandes* XXI, p. 3.

Marx, Karl (1977). *Capital, Volume One.* New York: Vintage Books.

Marx, Karl and Friedrich Engels (1964). *The Communist Manifesto,* translated by Samuel Moore. New York: Washington Square Press.

Mayr-Harting, H. (1975). "Functions of a twelfth-century recluse." *History* 60 (October), pp. 337-352.

McCormick, John (1987). "Diet for a poisoned planet." *Greenpeace* 12:3 (July-September), pp. 17ff.

McLaren, Angus (1990). *A History of Contraception: From Antiquity to the Present.* Oxford: Blackwell.

Mellaart, James (1967). *Çatal Hüyük: A Neolithic Town in Anatolia.* London: Thames and Hudson.

Menges, Karl H. (1968). *The Turkic Languages and Peoples: An Introduction to Turkic Studies.* Ural-Altaische Bibliotek XV, Wies-baden: Harrassowitz.

Mentley, Ruth (1988). Personal communication.

Merchant, Carolyn (1980). *The Death of Nature.* San Francisco: Harper and Row.

Mernissi, Fatima (1994). *Dreams of Trespass.* Reading, MA, and New York: Addison-Wesley Publishing Co.

Miller, Barnette (1931). *Beyond the Sublime Porte.* New Haven, CT: Yale University Press.

Miller, Jean Baker (1986). *Toward a New Psychology of Women,* Second Edition. Boston: Beacon Press.

Morgan, Robin (1984). *Sisterhood Is Global: The International Women's Movement Anthology.* Garden City, NY: Anchor Press, Doubleday.

———. (1989). *The Demon Lover: Or the Sexuality of Terrorism.* New York: Norton.

Müller, Valentin (1940). "Types of Mesopotamian houses." *Journal of the American Oriental Society* 60, pp. 151-180.

Mumford, Lewis (1961). *City in History: Its Origins, Its Transformations, and Its Prospects.* New York: Harcourt Brace Jovanovich.

Munroe, R. L., J. W. M. Whiting, and D. J. Hally (1969). "Institutional male transvestism and sex distinctions." *American Anthropologist* 71, pp. 87-90.

Murphy, Robert F. (1970). "Social distance and the veil [Tuareg]." In L. E. Sweet, *Peoples and Cultures of the Middle East,* Vol. 1 (pp. 290-314). Garden City, NY: The Natural History Press.

Musil, Alois (1928). *The Manners and Customs of the Rwala Bedouins.* New York: American Geographical Society.

Nafisi, Azar (2003). *Reading Lolita in Tehran: A Memoir in Books.* New York: Random House.

National Association for Single-Sex Public Education. Available at http://www.singlesexschools.org.

Needham, Rodney (1973). *Right and Left: Essays on Dual Symbolic Classification.* Chicago: University of Chicago Press.

———. (1979). *Symbolic Classification.* Santa Monica, CA: Goodyear Publishing Co.

Nelson, Cynthia (1974). "Public and private politics: Women in the Middle Eastern world." *American Ethnologist,* pp. 551-563.

Oates, Joan (1969). "Choga Mani, 1967-68: A preliminary report." *Iraq* 31:2(Autumn), pp. 115-152.

———. (1977). "Mesopotamian social organization: Archaeological and philological evidence." In J. Friedman and M. J. Rowlands, *The Evolution of Social Systems* (pp. 457-485). London: Duckworth.

O'Laughlin, Bridget (1975). "Marxist approaches in anthropology." *Annual Review of Anthropology* 4, pp. 341-370.

Ophuls, William (1977). *Ecology and the Politics of Scarcity: Prologue to a Political Theory of the Steady State.* San Francisco: W. H. Freeman.

Oppenheim, A. Leo (1948). "Catalogue of the cuneiform tablets of the Wilberforce Eames Babylonian Collection in the New York Public Library." *American Oriental Series,* Volume 32. New Haven: American Oriental Society.

———. (1964). *Ancient Mesopotamia: Portrait of a Dead Civilization.* Chicago: University of Chicago Press.

Ornan, Tallay (2002). "The queen in public: Royal women in neo-Assyrian art." In S. Parpola and R. M. Whiting, *Sex and Gender in the Ancient Near East: Proceedings of the 47th Recontre Assyriologique Internationale, Helsinki, July 2-6, 2001,* Volume 2 (pp. 461-477). Helsinki: The Neo-Assyrian Text Corpus Project, two volumes.

Ostrogorsky, George (1957). *History of the Byzantine State.* New Brunswick, NJ: Rutgers University Press.

Page, Hilary (1975). "Fertility levels: Patterns and trends." In J. C. Caldwell, *Population Growth and Socioeconomic Change in West Africa* (pp. 29-57). New York: Columbia University Press.

Pagels, Elaine (1979). *The Gnostic Gospels.* New York: Random House.

Palmer, Anne (1989). "Day-care infants more at risk to problems, says doctor." *The Salt Lake Tribune* (June).

Papanek, Hanna (1971). "Purdah in Pakistan: Seclusion and modern occupations for women." *Journal of Marriage and the Family* 33:3 (August) pp. 517-530.

———. (1988). "Caging the lion: A fable for our time." Afterword to B. Rokeya, *"Sultana's Dream" and Selections from "The Secluded Ones"* (pp. 58-85). Edited and translated by Roushan Jahan. New York: The Feminist Press at The City University of New York.

Parpola, Simo and R. M. Whiting (2002). *Sex and Gender in the Ancient Near East: Proceedings of the 47th Rencontre Assyriologique Internationale, Helsinki, July 2-6, 2001.* Helsinki: The Neo-Assyrian Text Corpus Project, two volumes.

Parsons, Talcott (1960). *Structure and Process in Modern Societies.* Glencoe, IL: Free Press.

Pastner, Carroll McC. (1972). "A social structural sand historical analysis of honor, shame and purdah." *Anthropological Quarterly,* pp. 248-261.

———. (1974). "Accommodations to Purdah: The female perspective." *Journal of Marriage and the Family* 36 (May), pp. 408-414.

Paulme, Denise (1971). *Women in Tropical Africa.* Berkeley: University of California.

Pauly, August Friedrich von (1894-1919). *Pauly's Real-encyclopädie der Classischer Altertumswissenschaft.* Stuttgart: J. B. Metzler.

Pearce, Joseph Chilton (1977). *Magical Child.* New York: E. P. Dutton, Inc.

Pearson, Carol Lynn (1992). "Healing the motherless house." In *Women and Authority: Re-Emerging Mormon Feminism,* edited by Maxine Hanks. Salt Lake City, UT: Signature Books.

Pehrson, Robert N. (1966). *The Social Organization of the Marri Baluch.* Chicago: Aldine Publishing Co.

Peirce, Leslie Penn (1993). *The Imperial Harem: Women and Sovereignty in the Ottoman Empire.* New York: Oxford University Press.

Pierce, Joe E. (1964a). *A Frequency Count of Turkish Words.* Georgetown: Georgetown University Language Program.

———. (1964b). *Life in a Turkish Village.* New York: Holt, Rinehart and Winston.

———. (1975). *Languages and Linguistics.* The Hague: Mouton.

Piggott, Stuart (1965). *Ancient Europe from the Beginnings of Agriculture to Classical Antiquity.* Chicago: Aldine Publishing Co.

———. (1972). "Conclusion." In P. J. Ucko, R. Tringham, and G. W. Dimbleby, *Man, Settlement and Urbanism* (pp. 947-952). Proceedings of a meeting of the Research Seminar in Archaeology and Related Subjects held at the Institute of Archaeology, London University. London: Duckworth.

Pitt-Rivers, Julian (1977). *The Fate of Sehchem, or the Politics of Sex: Essays in the Anthropology of the Mediterranean.* Cambridge: Cambridge University Press.

Plato (1920). *Republic, Parmenides* and *Timeaus* in *The Dialogues of Plato.* Translated by B. Jowett. New York: Random House, Inc.

Polanyi, Karl (1944). *The Great Transformation.* Boston: Beacon Press.

Pomeroy, Sarah (1975). *Goddesses, Whores, Wives and Slaves: Women in Classical Antiquity.* New York: Schocken Books.

Porter, Barbara Nevling (2002). "Beds, sex, and politics: The return of Marduk's bed to Babylon." In S. Parpola and R. M. Whiting, *Sex and Gender in the Ancient Near East: Proceedings of the 47th Recontre Assyriologique Internationale, Helsinki, July 2-6, 2001,* Volume 2 (pp. 523-535). Helsinki: The Neo-Assyrian Text Corpus Project, two volumes.

Postgate, J. N. (1972). "The role of the temple in the Mesopotamian secular community." In P. J. Ucko, R. Tringham, and G. W. Dimbleby, *Man, Settlement and Urbanism* (pp. 811-825). Proceedings of a meeting of the Research Seminar in Archaeology and Related Subjects held at the Institute of Archaeology, London University. London: Duckworth.

Pritchard, James B. (1969). *Ancient Near Eastern Texts Relating to the Old Testament,* Third Edition. Princeton, NJ: Princeton University Press.

————. (1975). *The Ancient Near East,* Vol II. Chichester, UK: Princeton University Press. Available at http://www.gatewaystobabylon.com/myths/texts/enheduanna/ninmesara.htm.

Rapoport, Amos (1969). *House Form and Culture.* Englewood Cliffs, NJ: Prentice-Hall, Inc.

Rappaport, Roy A. (1968). *Pigs for the Ancestors: Ritual in the Ecology of a New Guinea People.* New Haven, CT: Yale University Press.

————. (1977a). "Maladaption in social systems." In J. Friedman and M. J. Rowlands, *The Evolution of Social Systems* (pp. 49-17). London: Duckworth.

————. (1977b). "Normative models of adaptive processes: A response to Anne Whyte." In J. Friedman and M. J. Rowlands, *The Evolution of Social Systems* (pp. 79-87). London: Duckworth.

Rausch, Margaret (2000). *Bodies, Boundaries and Spirit Possession: Moroccan Women and the Revision of Tradition.* Bielefeld: Transcript Verlag.

Ravenholt, Albert (1973). "Man-land-productivity microdynamics in rural Bali." *American University Fieldstaff Reports. Southeast Asia Series.* XXXI(4).

Re'emi, S. Paul (1985). "The faithfulness of God: A commentary on the Book of Esther." In R. J. Coggins, *Israel Among the Nations: A Commentary on the Books of Nahum, Obadiah and Esther by S. Paul Re'emi* (pp. 103-140). Edinburgh: Handsel Press.

Reiter, Rayna R. (1975). *Toward an Anthropology of Women.* New York and London: Monthly Review Press.

Renfrew, Colin (1977). "Space, time and polity." In J. Friedman and M. J. Rowlands, *The Evolution of Social Systems* (pp. 89-112). London: Duckworth.

Renger, Johannes (1969). "Untersuchungen zum Priestertum der altbabylonischer Zeit." *Zeitshcrift für Assyriologie und Vorder-asiatische Archäologie,* NS 25.

Reuther, Oskar (1910). *Das Wohnhaus in Bagdad und anderem Städter des Irak.* Berlin: E. Wasmuth.

————. (1968). *Die Innenstadt von Babylon.* Osnabrück: Zeller.

Reyna, S. P. and Christian Bouquet (1975). "Chad." In J. C. Caldwell, *Population Growth and Socioeconomic Change in West Africa* (pp. 565-581). New York: Columbia University Press.

Reynolds, Vernon (1972). "Ethnology of urban life." In P. J. Ucko, R. Tringham, and G. W. Dimbleby, *Man, Settlement and Urbanism* (pp. 401-408). Proceedings of a meeting of the Research Seminar in Archaeology and Related Subjects held at the Institute of Archaeology, London University. London: Duckworth.

Rich, Adrienne (1979). *On Lies, Secrets and Silence.* New York: W. W. Norton.

Rindos, David (1984). *The Origins of Agriculture: An Evolutionary Perspective.* Orlando, FL: Academic Press.

Rokeya, Begum (1988). *"Sultana's Dream" and Selections from "The Secluded Ones."* Edited and translated by Roushan Jahan, afterword by Hanna Papanek. New York: The Feminist Press at The City University of New York.

Rosen, Lawrence (1978). "The negotiation of reality: Male-female relations in Sefrou, Morocco." In L. Beck and N. Keddie, *Women in the Muslim World* (pp. 561-584). Cambridge, MA: Harvard University Press.

Roux, Georges (1980). *Ancient Iraq,* Second Edition. Harmondsworth, Middlesex, England: Penguin Books.

Rubbo, Anna (1975). "The spread of capitalism in rural Colombia: Effects on poor women." In R. R. Reiter, *Toward an Anthropology of Women* (pp. 333-357). New York and London: Monthly Review Press.

Rushdie, Salman (1988). *The Satanic Verses.* New York: Viking.

Samons, Loren J., II (2004). *What's Wrong with Democracy.* Berkeley and Los Angeles: University of California Press.

Saunders, Barbara and Marie-Claire Foblets (2002). *Changing Genders in Intercultural Perspectives.* Leuven: Leuven University Press.

Schiffer, Michael B. (1984). *Advances in Archaeological Method and Theory,* Volume 7. Orlando, FL: Academic Press.

Schor, Juliet B. (2004). *Born to Buy.* New York: Scribner.

Schretter, Manfred (1990). *Emesal Studien: Sprach- und literaturgeschichtliche Untersuchungen zur sogenannten Frauensprache des Sumerischen.* Innsbruck: Innsbrucker Beiträge zur Kulturwissenschaft, Sonderheft 69.

Schwerdtfeger, Friedrich W. (1972). "Urban settlement patterns in northern Nigeria." In P. J. Ucko, R. Tringham, and G. W. Dimbleby, *Man, Settlement and Urbanism* (pp. 547-556). Proceedings of a meeting of the Research Seminar in Archaeology and Related Subjects held at the Institute of Archaeology, London University. London: Duckworth.

Sefati, Yitschak (1998). *Love Songs in Sumerian Literature.* Jerusalem: Bar-Ilan University Press.

Seidenberg, Robert and Karen DeCrow (1983). *Women Who Marry Houses: Panic and Protest in Agoraphobia.* New York: McGraw-Hill.

Severin, Tim (1985). "Jason's voyage: In search of the golden fleece." *National Geographic* 168:3 (September).

Seyrig, Henri (1934). "Antiquités Syriennes." *Syria* 15, pp. 155-186.

Shaker, Fatina Amin (1972). *Modernization of the Developing Nations: The Case of Saudi Arabia.* Ann Arbor, MI: University Microfilms International.

Shepherd, Gill (1978). "Transsexualism in Oman?" *Man* 13:1 (March), pp. 133-134.

Shepherd, Gill, G. Feuerstein, S. Al-Marzooq, and Unni Wikan (1978). "The Omani *xanith.*" *Man,* New Series, 13:4 (December), pp. 663-671.

Shibamoto, Janet S. (1985). *Japanese Women's Language.* Orlando, FL: Academic Press, Inc.

Silverstein, Roberta (2000). "Silicon Valley boardrooms still short of women." *Silicon Valley/San Jose Business Journal.* Available at http://sanjose.bizjournals .com/sanjose/stories/2000/08/07/focus3.html.

Silvestri, Domenico (1976). "Appunti sulla eme.sal sumerica." *Instituto orientale di Napoli, Annali* n.s. 26:2=36:213-221.

Simoons, Frederick J. (1979). "Dairying, milk use, and lactose malabsorption in Eurasia." *Anthropos* 74, pp. 61-80.

Sjöberg, Åke W. (1967). "Zu einiger Verwandtschaftsbezeichnungen im Sumerischen." *Heidelberger Studien zur Alten Orient* 237, pp. 201-231.

Slocum, Sally (1975). "Woman the gatherer: Male bias in anthropology." In R. R. Reiter, *Toward an Anthropology of Women* (pp. 36-50). New York and London: Monthly Review Press.

Smith, H. S. (1972). "Society and settlement in ancient Egypt." In P. J. Ucko, R. Tringham, and G. W. Dimbleby, *Man, Settlement and Urbanism* (pp. 705-719). Proceedings of a meeting of the Research Seminar in Archaeology and Related Subjects held at the Institute of Archaeology, London University. London: Duckworth.

Smith, M. G. (1972). "Complexity, size and urbanization." In P. J. Ucko, R. Tringham, and G. W. Dimbleby, *Man, Settlement and Urbanism* (pp. 567-574). Proceedings of a meeting of the Research Seminar in Archaeology and Related Subjects held at the Institute of Archaeology, London University. London: Duckworth.

Smith, Philip E. L. (1972). "Land-use, settlement patterns and subsistence agriculture: A demographic perspective" In P. J. Ucko, R. Tringham, and G. W. Dimbleby, *Man, Settlement and Urbanism* (pp. 409-425). Proceedings of a meeting of the Research Seminar in Archaeology and Related Subjects held at the Institute of Archaeology, London University. London: Duckworth.

Snyder, Gary (1980). *The Real Work*. Edited with an introduction by William Scott McLean. New York: New Directions Publishing Corp.

Solzhenitsyn, Aleksandr I. (1975). *The Gulag Archipelago,* Volume II. New York: Harper and Row.

Spain, Daphne (1992). *Gendered Spaces*. Chapel Hill and London: University of North Carolina Press.

Spooner, B. (1972). *Population Growth: Anthropological Implications*. Cambridge, MA: University Press.

Springer, Sally P. and George Deutsch (1981). *Left Brain, Right Brain*. San Francisco: W. H. Freeman and Co.

Stanley, Autumn (1981). "Daughters of Isis, Daughters of Demeter: When women sowed and reaped." *Women's Studies International Quarterly* 4:3, pp. 289-304.

Starhawk (1979). *Spiral Dance*. San Francisco: Harper and Row.

Steinmueller, John E. and Kathryn Sullivan (1959). *Catholic Biblical Encyclopedia*. New York: J. F. Wagner, two volumes.

Stewart, Desmond et al. (1967). *Early Islam*. New York: Time Incorporated.

Stigers, Eva Stehle (1981). "Sappho's private world." In H. P. Foley, *Reflections of Women in Antiquity* (pp. 45-61). New York: Gordon and Breach Science Publishers.

Stone, Merlin (1976). *When God Was a Woman*. New York: Harcourt Brace Jovanovich.

Strecker, Ivo (1996). "Do the Hamar have a concept of honor?" In *Proceedings of the Xth Conference of Ethiopian Studies* (pp. 419-429). Ed. by Eric Godet et al. Paris. Available at http://www/ifeas.uni-mainz.de/ethno/kulturanthro_afrika/ concept_of_honor.html.

Suggs, David N. and Andrew W. Miracle (1993). *Culture and Human Sexuality: A Reader*. Pacific Grove, CA: Brooks/Cole Pub. Co.

Sweet, Louise E. (1970). *Peoples and Cultures of the Middle East,* Volumes I-II. Garden City, NY: The Natural History Press.

Tainter, J. A. (1988). *The Collapse of Complex Societies*. Cambridge, UK: Cambridge University Press.

Tannen, Deborah (1990). *You Just Don't Understand: Women and Men in Conversation*. New York: William Morrow.

Tate, William Edward (1967). *The English Village Community and the Enclosure Movements*. London: Gollancz.

Tavard, George H. (1973). *Woman in Christian Tradition*. Notre Dame, IN: University of Notre Dame Press.

Tellenbach, Gerd (1959). *Church, State and Christian Society at the Time of the Investiture Contest*. New York: Harper and Row.

Tertullian (1956). *De oratione et De virginibus velandis libelli*. Ed. by G. F. Diercks. Ultraiecti: In aedibus Spectrum.

Thayer, James Steel (1980). "The berdache of the Northern Plains: A sociological perspective." *Journal of Anthropological Research* 36:3 (Fall), pp. 287-293.

Thesiger, Wilfred (1959). *Arabian Sands*. London: Longmans.

Thompson, Thomas L. (1999). *The Mythic Past*. London: Basic Books.

Thorne, Barrie and Nancy Henley (1975). *Language and Sex: Difference and Dominance*. Rowley, MA: Newbury House Publishers.

Törries, F. (1963). *Community and Society, Gemeinschaft und Gesellschaft*. New York: Harper and Row.

Trigger, Bruce G. (1968). *Beyond History: The Methods of Prehistory*. New York: Holt, Rinehart and Winston.

―――. (1972). "Determinants of urban growth in pre-industrial societies." In P. J. Ucko, R. Tringham, and G. W. Dimbleby, *Man, Settlement and Urbanism* (pp. 575-600). Proceedings of a meeting of the Research Seminar in Archaeology and Related Subjects held at the Institute of Archaeology, London University. London: Duckworth.

Trudgill, Peter (1972). "Sex, covert prestige and linguistic change in the urban British English of Norwich." *Language in Society* I, pp. 179-195.

Turner, Bryan S. (1984). *Capitalism and Class in the Middle East: Theories of Social Change and Economic Development*. London: Heinemann.

Turner, Michael (1984). *Enclosure in Britain 1750-1830*. London: Macmillan Press.

Uchitel, Alexander (1984a). "Daily work at Sagdana millhouse." *Acta Sumerologica* 6, pp. 75-98.

———. (1984b). "Women at work: Pylos and Knosses, Lagash and Ur." *Historia* 33, pp. 257-282.

Ucko, Peter J., Ruth Tringham, and G. W. Dimbleby (1972a). "Preface" in *Man, Settlement and Urbanism.* Proceedings of a meeting of the Research Seminar in Archaeology and Related Subjects held at the Institute of Archaeology, London University. London: Duckworth.

———. (1972b). *Man, Settlement and Urbanism.* Proceedings of a meeting of the Research Seminar in Archaeology and Related Subjects held at the Institute of Archaeology, London University. London: Duckworth.

Uluçay, M. Çağatay (1959). "The harem in the XVIIIth century." *Akten des Vierundzwanzigsten Internationaler Orientalisten-Kongresses, München, 28. August bis 4. September, 1957.*

Venarde, Bruce L. (1996). "*Praesidentes negotiis:* Abbesses as managers in twelfth-century France." In S. K. Cohn and S. A. Epstein, *Portraits of Medieval and Renaissance Living: Essays in Memory of David Herlihy* (pp. 189-205). Ann Arbor: University of Michigan Press.

Villiers, Alan (1970). "Some aspects of the Arab dhow trade." In L. E. Sweet, *Peoples and Cultures of the Middle East,* Vol. 1 (pp. 155-172). Garden City, NY: The Natural History Press.

Volterra, Vito (1931). *Leçons sur la Théorie Mathématique de la Lutte pour la Vie.* Paris: Gauthier-Villars et Cie.

von Bertalanffy, Ludwig (1968). *General System Theory: Foundations, Development, Applications.* New York: George Braziller.

von Oppenheim, Max F. (1908). "Tell-Halaf und die verschleierte Göttin." *Die Alte Orient* X, 1, pp. 36-43.

Vreede-de Stuers, Cora (1968). *Parda: A Study of Muslim Women's Life in Northern India.* Assen: Van Gorcum.

Wachtel, Paul L. (1989). *The Poverty of Affluence.* Philadelphia: New Society Publishers.

Warner, W. L. (1964). *A Black Civilization.* New York: Harper.

Washburn, S. L. and Ruth Moore (1974). *Ape into Man: A Study of Human Evolution.* Boston: Little, Brown and Co.

Wasilewska, Ewa (1987). Personal communication.

Watt, William Montgomery (1956). *Mohammad at Medina.* Oxford: Clarendon Press.

Watts, Alan (1958). *Nature, Man and Woman.* New York: Pantheon Books, Inc.

Weadock, Penelope (1975). "The Giparu at Ur." *Iraq* 37, pp. 101-137.

Weidner, Ernst (1954-1956)."Hof- und Harems-Erlasse assyrischer Könige aus dem 2. Jahrtausend v. Chr." *Archiv für Orientforschung* 17, p. 273.

Weinbaum, Batya (1977). "Redefining the question of revolution." *Review of Radical Political Economics* 9, pp. 54-77.

West, W. A. (1972). "The effect of private and public law in the use and development of land." In P. J. Ucko, R. Tringham, and G. W. Dimbleby, *Man, Settlement and Urbanism* (pp. 477-486). Proceedings of a meeting of the Research Seminar in Archaeology and Related Subjects held at the Institute of Archaeology, London University. London: Duckworth.

Wheatley, P. (1972). "The concept of urbanism." In P. J. Ucko, R. Tringham, and G. W. Dimbleby, *Man, Settlement and Urbanism* (pp. 601-637). Proceedings of a meeting of the Research Seminar in Archaeology and Related Subjects held at the Institute of Archaeology, London University. London: Duckworth.

White, Tim D. and Gen Suwa (1987). "Hominid footprints at Laetoli: Facts and interpretations." *American Journal of Physical Anthropology* 72 (April), pp. 485-514.

Whittaker, Gordon (2002). "Linguistic anthropology and the study of Emesal as (a) women's language." In S. Parpola and R. M. Whiting, *Sex and Gender in the Ancient Near East: Proceedings of the 47th Recontre Assyriologique Internationale, Helsinki, July 2-6, 2001*, Volume 2 (pp. 633-644). Helsinki: The Neo-Assyrian Text Corpus Project, two volumes.

Wikan, Unni (1977). "Man becomes woman: Transsexualism in Oman as a key to gender roles." *Man,* New Series, 12:2 (August), pp. 304-319.

———. (1978). "The Omani *xanith*: A third gender role?" *Man* 13:3 (September), pp. 473-475.

Wilson, Peter Lamborn (2003). Personal communication.

Winkler, Jack (1981). "Gardens of nymphs: Public and private in Sappho's lyrics." In H. P. Foley, *Reflections of Women in Antiquity* (pp. 63-89). New York: Gordon and Breach Science Publications.

Wirth, L. (1938). "Urbansim as a way of life." *American Journal of Sociology,* 44.

Wood, Michael (1985). *In Search of the Trojan War.* New York: Facts on File Publications.

Woodburn, James (1972). "Ecology, nomadic movement and the composition of the local group among hunters and gatherers." In P. J. Ucko, R. Tringham, and G. W. Dimbleby, *Man, Settlement and Urbanism* (pp. 193-206). Proceedings of a meeting of the Research Seminar in Archaeology and Related Subjects held at the Institute of Archaeology, London University. London: Duckworth.

Woodham-Smith, Cecil (1962). *The Great Hunger: Ireland 1845-1849.* New York: Harper and Row.

Woolfson, Charles (1982). *The Labour Theory of Culture.* London: Routledge and Kegan Paul.

Wright, G. R. H. (1985). *Ancient Building in South Syria and Palestine,* Volume I-II. Leiden-Köln: E. J. Brill.

Wright, Henry T. (1969). "The administration of rural production in an early Mesopotamian town." *Museum of Anthropology, University of Michigan, Anthrological Papers,* no. 38.

Yellen, John and Henry Harpending (1973). "Hunter-gatherer populations and archaeological inference." *World Archaeology* 4, pp. 244-253.

Young, Gavin (1980). *Iraq: Land of Two Rivers*. London: Collins.

Young, T. C., Jr. (1972). "Population densities and early Mesopotamian urbanism." In P. J. Ucko, R. Tringham, and G. W. Dimbleby, *Man, Settlement and Urbanism* (pp. 827-842). Proceedings of a meeting of the Research Seminar in Archaeology and Related Subjects held at the Institute of Archaeology, London University. London: Duckworth.

Youssef, Nadia H. (1978). "The status and fertility patterns of Muslim women." In L. Beck and N. Keddie, *Women in the Muslim World* (pp. 69-99). Cambridge, MA: Harvard University Press.

Zagarell, Allen (1986a). "Reply" In A. Zagarell, "Trade, women, class and society in ancient Western Asia." *Current Anthropology* 27:5, pp. 426-428

———. (1986b). "Trade, women, class and society in ancient Western Asia." *Current Anthropology* 27:5, pp. 415-420.

Zborowski, Mark and Elizabeth Herzog (1952). *Life Is with People: The Culture of the Shtetl*. New York: Schocken Books.

Ziffer, Irit (2002). "Four new belts from the Land of Ararat and the Feast of Women in Esther 1:9." In S. Parpola and R. M. Whiting, *Sex and Gender in the Ancient Near East: Proceedings of the 47th Recontre Assyriologique Internationale, Helsinki, July 2-6, 2001,* Volume 2 (pp. 645-657). Helsinki: The Neo-Assyrian Text Corpus Project, two volumes.

Zipes, Jack David (1983). *The Trials and Tribulations of Little Red Riding Hood: Versions of the Tale in Sociological Perspective*. South Hadley, MA: J. F. Bergin Publishers.

Zwettler, Michael (1978). *The Oral Tradition of Classical Arabic Poetry*. Columbus: Ohio State University Press.

Index

Page numbers followed by the letter "i" indicate illustrations.

A History of Women's Seclusion in the Middle East
Published by the Haworth Press, Inc., 2006. All rights reserved.
doi:10.1300/5666_25